KENVIN

AN ARTIST'S KITCHEN

FOOD, ART & WISDOM OF A BOHEMIAN COWBOY

RECIPES, STORIES & ARTWORK BY KENVIN LYMAN

GIBBS SMITH

TO ENRICH AND INSPIRE HUMANKIND

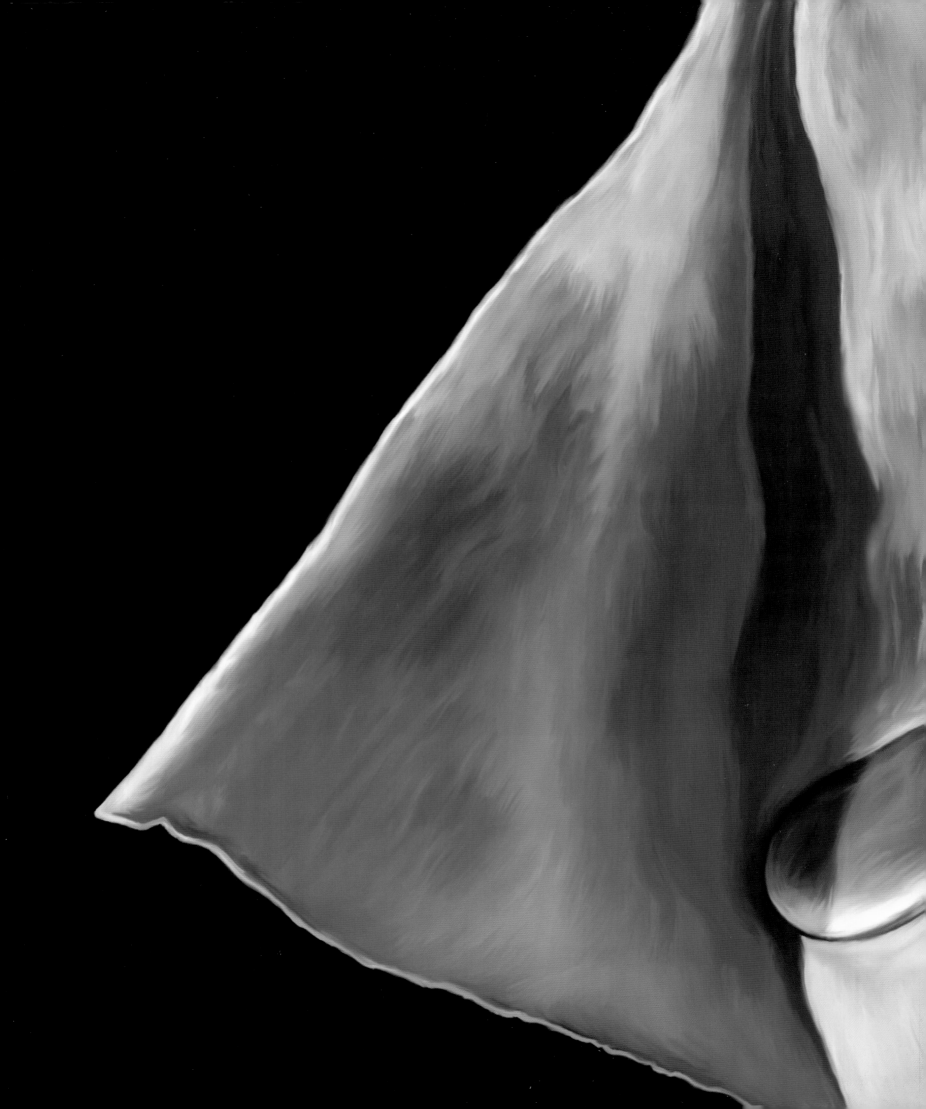

THE GENESIS OF THIS BOOK

On Saturday morning March 28, 1998, my mother launched the creation of this book. With her characteristic humility she asked if I would write down the recipes that I had created over the years so she could include them in our family history. It was a simple request that I assumed I could knock out in a few hours. Eventually it became this book and turned into twelve richly textured years. My mother, a truly angelic woman, died in 2007.

She never did see the results of her encouragement. It was her food and love that made this book and all my life's work possible. The roots of my relationship with food began with her and my dad and back through generations of Pioneer ancestors—farmers and ranchers who tilled the soil with their hands, animals and machines, and then respectfully prepared and enjoyed the bounty of their labors.

It was an honest relationship with the land. Almost everything they consumed they grew themselves. Traditional farm food is the prototype for today's local, sustainable food movement.

Contents

In the romantic visions of my youth I imagined the place where I grew up to be Provence. Down the country lanes under the shade of poplar and black willow there were streams of pure water flowing across the land with happy cows in lush pastures. I was Cézanne in Aix, Rimbaud in the Ardennes and Django in the Gypsy camps of Paris. I saw the purity of the past and the precious gifts of nature before the cruel hand of efficiency crushed them and covered their bones with the counterfeit veneer of civilization.

INTRODUCTION

Among other things, this book is my personal definition of Utah as a culinary region. The recipes here are almost entirely based on what grows within the boundaries of this state—mostly what my wife and I have grown here over the years. The general exceptions to that self-imposed rule are citrus, olives and their oil, chocolate, coffee and spices. We believe our best food is prepared from what we grow ourselves and what grows locally. A great deal of this book takes place inside our humble cottage kitchen and on the little plot of land that surrounds it. Our kitchen garden is our secret weapon. We have entertained some excellent cooks and chefs without intimidation because we know the advantages we have that most of them don't. Even most of the very good chefs in this country work with what we consider to be medium-quality ingredients: among other things, under-ripened tomatoes and peaches that are often hard and barely sweet.

Utah has been a liquor control state since 1935. Most of the control has emanated from the state's political system. In the first years of the territory before it became a state, wine was produced and enjoyed with the simple country food of the mostly European immigrants. As time passed, wine production was outlawed. Eventually it was allowed but with an oppressive tax that amounted to over 50 percent, making it impossible for Utah winemakers to compete in the world market. Thanks to a rational and progressive Gov. Jon Huntsman Jr., that tax was lifted in 2007 and replaced with one that will allow Utah winemakers to conduct their business on a level playing field. This change has effectively opened up a

huge virgin wine region—the entire state of Utah. The implications are very exciting. Besides hunger, nothing stimulates the joy and evolution of good food like wine does. Nothing brings money to both urban and rural areas like a healthy hospitality industry and nothing stimulates the hospitality industry like a healthy local wine industry. Until now it has been a conspicuously absent piece of the rural economic puzzle in the state, but now that piece is in place. With dire economic conditions becoming apparent in 2008, most of us began spending a lot of time entertaining at home, and that is the emphasis of this book. The economic recovery may take years, and it will take years for a new wine industry to realize the great potential within the borders of this neglected region. With economic recovery and the spread of new culinary gospels like Alice Waters' "Delicious Revolution" and the birth of a new wine industry, I see Utah on the verge of a culinary and perhaps even a rural economic renaissance. Until then, I suggest we all hunker down, improve our cooking skills and enjoy our own personal renaissance.

Using home food at its center, this book is a simple story—a personal glimpse into Utah's rural past and the way my wife and I live in our 1600 square foot Queen Anne cottage on a quarter acre in Salt Lake City in a state not yet recognized for its place in progressive American culture. Perhaps part of its reputation is deserved, but we don't waste time worrying about that. In fact Utah is endowed with some of the world's richest landscapes and a cornucopia of local foods which we explore in our kitchen.

Our home life is centered around our kitchen stove and a hearth shared with family and friends. Our life is made richer because of the pleasure of sharing. In our quest for knowledge and the various processes of our chosen lifestyle, our lives have evolved toward an unusual degree of self-containment. We grow most of our food on our own property; a wide variety of garden produce in the warm months, greens and roots the entire year. We make our own butter. We grind our own grain. We grow our own grapes and make our own wine. We preserve fruit for the winter months and make a year's supply of prepared horseradish in the fall. We invent and, with the help of our friends, test our own recipes. Undoubtedly it would be more convenient to order in and watch TV with dinner, but the pleasure of these processes gives a depth and meaning to our lives. This is why we live the way we do.

Pretty much everything in our lives revolves around growing, preparing and eating food with friends and family and the entertainment that either precedes or follows meals. Depending on who's around, the creative impulse can happen anytime, but after dinner is when we usually have the most fun.

Here is a typical example of the way we live: Last night I assumed head-cook duties and taught Ina, our eleven-year-old niece, and her eleven-year-old friend Caleb, both from the West Village in New York City, the essentials of a good fish salad. After an unsuccessful search for local trout we picked up a few cans of decent tuna from a local market. It was the best we could do. To give it a cleaner flavor, we gave it a quick rinse in water, marinated it in lemon juice infused with new garlic then surrounded it with a cornucopia of vegetables from our garden, including a bed of immature lettuces and slivers of sweet onion; new potatoes; tiny green beans; cucumbers; vine-ripe tomatoes; perfectly boiled eggs still moist in their centers, freshly gathered from our own chickens; a generous scattering of olives and a dressing of extra virgin olive oil infused with crushed tarragon, all seasoned with our favorite local salt and a few grinds of black pepper. We served it on an oversized platter in the center of the table so everyone could enjoy the way it looked and have the pleasure of serving themselves. Local trout would have improved the dish but even so we couldn't stop ourselves until it was completely gone. It was beautiful and quite delicious.

After dinner Caleb did a standup routine of "Mickey the Chimney Sweep," a character he invented on the spot. It was hilarious. I performed a new song I was still writing called "Sharky" about a pan handler I met in San Francisco. Then everyone joined in and we performed it together. The evening turned into a hat party when everyone chose a hat from our in-house collection to anchor their character. Like all the others, last night was unique and it will never come again. It all started with food from the garden and ended with the sweet satisfaction that only comes from exploring the great creative unknown.

We are carrying on the Bohemian tradition of celebrating life with the full force of our creativity just as generations have done before, but there is one major difference—we do almost all of our creative/philosophical explorations at home rather than the bistros and cafes of the Fauves or Impressionists. One reason is that America has never created an affordable infrastructure to support the nighttime Bohemian experiment. An evening in an American cafe or restaurant can cost more than an average day's wages. For us it is much more cost effective and satisfying to live our creative lives at home. It is also our contribution to the global environment. With driving becoming more expensive both to our budget and our environment, we think the best place for our car is at home where the most pleasurable evenings also happen.

— KENVIN LYMAN

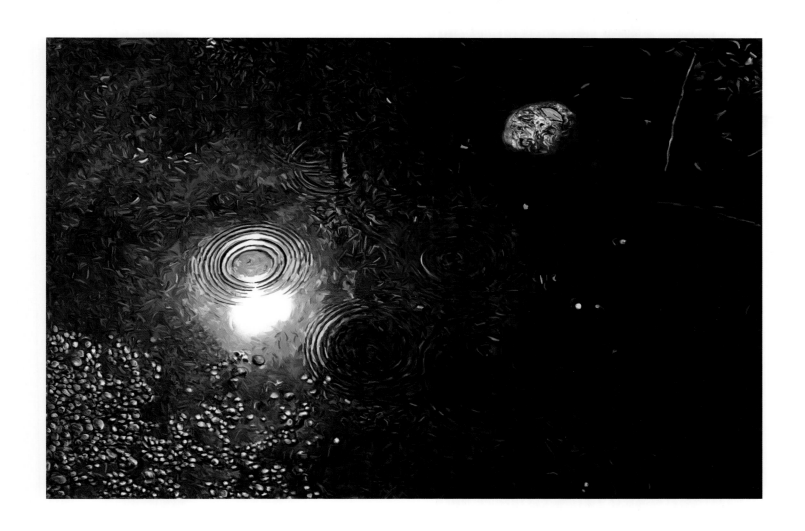

To a desert
Rain is more precious than gold
Whenever it falls through the hot dry air of day
It disappears like it would on a hot skillet
So that by the time it reaches the earth
It lands with the delicacy of an angel's breath
But at night when it rains, for a precious few hours, it accumulates
And when the full moon lights the puddle
And the rain ripples its surface
The desert shaman sees the face of God

Hooper   Keith

A NOTE OF GRATITUDE TO MY ANCESTORS

On both sides as far back as I can see, it feels like my ancestors live with me day-to-day.

Some of them were conservative; some were wild-eyed dreamers.
Some were saints and some were sinners.
Some of them tell me to go for broke and some tell me to hold back.

Whatever their differences the one thing they all have in common was their love of family,
friends and a willingness to help total strangers. Another thing they have in common
is their closeness to the Earth. Most of them were ranchers or farmers—herders or tillers of the soil.

They encouraged me, in their own way, to write this book and their spirit lives on in my life more
vividly as time passes. I tip my hat to them and send heartfelt gratitude. I feel them in my bones.

Good Butter Begins in the Pasture

{ DAIRY }

GOOD BUTTER BEGINS IN THE PASTURE

My mother's butter was the best I've ever tasted—and that's even accounting for nostalgia. It was made from the milk of Jersey or Guernsey cows that grazed the high mountain valleys of Utah in the late 1940s. She churned it only once a week from the cream she skimmed each morning from the previous day's milk.

By week's end its contents had mellowed and matured in the ranch "refrigerator," a log enclosure built over a spring. I remember the cold, crystal clear water that flowed upward from the sandy bottom of the spring to be about 50° F. By churning day, the week's cream had transformed into a pastoral scented elixir.

In 1998 when I began writing this book I began thinking about how to re-create that indescribably rich butter. Mixing a culture with cream seemed like the obvious way to duplicate what happened naturally, with the spring house cream.

Each culture I tried imparted a slightly different flavor. I tested buttermilk, kefir, yogurt and a dairy culture from Canada called Bio-K+ (see resources). Separately or mixed, I realized they all worked quite well.

The DeLaval No. 10 Cream Separator is a bona-fide, hard working, day-in day-out farm machine—an example of Victorian technology at its best. The one we have is over eighty years old and still in good working order. Essentially it is a carefully designed, proudly constructed, hand-cranked centrifuge. Separating milk with a cream separator—its deeply resonant whirring, its bell ringing, skim milk and cream pouring into their shiny silver buckets—is very exciting, especially when there is a gaggle of wide-eyed children looking on. It's a theatrical event and a romantic vision—like a cross between a Paul Klee Twittering Machine and a miniature Niagara Falls.

SOUR CREAM BUTTER

Here are four contemporary methods for making my favorite butter:

1. Whisk
2. Kitchen mixer
3. Kitchen blender
4. Home churn

Culturing improves cream for churning in two ways:

First, the flavor is greatly enhanced by this simple process, which brings out and accentuates plant aromatics from the cows' feed.

Second, those same friendly cultures also protect the butter against microorganisms that would cause spoilage. The method makes a surprisingly rich butter even with less than perfect cream. The pinnacle of butter, however, can only be reached using free-range organic cream from cows grazed on pasture in the summer months during the most vigorous bloom.

Of course you can use this butter in all the ways you normally use sweet cream butter. Because of the effort involved I usually save it for special purposes.

GOOD BUTTER BEGINS IN THE PASTURE

THE FOLLOWING INGREDIENTS AND STEP 1 APPLY TO ALL FOUR BUTTER METHODS

1 quart heavy cream

6 tablespoons mixed cultures such as buttermilk, kefir, yogurt or Bio-K+ (see resources)

Ice chips as needed for blender butter and mixer methods only

MAKES ABOUT 1 LB.

STEP 1 (Illustrations 1 & 2)
Prepare a colander or large sieve lined with cheesecloth. Put the cream in a large nonreactive bowl — glass or stainless steel. Stir all of the cultures into the cream, cover the bowl with plastic wrap and place in a 55° F to 60° F environment for 12 to 48 hours. (A wine cellar works splendidly for this). Leaving it longer increases the sour cream flavor. When finished, refrigerate for a few hours until it's completely cold (about 40° F). From there, you can make the butter using the four methods that follow.

WHISK METHOD (Illustrations 3, 4, 5, 10, 11 & 12)
The modified balloon whisk method is the simplest and most athletic of the four, requiring about a half-hour of quite vigorous whisking. A balloon whisk will trap whipped cream when it becomes stiff and will completely fill as the whipped cream turns to butter. To make a modified balloon whisk, clip about half of the wires from the whisk and file down the sharp edges. (See right two whisks in Illustration 3; the unmodified whisk is on the left, and modified version on the right.)

Whisk cream through the stiff whipped cream stage until granular clusters of butter begin to form, separating from the thin liquid called "whey." When it becomes so stiff that you can no longer whisk it, transfer butter and whey into a cheesecloth-lined colander or large cheesecloth-lined sieve to drain out the whey. Wash butter with cool water. Squeeze the butter against the side of the bowl with a wooden spoon or paddle, forcing most of the remaining water out. The butter can be salted at this stage if desired, approximately one teaspoon per pound.

BLENDER METHOD (Illustrations 6, 7, 10, 11 & 12 on p. 21)

For the standard consumer blender, you will place 1/2 to 1 cup at a time of the cultured cream mixture in the blender. If the stiffened cream traps air, holding it away from the blades, it probably means there is too much cream. Take some of it out.

Set blender speed to approximately medium-low and blend until the butter granular clusters separate from the whey. Ice chips can help if the butter granules need a boost toward the end of the process. It may take up to 5 minutes for the butter to form. Turn each batch out into a cheesecloth-lined strainer that's placed in the fridge while you process the next batch.

Repeat. After all the batches are completed and in the strainer, pour a generous amount of cool spring or filtered water over the butter to wash away any cream residue. Squeeze the butter against side of the bowl with a wooden spoon or paddle forcing most of the remaining water out. The butter can be salted at this stage if desired, approximately one teaspoon per pound.

KITCHEN MIXER METHOD (Illustrations 8, 10, 11 & 12 on p. 21)

A heavy-duty mixer works well for churning butter. As with blenders, the ingredients need to be completely chilled. Ice chips can help if the butter granules need a boost toward the end of the process. Mixers are gentle and take longer than the blender method.

Chill the mixer bowl and paddle in the refrigerator until cold. Pour the cultured cream into the bowl and begin blending on medium. Depending on your mixer, you may want to use a higher setting as you would for whipping cream. When the butter granules begin to form, slow the speed down as needed until the butter is completely separated from the whey.

Repeat. When it has gone as far as it will go and the mixer barely moves, pour off the butter and whey into a cheesecloth-lined colander or large cheesecloth-lined sieve and wash the butter with cool water. Squeeze the butter against side of the bowl with a wooden spoon or paddle forcing most of the remaining water out. The butter can be salted at this stage if desired, approximately one teaspoon per pound.

CHURN METHOD (Illustrations 9, 10, 11 & 12 on p. 21)

Churns are an easy, time-tested method from the past. Simply place a quart of cultured cream in a churn and crank the handle until the cream turns to butter. When the cream stiffens and has gone as far as it will go, pour off the butter and whey into a cheesecloth-lined colander or large cheesecloth-lined sieve and wash the butter with cool water. Squeeze the butter against side of the bowl with a wooden spoon or paddle forcing out most of the remaining water. The butter can be salted at this stage if desired, approximately one teaspoon per pound.

FOR ALL METHODS

Unsalted, sour cream butter will keep about 3 weeks in the refrigerator, longer when salted.

You may mold the butter into a rounded half circle and place on a plate or press it into a wooden butter mold (these can often be found in antique stores) before refrigerating.

To further enhance flavor of finished butter, allow it to ripen in a tightly covered container in the refrigerator for a few days. Test it every day or two to get a sense of how the flavor is changing.

Serve this delicately balanced butter with crusty Home Bread (p. 51) and a lightly chilled brut Champagne or sparkling wine as a simple appetizer.

WATERCRESS BUTTER

This butter brings back the best of childhood food memories for me. A secret rendezvous with flowing wells, quiet moments and lush stands of wild watercress. It is rich, peppery and delicious on full-flavored breads, such as whole grain walnut bread, preferably crusty and fresh from the oven. This combination stands up beautifully to most hearty soups.

1/2 cup finely minced watercress

1 pound Sour Cream Butter (p. 20) or unsalted butter

MAKES ABOUT 1 LB.

NOTE: To revive a loaf of bread that isn't perfectly fresh, put it in a damp paper bag in a 400° F oven for 10 minutes just before serving.

With a wooden spoon or butter paddle fold the watercress into cool but slightly soft butter until evenly mixed, taking care to not overwork it. Pat the mixture into a generous mound on a plate and garnish with a pristine sprig or two of watercress.

BEVERAGE RECOMMENDATION

This butter on walnut bread also goes well with most sparkling wines. Another good match, if you can find it, is a bottle of David Fulton Petite Sirah from St. Helena in Napa Valley.

In the winter, when I was a boy, sometimes the fog would settle in around the wetlands by our farm creating a soft, silent world. Whenever all the conditions were right, I would slip away from the day's chores and walk to the flowing wells where I could spend an hour or two alone in that enchanted environment. Besides the soft hypnotic flow of water, the only sound might be an occasional duck landing on the little fog-shrouded pond fed by the wells.

Watercress proudly defied the winter cold and grew in the running water around the well pipes creating miniature Zen gardens waiting to be picked, crushed into sour cream butter and spread on warm slices of homemade whole-wheat bread.

Farmer's Cheese with Olive Oil and Freshly Ground Peppercorns

In texture this cheese is similar to Ricotta, but with a more delicate, fresh flavor. Excellent as an appetizer on Flatbread (p. 45) with smoked trout and a pinch of minced, fresh dill.

2 quarts whole milk

5 tablespoons buttermilk, kefir or yogurt

Salt

1 teaspoon fresh lemon juice (optional)

Extra virgin olive oil to taste

Black, green and red peppercorns ground fresh to taste

MAKES ABOUT 1 LB.

NOTE: It is important in cheese making to use raw, free-range milk if at all possible. Depending on the degree to which it was processed, conventional supermarket milk is not always reliable. An option is to use whole, organic, free-range milk.

In a double boiler slowly heat the milk to 80° F. Add the buttermilk, kefir or yogurt. For more tang, lemon juice can be added at this point. Remove the mixture from the stove, cover with plastic wrap and leave at room temperature for about 24 hours.

When curds form and pull away from the surrounding whey, place them in a colander lined with 2 or 3 layers of cheesecloth. Cover with another layer of cheesecloth, letting the whey drip into a bowl for 4 or 5 hours. Pull the corners of the cheesecloth together and tie securely with a cotton string.

Hang the bag on a hook or wire hanger and allow it to drain further for a few more hours until it achieves the firmness you want. (It will take up to 24 hours for firm curd.) Put a bowl under the bag to catch the dripping whey.

Take the bag down, untie the string and open it to test for firmness. When it reaches the texture you like, turn it out of the bag and either serve it or refrigerate until ready to use. Drizzle the olive oil and grind the peppercorns over it when served.

BEVERAGE RECOMMENDATION

A flinty, dry Arbolitos Pinot Gris from Argentina or a jammy Zinfandel.

Nothing showcases the aromatic beauty of freshly ground pepper and good olive oil like fresh homemade farmer's cheese.

SPICY WHITE CHEDDAR CHEESE IN GRAPE LEAVES

My grandmother made cheddar cheese in an old tin vat outside her farmhouse where I later grew up. In those days, home cheese-making was a common way to turn milk into a value-added commodity.

The addition of toasted garlic, fresh chives and crushed red peppercorns also yields flavors that penetrate the cheese as it ages in the lemony grape leaf packets. The oil, in which it is aged, takes on a mellowed spiciness. It is nice brushed on Flatbread (p. 45) covered with cheese shavings served alongside niçoise olives or Marinated Olives (p. 211).

4 quarts whole milk

4 rennet tablets

2 tablespoons spring water to dissolve rennet

6 medium cloves garlic with husks left on

3 tablespoons finely chopped fresh chives

2 teaspoons red or black peppercorns, finely crushed

1 teaspoon salt or to taste

Grape leaves to create single leaf packets large enough to contain the cheese mixture, fresh or canned

Cotton string for tying the packets

Extra virgin olive oil to cover the packets

2 whole garlic cloves, peeled

1 bay leaf, fresh or dried

1 small dried chile pepper such as ancho

MAKES ABOUT 1 LB.

NOTE: It is important in cheese making to use raw, free-range milk if at all possible. Depending on the degree to which it was processed, conventional supermarket milk is not always reliable. An option is to use whole, organic, free-range milk.

In a double, nonreactive boiler, heat the milk to 110° F. After it reaches this temperature crush the rennet tablets in spring water and stir mixture into the milk. Set the covered double boiler in a warm place and leave it undisturbed for 1 hour. By this time a firm curd should have formed. If it hasn't, the milk has either been overcooked during pasteurization, ultra-homogenized, you have not controlled the temperature carefully enough, or there was not enough rennet. You will have to discard and start again. If the curd is soft instead of firm continue anyway. The cheese will be softer than it should have been but will still be good.

Make a 2-inch grid and cut through the curd with a sharp knife. Gently turn out the long rectangular pieces on a cutting board. Cut the rectangles into two-inch cubes and transfer to a cotton cheesecloth-lined colander placed over a large pan to collect the whey that will drip from the curd. After about two hours gather up the corners of the cheesecloth and tie it with cotton string in a bow, which will allow you to untie it later.

Hang the bag where it is warm and airy. Place a pan underneath the bag to catch the dripping whey. The curds will lose more whey as they get firmer. To speed up the process gently squeeze the bag with both hands and force the whey from the curds. Don't squeeze too hard or the bag will tear. After the curds are quite firm (about 48 hours), remove them from the bag and chop them with a sharp knife or put in the food processor to reach a grain-sized texture.

Place the garlic cloves in a dry frying pan over medium heat. Stir and turn them until their husks turn a deep golden brown and their flesh begins to soften (approximately 10 minutes). Remove the husks. Crush the garlic, peppercorns and salt to a paste with a mortar and pestle. Scrape the garlic mixture from the mortar with a rubber spatula into the cheese. Mix well.

If you have one, line a wooden cheese mold that has a few holes in the bottom or a small plastic basket with 2 layers of cheesecloth. Press the curds into the mold with your hands, pushing out any air pockets. There should be about 3 cups total.

Fold the cheesecloth over the cheese and set it in a large pan to catch the whey that will be released. Place a rectangular piece of clean untreated wood on top of the cheese. It should rest on the cheese as close to the edges of the mold as possible but not touch the edges. Place a 2 or 3 pound weight on the wood. Books or bricks work well. The weight will compress the cheese and force out any residual whey. As the whey drips from the cheese, the cheese will lose volume. Leave the cheese weighted until it is reduced by about 1/3 (about two cups and about one day).

Remove cheese from the mold and remove the cheesecloth. Drape a dish towel over the cheese and allow it to dry in a warm place for another day or two. Cut it into six or eight equal cubes. Neatly wrap each piece in a large grape leaf and tie cotton string around the center in both directions.

Put the packets in a glass container and cover with olive oil. Add the whole garlic cloves, bay leaf and chile pepper. Seal with a tight lid. Place the container in the refrigerator to age and mellow. It will continue to improve for several weeks.

BEVERAGE RECOMMENDATION

La Riva Tres Palmas fino sherry provides a rich, nutty balance to the spicy flavors of this cheese. Another less orthodox but equally good match is a Manzanilla La Gitana, a light sherry with a special delicacy and a slight tang of ocean salt on the aftertaste.

Aunt Teresa's Unchurned White Butter

A novel non-recipe for those who have access to clotted cream or a cream separator and free-range milk.

My Uncle Roy and Aunt Teresa and my cousins Bob, Jerry and Kim lived on a farm about a mile from ours. There was a special charm about their lifestyle that I always admired. For one thing Aunt Teresa was a good cook with original ideas.

One idea was an unchurned butter she made from unusually rich cream obtained by setting the adjusting screw on their nicely worn DeLaval cream separator to its richest setting. The warm cream was so thick it would barely run out of the cream spout. She placed a rectangular glass dish under the spout, filled it with cream, covered it and put it in the refrigerator. Remarkably, as it cooled, it solidified into a delicate, silky-white, unchurned butter. It is especially good on toast with Green Tomato and Caramelized Orange Jam (p. 242).

1 pint of extra-heavy cream from a free-range cow

MAKES ABOUT 1 LB.

Fill a large glass dish with the cream and refrigerate until firm.

BEVERAGE RECOMMENDATION

Serve a dry, sparkling wine such as Segura Viudas Brut Reserva or rich, black Colombian coffee.

*For us it makes more sense to focus on the quality of life than the size
of our bank account so raising a garden is a good fit for our lifestyle.*

NEW MILK

Whole milk is one of the world's most versatile foods. With the age-old ingenuity of the human hand it can become so many things: skim milk, whey, half-and-half, cream, butter, yogurt, kefir, cream cheese, cottage cheese, quark, fermented milk and a long list of hard and soft cheeses including: *Harzer, Mainzer, Mato, Queso Camerano, Brossat, Recuit, La Dama Blanca, Moli de l'Alzina, Gouda, Asiago, Gruyere, Provolone, Jarlsberg, Fontina, Noekkelost, Appenzeller, Mimolette, Pecorino Romano, Derby, Cheshire, Cheddar, Stilton, Caerphilly, Raclette, Ricotta Salata, Danbo, Edam, Gjetost, Cantal, Parmesan, Emmentaler, Sapsago, Camembert, Pont l'Evêque, Livarot, Chèvre, Roquefort, Gorgonzola, Maroilles, Wensleydale, Tomme de Savoie, Stracchino, Morbier, Farmer Cheese, Reblochon, St. Nectaire, Taleggio, Caerphilly, Pelardon, Chaource, Pouligny Saint-Pierre, Brillat-Savarin, Salers, Beaufort, Bethmale, Ossau* and *Brie.* In one form or another, it is also used in endless ways: in an endless number of sauces, soups, baked goods, desserts, entrees and appetizers. I say "endless" because every day new dishes are invented using some form of milk.

Freshly churned butter made from free-range cream has a sweet, complex flavor enhanced by culturing before it goes into the churn.

GOOD BUTTER BEGINS IN THE PASTURE

TOASTED SHALLOT BUTTER

This is a sumptuous compound butter with the rich, caramelized flavors of onion. It is especially good when made with Sour Cream Butter. Delicious on crusty bread as an appetizer or served with hearty soups.

2 medium shallots, peeled

Pinch or two of salt

1/2 pound Sour Cream Butter (p. 20) or unsalted butter

MAKES ABOUT 1/2 LB.

Flatten shallots with the side of a knife. Place them in a small dry frying pan over medium heat, occasionally stirring, until they turn golden brown, about 6 to 10 minutes. Don't let them blacken. Chop them fine, then grind to a smooth paste with a pinch or two of salt in a mortar with a pestle, or process in a small food processor until smooth. Thoroughly blend the paste into cool, soft butter with a wooden spoon.

BEVERAGE RECOMMENDATION

A dry California Chardonnay such as a Neyers Carneros.

Of all designed objects, few give me as much pleasure as a hand-carved peg of wood keeping the door of a finely weathered farm shed.

GOOD BUTTER BEGINS IN THE PASTURE

Zesty Chipotle Butter

This is a full-flavored, hot, racy butter that goes well with almost any Mexican dish that benefits from butter.

1 teaspoon dried or canned chipotle peppers chopped, without seeds or ribs

1 clove garlic, chopped

1 tablespoon chopped cilantro

1/2 teaspoon lime zest

1 teaspoon fresh squeezed lime juice

1/2 pound Sour Cream Butter (p. 20) or unsalted butter

MAKES ABOUT 1/2 LB.

Crush the peppers, garlic, cilantro and lime zest to a smooth paste in a mortar and pestle. Stir the lime juice into the paste. Thoroughly blend into the butter with a wooden spoon.

Form into an attractive round or oval shape. Goes well with fresh corn on the cob.

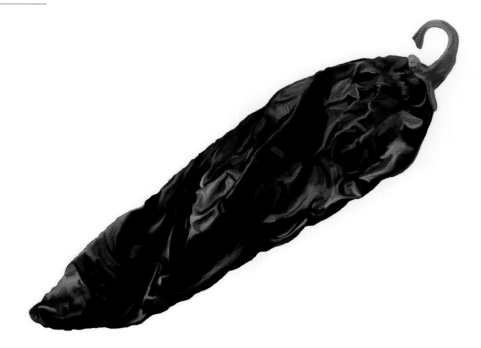

An Enchanted Table

{ BREAD }

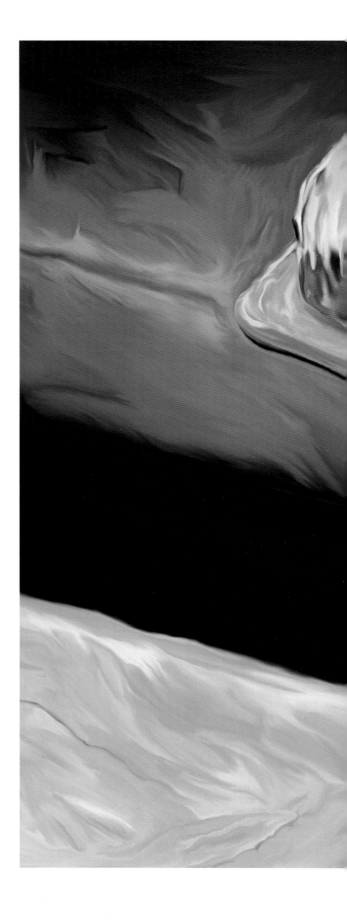

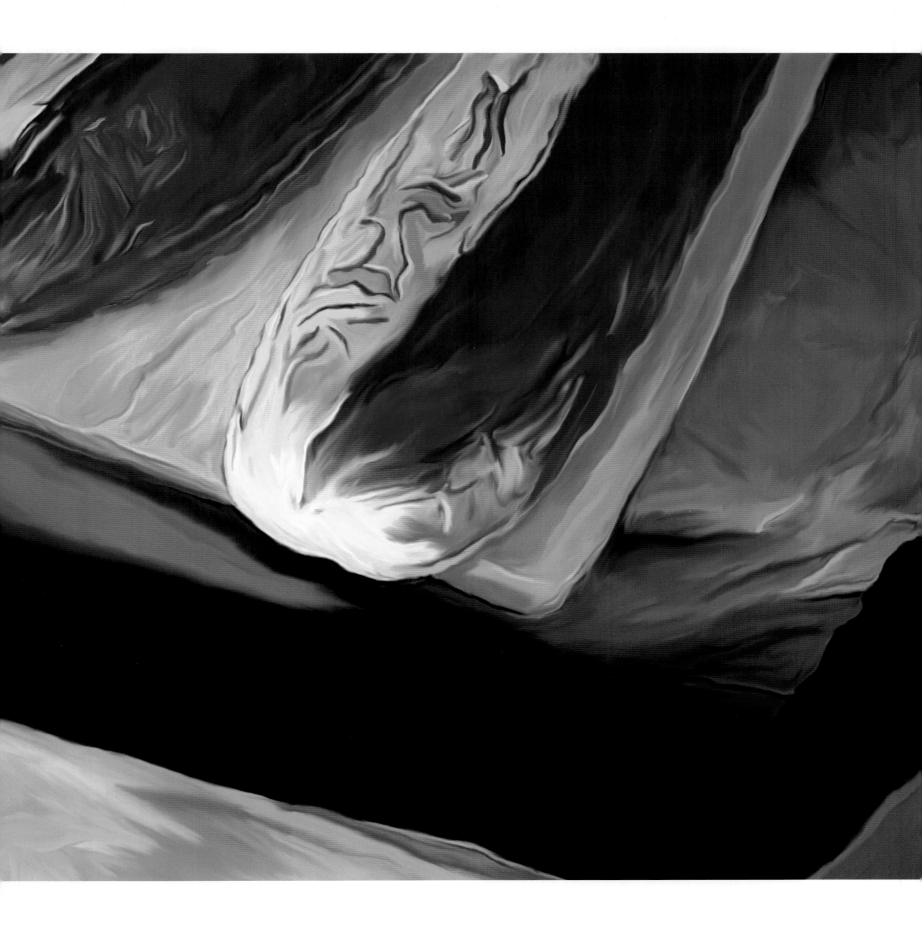

AN ENCHANTED TABLE

This table has witnessed parts of three centuries in our kitchen yet remained there, in that same place, under that same window. It was there when the Flowers family moved into their new home in 1892 as it was when I first walked into that room in 1967. As I write this at the end of 2010 it is still there. My first wife and I raised our kids around it on heavy peasant loaves from wheat we grew on the family farm and then ground into coarse flour with an old, red, hand-cranked, cast-iron, grain grinder mounted, as needed, on one of the table's corners.

At night, after the kids were in bed, it became my night studio where I worked into the early hours of the morning. It was on this table in the late sixties that I wrote my declaration of independence with and without words. Writing and creating art for posters on the backs of other posters, to avoid having to buy illustration board. And I worked on tiny glass slides that propelled me into a world of shimmering light shows with, over the next decade, two different light show companies, two different partners and some of the most legendary bands in the world.

Some of my favorite moments were when I designed posters for some of those bands. Two for Led Zeppelin on the table's richly textured surface that still brings forth memories of long ago meals and projects. Those Led Zeppelin commissions came from The Family Dog, one of the two great venues for rock shows in San Francisco in the sixties. I was paid $75 each and had no idea that some day the band would become legendary and those posters would rise to become favorites of the band. I sketched hundreds of ideas and wrote songs, prose and poetry on an old Remington typewriter here. I learned to cook in this kitchen where this table still stands and where I have enjoyed countless meals with people who told tales of kings and queens, artists, mountain climbers, rock stars, beggars, madness and hope. How could a simple old Mormon pine table play such an important role in a person's life? It must be enchanted.

The inside walls of our kitchen are a painting. Art doesn't end anywhere in particular for me. I view most things as having the potential of being elevated to that status including the process of cooking, raising a garden, making a bottle of wine, setting a table, plowing a field, writing a song, performing a light show or making objects and images, still or moving. First, art is in the mind of the creator then the beholder.

SWEET CORNBREAD

A rich, crusty cornbread that goes well with smoked meats, eggs, beans and chiles. Fresh sweet corn with the milk scraped from the cobs after the corn kernels have been cut off gives it a mildly sweet, aromatic, fresh corn flavor. The binder in most cornbread is provided by wheat flour. Replacing the flour with cornstarch and masa harina gives it a richer and more harmonious flavor.

Serve hot with plenty of good butter.

---

1 cup yellow cornmeal
(stone-ground is better)

1 cup masa harina (found in the
baking section or Mexican food
section of most markets)

1 level tablespoon cornstarch

1 level tablespoon baking powder

1 teaspoon salt

2 ears fresh, sweet corn kernels cut
from the ears and the milk scraped
from the cobs with a sharp knife

1 egg, beaten well

1/3 cup corn oil or safflower oil

Spring water to make 2 cups
including corn kernels, oil and egg

Bacon fat, butter or nonstick spray
to coat pan

SERVES 4 TO 6

Preheat oven between 400° F and 450° F depending on how brown and crusty you want the top of the cornbread to be.

Mix dry ingredients together. Set aside.

In a blender, process 3/4 cup spring water and corn to make about 1 cup liquid. If your blender doesn't completely break down the cellulose, strain it out. Add the wet ingredients together— including the egg and oil. Add enough spring water to bring mixture up to 2 cups and mix well. Pour the wet ingredients into the dry ingredients in a large mixing bowl and stir together quickly with a wooden spoon. Don't overwork it or the finished bread will toughen. If necessary add a little more spring water to make the batter pourable.

Liberally grease or oil an ovenproof, iron skillet or heavy cake pan and place in the preheated oven until sizzling hot. Quickly remove the skillet, add the batter and bake in the oven for about 25 minutes. Check it at 20 minutes by inserting a toothpick. If it is done it will come out clean. If not, put it back in the oven for a few more minutes then retest. Don't overbake it or it will dry out. Cut into squares, place in a basket lined with a clean dish towel and cover to keep it hot.

Serve immediately.

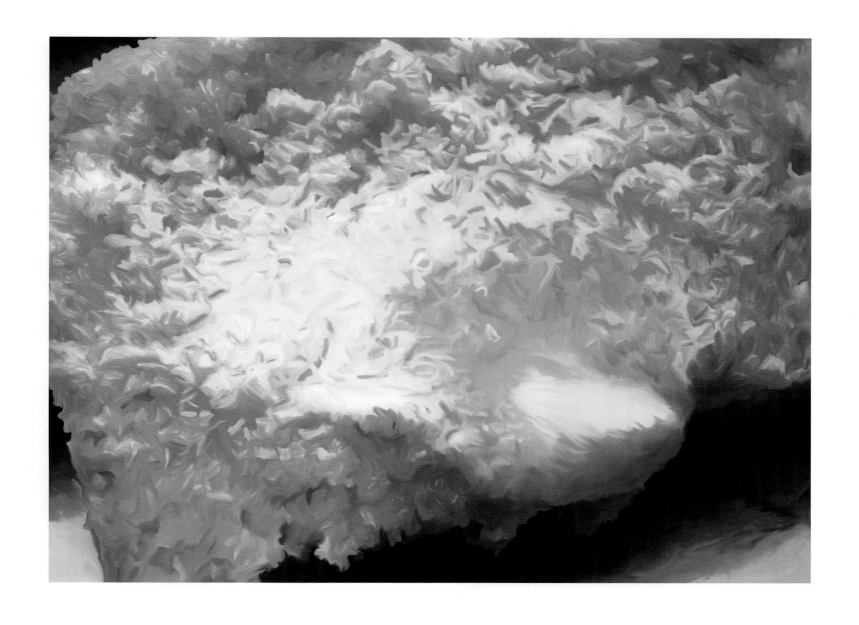

CORN LACE CAKES

Serve these crepe-like cakes for breakfast as you would pancakes, as a side dish with game such as leg of venison or elk tenderloin accompanied by Brown Sauce (p. 260) or with an assertive vegetable such as grilled asparagus.

2 cups red, yellow or blue stone-ground corn flour

2 cups spring water

1 to 2 tablespoons hazelnut oil (see resources) or other vegetable oil

Salt to taste (about 1 teaspoon)

1 teaspoon baking powder

2 tablespoons grapeseed oil for griddle

MAKES 16 TO 20 4-INCH DIAMETER CAKES

Mix all ingredients but baking powder and grapeseed oil. Let stand for a half hour or more. Add the baking powder just before cooking the cakes. The mixture should be about as thick as heavy whipping cream. If it is too thick, thin with a little spring water.

When the griddle is hot, coat it with a little grapeseed oil. When it begins to smoke, pour enough of the batter on the griddle to make a 4-inch diameter test cake. When many bubbles appear on top, turn it over and place a small pat of butter on the cooked side, if desired.

BEVERAGE RECOMMENDATION

A good wine for the venison or elk meal is a full-flavored Shiraz.

FLATBREAD

An ancient, richly aromatic bread. With freshly ground flour it is nearly as satisfying as meat. It goes well with Smoky Squash Soup (p. 103) and chèvre, sheep's milk feta or buffalo mozzarella.

It is also a good base for a wide range of appetizers such as fresh goat cheese with herbs, smoked trout, and scrambled eggs with sautéed mushrooms.

3 cups freshly ground whole wheat or spelt flour

1 teaspoon salt

4 tablespoons extra virgin olive oil

Olive oil as needed to brush on bread before turning

1 1/4 cups boiling spring water

1 medium yellow Spanish onion, chopped medium-fine (optional)

Grapeseed or any oil with a high smoking point to oil the griddle

MAKES 10 TO 12 7-INCH
ROUND FLATBREADS

In a large mixing bowl, mix the flour and salt together, then the olive oil. Work the mixture with your hands until the oil is evenly distributed and the blend resembles cornmeal. Add the boiling spring water and mix with an oiled wooden spoon until the flour and water stick together. If the mixture is too sticky to knead by hand or roll out with an oiled rolling pin, sprinkle with and work in a little more flour. The hot spring water brings out the gluten very quickly so the dough doesn't have to be worked much or rest for a long time. Knead the dough a little on a floured surface, until it loses its stickiness but remains soft and moist. Put it back in the mixing bowl and cover with a moist cloth or paper towel.

Pull off pieces of dough about the size of a chicken's egg and roll them smooth with your oiled hands. On an oiled surface with an oiled or floured rolling pin, roll into 7-inch circular disks 1/16 to 1/8 inch thick. Cook on a hot griddle oiled with a drizzle of oil spread evenly with a spatula.

For onion flatbread, press a pinch of the chopped onion into one side of the flattened dough with your hand or rolling pin before frying. Remove the bread from the griddle while still soft and pliable with golden brown, mottled surfaces. Because the first surface absorbs the oil from the griddle, brush a little oil on the top before you turn it over, giving both sides an even surface texture.

Put the finished bread on a warm plate covered with a soft cloth or a couple of paper towels. Cover the bread with a soft cloth or a couple of paper towels to keep it warm as you cook more. Leftover bread keeps well for a day or two if you store it in a plastic bag in the refrigerator.

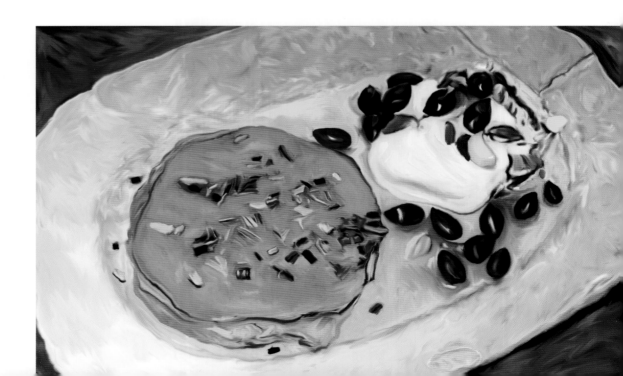

WILD RICE CAKES

Freshly ground, new crop wild rice flour (see resources) has the wonderfully complex flavors of buckwheat, hazelnut and the earthiness of the forest floor in late fall. Fresh ground wild rice flour is another good reason to have a grain grinder (see resources). It is also gluten-free.

These cakes are delicious with butter and maple syrup for breakfast. For dinner they are delicious with a quick, savory sauce made from reduced Wild Mushroom Stock (p. 126) mixed with pan liquid from the braised meat it will be served with. It can be further enriched with a pat or two of butter and a pinch of minced herbs such as chervil mixed with marjoram and parsley.

These cakes are also much better if made just before serving. If you can't do that, make them ahead and keep them in a warm oven until served and serve them on hot plates. Cakes made ahead though will never be as good as those hot off the griddle. (I like to serve them at the table next to the kitchen stove and ritualistically cook them as the guests watch and consume them in their meltingly perfect state).

1 cup finely ground wild rice flour

1 1/2 cups spring water

1/2 teaspoon salt

1 1/2 tablespoons hazelnut oil or a mild oil like safflower for the batter

1/2 teaspoon non-aluminum baking powder

Grapeseed oil for the griddle

MAKES 20 4-INCH
DIAMETER CAKES

Mix all ingredients except baking powder and grapeseed oil together and stir until well blended. Let stand for 15 minutes so the flour absorbs the spring water and thickens a little.

With a spatula, spread a few drops of grapeseed oil on a griddle over medium-high heat. Stir in the baking powder. When the griddle starts to smoke, pour a small ladle of the batter in the center for a tester. The mixture should be the consistency of very heavy whipping cream. If too thick, thin with a little more spring water. If too thin add flour. When many bubbles appear, turn the cake over and place a small pat of butter on it, if desired. When the first cake is finished, taste and make the necessary corrections before continuing.

Luxuriously Simple Crepes

These are the simplest and my favorite of all crepes. They have a rich, nutty flavor and they can morph to accommodate about any filling, sweet or savory.

For savory, brush one side with olive oil and serve with paper-thin prosciutto or spread with any number of soft cheeses and a pinch of freshly minced herbs. For sweet, spread with butter and Fruited Syrup (p. 245) and stack six or so high. Cut into pie-shaped wedges, say, eight to the circle, and serve with whipped cream. Sprinkle with powdered sugar or cinnamon if desired.

1 cup whole wheat pastry flour

1 1/2 cups spring water

1/4 teaspoon salt

1 tablespoon fresh walnut oil (safflower can be substituted)

Grapeseed oil as needed for the griddle

MAKES 10 TO 12 6-INCH CREPES

Mix all of the ingredients, except grapeseed oil, together and whisk until there are no lumps. It should be the consistency of cream. Allow the mixture to stand for a few minutes so the flour granules fully absorb the moisture. Spread a few drops of oil with a spatula on a nonstick 7-inch frying pan. When it smokes, put a ladle of about 2 or 3 tablespoons batter on the griddle and roll it around to increase its diameter to about 6 inches. When bubbles appear on top, leave it for another minute till finished. Turn the cake and cook until cooked through and brown. It should take about 2 minutes per side. If it is too thick and takes longer, thin the batter a little and use less.

AN ENCHANTED TABLE

Uncle Mel's Sourdough Biscuits

My late uncle Mel King was the quintessential sheepman and a good cook. Back in the late forties, whenever we visited him at the sheep herd, he welcomed us into a simple but richly textured world that now barely exists on the fringes of the Old West.

To this day the sheepherder's house of choice is the "sheep wagon." The ones I remember from those days were branded as "Home on the Range" and many are still in use. They are compact, portable little units with a special stove that doubles as furnace and kitchen stove. When it's chilly and someone's in camp, the stove is always radiating a hospitable warmth fed by pinion and quaking aspen and ready for its central role in the next meal's preparation.

The three constants in the sheepherder's diet are the ever-present pot of black coffee, sourdough biscuits and of course mutton, which is always available and affordable.

STARTER – FIRST STAGE

2 cups unbleached all-purpose flour

1 cup lukewarm spring water

1 cup lukewarm milk

1 teaspoon raw sugar

1 package dry yeast

With a wooden spoon stir together flour, water, milk, sugar and yeast. Let stand, in a large, loosely covered jar, in a warm place for 3 or 4 days or up to a week if necessary. It will bubble and smell sour when it is ready.

STARTER – SECOND STAGE

2 cups unbleached all-purpose flour

2 cups lukewarm spring water

With a wooden spoon stir 2 cups flour and 2 cups spring water into the first stage mixture and let stand overnight in a warm place. The batter will expand up to three times its original volume so make sure the jar is large enough. (If fed regularly sourdough starters can be kept in the refrigerator indefinitely. I've seen starters that are over 100 years old.)

(recipe continued on page 50)

SHEEPHERDER VERSION (use first & second stage starter from the Home Version)

FOR THE BISCUITS

1 1/2 cups starter

1/2 cup buttermilk

**2 cups all-purpose flour
plus some for kneading surface**

1 teaspoon salt

1 teaspoon baking soda

**Mutton tallow, butter
or vegetable oil for pan**

MAKES APPROX. 6 BISCUITS

*For an experienced camp cook, judging an oven's
temperature is a matter of experience, instinct,
smell and sensing the stove's radiant heat or
feeling the oven's temperature with the quick
check of a hand inserted into its interior.

NOTE: The sheepherder's version is an account of how
uncle Mel made his biscuits and is intended to serve
as a recipe for anyone who wants to duplicate his
methods. (It may seem terribly imprecise, but after
a few batches you will get the hang of it, developing
a sense and feeling for it.

Uncle Mel's method for making sourdough biscuits was a time honored one employing an uncanny economy of means. He would use a sack of flour itself as his mixing bowl, first rolling the top of the sack down to a little above the level of the flour. Then he would dig a hollow impression in the flour about the size of his two cupped hands and pour in enough starter to make a batch of biscuits. Next he sprinkled in soda and salt then worked enough flour in, from the sides, to make a soft dough. After the dough reached the desired consistency, he pinched off egg-sized pieces, patted and shaped them in a steel baking pan called a "dripper" lightly greased with mutton tallow (mutton tallow is what's left from cooking the daily mutton and serves as an all-purpose cooking lubricant). After they were shaped, he flipped them over and coated the other side with a little of the melted tallow then left them to raise. Once they had puffed up to the proper size he popped them into the oven from which they emerged, twenty minutes or so later, piping hot, golden and smelling like a combination of hot bread and richly scented mutton tallow. It's one of my favorite cooking aromas.

Sourdough biscuits are an embodiment of the Old West — folklore brought to the sheepherder's table where they still accompany everything from mutton stew to the meal's final cup of black coffee. For dessert, I remember them served with chunky strawberry jam, the sheepherder's favorite. That jam on a hot biscuit was, and still is, a simple, satisfying dessert — the perfect ending to a good mutton dinner.

HOME VERSION

Preheat oven to 350° F (or adjust for altitude — see below).

Put starter and buttermilk in mixing bowl. Add 2 cups flour, salt and soda. Stir together. Sprinkle a little flour onto a kneading surface. Turn the dough out of the bowl onto the kneading surface. Knead into a soft dough working in enough flour to take the stickiness out of the dough but not enough to make it stiff. Sprinkle the surface with a little more flour then roll out the dough to about 1/2 inch thick and cut as many biscuits with a biscuit cutter or a tin cup as you can. Then gather up what's left of the dough, roll it out and repeat until all of the dough is used. Coat both sides of each biscuit with tallow, butter or oil. Arrange them in a greased pan leaving enough room for expansion.

If you want the authentic sheepherder's version, make a dough that is slightly softer so you can easily pinch off egg-size chunks and shape them in a greased pan with your hands. With either method, they should rise in a warm place for 15 to 30 minutes. Bake in a 350° F (at sea level) oven for 20 to 30 minutes until golden brown. With every 1,000 foot increase in altitude add 5° F and decrease the amount of soda by 5 percent. At sea level if you bake something at 350° F., it would be necessary to bake it at 400° F and decrease the soda by 50 percent to get about the same results at 10,000 feet. Exact results are harder to get at high altitudes. Experience is always the best teacher.*

Home Bread

This is truly great bread that anyone can make (based on a recipe from Jim Lahey, head baker from Sullivan Street Bakery in Manhattan). By baking in a covered cast-iron pan inside the larger oven you trap and increase the humidity yielding a very crusty bread. Fresh from the oven it's nearly as good as anything you can buy in Paris. Still warm, it's at its best with Sour Cream Butter (p. 20).

4 cups all-purpose flour, or for an earthier version use up to 25 percent whole wheat pastry flour

1/2 teaspoon dry instant yeast

1 1/2 teaspoons salt

2 cups spring water

MAKES 1 LOAF

Mix all dry ingredients together then add the spring water and quickly stir until it comes together. Cover with plastic wrap. Use more than one piece if necessary to lap over the edges so the bread won't dry out. Set aside for 24 hours in a warm place (around 70° F).

Preheat oven between 500° F and 515° F; preheat cast-iron pan lid as well.

Turn dough out onto a dry cloth generously sprinkled with flour. Use an oiled rubber spatula to scrape out any remaining dough and add. Fold the dough up from the four sides. Lifting one edge of the cloth at a time helps you fold it over onto the top of itself. Sprinkle the top with flour. Slip one hand under the cloth and pick it up with the dough. Turn the folded dough over into your free, freshly floured hand and drop it into the preheated cast-iron pan with folded side up.

Cover with preheated lid and place in hot oven. Bake with lid on for 50 to 60 minutes. Check for brownness after 40 or so minutes and adjust heat if necessary. Remove the loaf from pan as soon as it is finished or it will soften and take on a metallic flavor. Let cool on a wire rack until slightly warm or room temperature before slicing or pulling apart with your hands.

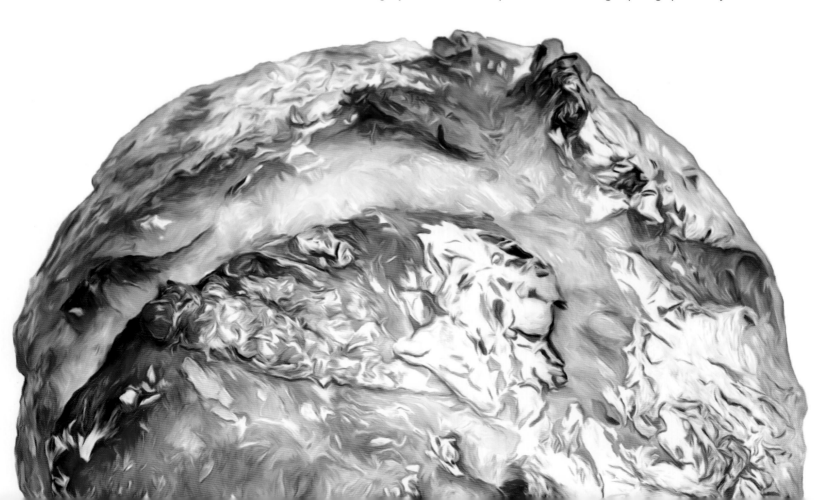

STRAWBERRY RANCH

STRAWBERRY RANCH

Some of my most vivid childhood memories are of a 65,000-acre cattle ranch on the eastern edge of the Wasatch Range in a high mountain valley called "Strawberry." That's where my father was a hired hand and our family lived during the high-mountain summers for most of my youth. The ranch had a big, extravagant, movie-set quality and my dad was the leading man. He had finely chiseled features and more cow and horse sense than any man I ever met. For him to be called a cowboy was a badge of honor handed down through generations of accumulated knowledge and thousands of bone-hard hours in the saddle.

We lived in a whitewashed two-room cabin that sat proudly in an open meadow—miles from our nearest neighbor. We were completely off the grid—no gas heat, no plumbing or electricity—things we apparently didn't need since somehow we managed to live quite well without them. We used coal-oil lamps for light and kept our food cool in a spring house, and my mother cooked honest, simple meals on a big wood-burning range that also served as the cabin's central heater.

As if it had happened only yesterday, I remember the aroma of breakfast cooking in that old kitchen and the mixed aromas of a crackling wood fire and the crisp mountain air. Waking up to those aromas was heaven to hungry young kids.

To put meat on the table, my father would go out to sheep country where the herds grazed the quaky-covered hills. It was a few miles south of the cattle ranch where my uncle Mel lived in a tin-covered, "Home-on-the-Range" sheep wagon. Dad would bring home a whole mutton that he had already cleaned and dressed, and hang it high from the granary roof at night in the cold mountain air. In the morning he would take it down from its perch and carry it into the kitchen table where he'd cut off another day's supply of meat with a blonde-handled meat saw and a well-worn butcher knife. Then he would put it back in its cotton sack, wrap it in a tattered old quilt and put it under the covers of his and mother's bed to keep it away from the warmth of another day. Our kitchen was the center of our lives on that ranch and it seems like it was always filled with the rich aromas of a well-run ranch kitchen.

The best part of sheep ranching is definitely not the money — but rather the solitude, beauty, independence, wide-open spaces and the best damn meat money can buy.

POACHED EGGS IN FLOWER PETAL SOUP

When Sofia, my wife of Chinese extraction, came to live with me a few years ago I began experimenting with dishes that were inspired by her noble culture. This one is endlessly variable and for me conjures Asian breakfast soups. Serve with steamed rice, cucumber pickles in soy sauce or takuan (pickled daikon radish found at Asian markets), and steaming cups of good oolong tea.

4 large eggs

Water to cover eggs

1 tablespoon mild oil, such as safflower

Few drops toasted sesame oil or to taste

1 small yellow onion, chopped fine

2 quarts Wild Mushroom stock (p. 126), or chicken stock

2 heaping tablespoons miso paste such as red barley, brown rice or dandelion leek

4 servings bean thread noodles or rice noodles (at Asian markets)

Chile Oil (p. 250) or chile paste (at Asian markets) to taste

Bragg Liquid Aminos to taste (see resources)

Rice vinegar to taste

Fish sauce to taste

Black bean paste to taste

Cilantro leaves to taste

1/2 cup edible flower petals such as violets or calendula, sunflower or rose, whole or chopped medium

SERVES 4

Gently break eggs into a large saucepan of simmering water to cover by at least 2 inches. Turn off heat and cover with lid. When the whites are firm and yolks still soft (3 to 6 minutes), carefully remove them with a slotted spoon and place in a pan of cool water.

Add the oils and onion to a saucepan. Cover and cook over low heat for a few minutes, stirring occasionally, to soften. Add the stock and miso. Whisk until smooth. Raise the heat to medium. When it reaches a simmer, add the noodles and cook until tender. Lower heat to low. Add the other ingredients, except the flower petals, and correct the flavors. Remove from heat. Add the flower petals. Let them wilt in the hot liquid for a minute or two. Put one poached egg into each of four large, Japanese-style noodle bowls (found at Asian markets), gently ladle one fourth of the soup mixture over each egg and serve immediately.

STRAWBERRY RANCH

The Perfect "Fried" Egg with Tarragon

1 tablespoon olive oil, butter or bacon fat

2 large, fresh eggs

2 tablespoons spring water

A big pinch of minced fresh or dry tarragon (other herbs, such as thyme, marjoram or chervil may be substituted)

Salt and freshly ground pepper to taste

SERVES 1

Instead of just fried, these eggs are both fried and steamed, at the same time, in a tightly covered pan. This method yields a smooth, evenly cooked egg with rich tarragon flavor great for a Sunday brunch. For a substantial breakfast serve with bacon or chicken sausages, toast, and coffee or tea.

Use low heat and a pan that has a tight lid so the steam can cook the top surface of the yolks before their bottoms harden. Heating the lid before placing it on the pan also helps. Put the olive oil in a pan, coating its bottom evenly. Crack and open the eggs into the pan. Add the spring water. Sprinkle with tarragon. Put on the lid. Lower the heat to low and steam to desired doneness (3 to 5 minutes). Season with salt and pepper and serve.

As far as protecting its agricultural base America is asleep at the wheel.

STRAWBERRY RANCH

BREAKFAST BEAN CURD

This recipe is for breakfast eaters who crave variety—there are endless possibilities to what you can do with this recipe. Like most cooking, once you get the hang of it, you should experiment with your own ideas. . . . it's more fun. By pushing the recipe's limits and experimenting with new variations you'll develop your own favorite versions much faster. Think of this version as a starting point.

1/2 yellow onion, chopped medium

2 tablespoons olive oil

1 medium vine-ripened tomato, chopped medium (or about the same amount of canned crushed tomato)

1/2 pound firm bean curd

1 tablespoon straight or mixed finely chopped fresh herbs such as tarragon, parsley, thyme, cilantro, basil and lovage

2 tablespoons roasted, skinned and seeded red pepper, chopped fine

Squeeze or two of lime juice

Cayenne pepper, Chile Oil (p. 250) or chile paste to taste (optional)

1/4 cup canned coconut milk (optional)

Bragg Liquid Aminos to taste (see resources)

SERVES 2

Sauté the onion in a tablespoon of olive oil. Add the tomato and cook 3 or 4 minutes more. Firmly grip the block of bean curd and squeeze it through your fingers into the onion mixture. The texture should resemble scrambled eggs. Break up any large chunks with a spatula.

Add the other ingredients and stir. Correct seasoning with Bragg Aminos and drizzle the rest of the olive oil over the mixture. Turn off the heat and leave covered for 2 or 3 minutes to allow the flavors to develop and mix before serving.

For a hearty vegetarian breakfast serve with Spicy Potato Cakes (p. 203) and buttered toast.

BEVERAGE RECOMMENDATION

Coffee or Tea

Cornmeal Trout with Bacon & Spicy Cottage Fries

There are many ways to cook a trout. This is one of the simplest and most honest. The cornmeal coating fries to a crisp crust and keeps the trout's flesh moist during the time it takes to cook. By repeating the dipping and dredging process, the cornmeal coating and its effects can be increased, but it must dry between coatings.

FOR THE FISH

4 fresh whole trout, approximately 8 inches long, gutted and washed with heads and tails intact

1 cup milk

1 egg

1/2 cup yellow cornmeal mixed with salt and pepper to taste

12 strips bacon

2 cups mild oil such as safflower or grapeseed

FOR THE COTTAGE FRIES

1 medium yellow onion, chopped fine

1 red or green bell pepper, chopped medium

1 vine-ripened tomato, chopped medium or same amount of canned tomatoes drained and chopped medium

4 medium red potatoes with skins on, gently simmered until nearly tender, peeled and cut into 1/2-inch dice

Salt and fresh ground black pepper to taste

Cayenne pepper to taste

Fresh squeezed lemon juice

Fresh pine needles or rosemary needles for garnish (optional)

SERVES 4

In this recipe the freshness of the fish is of paramount importance. Also of critical importance is its cooking time and temperature. Too cool a pan makes the cornmeal coating heavy and oily. Too hot and it will scorch, ruining the delicate flavors.

Blot trout dry with paper towels. In a medium-sized mixing bowl add milk and egg and whisk until smooth. Pour cornmeal mixture onto a plate. One at a time, dip trout first in the egg mixture, taking care to completely coat each fish. Then dip in seasoned cornmeal mixture — again, completely coating the outside surface of each fish. After trout has been coated once and dried, repeat both steps for a second coating. Set aside on a wire rack to dry while you fry the bacon.

Pour the 2 cups of oil in a 12-inch frying pan. The oil should be about 1/2 inch deep, which will submerge the bacon, eliminating over- and undercooked areas. Heat oil over medium-low heat until hot and place bacon in hot oil, taking care to prevent scorching. Turn as needed until thoroughly cooked and crisp. Your sense of smell is a good indicator of the proper frying temperature. Remove bacon to a plate covered with paper towels and place in a warm oven.

If you have three frying pans, divide the bacon fat/oil mixture among the three. Add enough to the two trout pans to bring their levels up to 1/4 inch. If you only have one or two pans cook the bacon first then the potatoes and put them in a warm oven while you cook the trout. Over medium-low, heat the bacon fat/oil mixture to well below the smoking point and put the coated fish into the pan. Watch closely to determine if the heat needs to be adjusted. Cook the trout, turning once, until the meat is done but still moist and the skin crisp. Over medium-low this takes about 10 minutes for each inch of thickness (5 minutes per side — measured from side to side through its thickest part).

To prepare the potatoes, sauté the onion for a minute or two in 2 tablespoons of the bacon-flavored oil then add the bell pepper, tomato and potatoes. Season with salt, pepper and cayenne pepper to taste. Cook until potatoes are tender and turning golden brown. Squeeze a little lemon juice over both the potatoes and the trout and serve with the bacon. Garnish with fresh pine needles or fresh rosemary needles, if desired.

Trout prepared this way accompanied with bacon and potatoes makes a satisfying breakfast. Serve with lemon wedges, buttered toast, Fresh Ripe Tomato Salsa (p. 245) or Tomatillo Salsa (p. 255).

BEVERAGE RECOMMENDATION

Coffee or Tea

During the years we lived on the ranch in Strawberry our relatives would visit and fish the legendary Strawberry Reservoir. At day's end they would bring back big bright-eyed, native trout that my mother would dredge in yellow cornmeal, pan fry and serve with hot, baking-powder biscuits and brown eggs for breakfast. To this day I don't think I've eaten better food than that was to my young senses.

What poet could resist
writing about a sunny,
cold Spring morning with
a sap bucket hanging on
a great maple and its
dripping essence finding
its way into the great
American Breakfast?

And when the sap is
boiled down and day is
done, there is fine Whiskey
to be sipped before
a maplewood fire.

Eggs in Ramekins with Herbs & Buttered Crumbs

To achieve moist, even results, these eggs are first poached then baked. The finished dish has a crisp, golden crumb topping with flavors married in the heat of the oven. For a nice weekend brunch or breakfast serve with good country ham and buttered toast.

4 tablespoons butter plus some for the ramekins

1/2 cup plain whole grain or white breadcrumbs

1 tablespoon fresh minced herbs such as chives, thyme, chervil or tarragon

8 large fresh eggs

2 tablespoons white wine vinegar

1/2 cup half-and-half at room temperature

Salt and pepper to taste

Strained juice of 1 lemon

Cayenne pepper

SERVES 4

Preheat oven to 450° F.

To poach the eggs: Bring 3 or 4 inches of water and vinegar to a boil in a wide saucepan that has a tight-fitting lid. Once the water has boiled, turn the heat off and gently break open 4 of the eggs, one at a time, into a large soup ladle and gently lower each one into the water so it won't break. Cover with the lid. Fill a large dish with cool water and set aside. After about 3 minutes remove the lid from the eggs and check to see if the whites are opaque. Since they will be finished in a hot oven, they should have enough solidity to hold together but still be underdone. Remove them, one at a time, from the hot water to the cool water with a slotted spoon then repeat with the other 4 eggs.

To assemble the dish: Rub 2 tablespoons of the butter into the crumbs until they are evenly coated, then toss them with half of the herbs. Set aside. Coat the inside of four ceramic ramekins with a little butter and preheat in the 450° F oven for approximately 60 seconds. Remove ramekins and set two of the poached eggs in each. Pour off any excess water that may have collected in the bottom of the ramekins. Season the eggs with salt and pepper to taste.

Pour 1/4 (2 tablespoons) of the half-and-half over the eggs in each ramekin. Evenly divide and sprinkle the buttered breadcrumbs over the eggs. Place the ramekins back in the 450° F oven and bake until the eggs are cooked to desired doneness and the breadcrumbs are a light golden brown (approximately 3 to 7 minutes depending on the size of the ramekin and the eggs). It is better to err on the side of underdone as they will continue to cook from the residual heat and may dry out if not served immediately.

Just before removing the ramekins from the oven, gently melt the rest of the butter. Remove the ramekins and drizzle the melted butter over the eggs before serving. To brighten the flavors sprinkle a few drops of freshly squeezed lemon juice over the eggs and crumbs in each ramekin. Sprinkle the remaining herbs and a whisper of cayenne pepper over each and then serve.

BEVERAGE RECOMMENDATION

For breakfast or brunch serve with Spanish Valley Gewurztraminer. This is an honest, well made wine from Utah's premiere winery in Moab.

Indian Porridge with Pecans & Maple Syrup

We have our own strain of red corn that I have been selecting and growing for over 35 years. It makes a richly flavored porridge. We remove the dried kernels from their cobs and grind it fresh just before using it. The rich fragrance and flavor of corn is at its peak then. If you don't have a grain grinder, blue cornmeal can usually be found in a good grocery store and yellow always — although the instant yellow is usually genetically modified and overprocessed. It still makes a decent porridge. Cornmeal cereal was my mother's favorite and one of mine.

1 cup fine, stone-ground corn

4 cups spring water

Salt to taste

Maple syrup to taste

1/8 cup pecans, chopped

SERVES 4

This is a good dish for a leisurely breakfast. It goes well with whole-grain buttered toast and keemun black tea or good coffee. Drizzle maple syrup over each serving. Sprinkle pecans on top and serve with coconut milk or half-and-half. Peaches and berries are also good scattered over the top.

Whisk the cornmeal and cold spring water together in a saucepan, making sure there are no lumps. Bring the mixture to a simmer. Turn the heat to low and stir often while cooking to prevent scorching. Stirring constantly is even better. Thin with additional spring water if necessary. Cook until all taste of rawness is gone (about 15 minutes for whole-grain cornmeal). Add salt, stir and let sit for a minute or two to allow the salt to dissolve. Stir again, taste and add more if necessary. (If it tastes flat it needs more salt, but it should not taste salty.) Ladle into bowls and let cool for a few minutes before serving.

CODDLED EGGS WITH FRESH TOMATO SALSA FOR A DOZEN PEOPLE

This recipe is visually appealing, delicious, satisfying, quick and simple, so it makes an excellent casual breakfast for a large number of people. The challenge is to serve twelve people before the eggs cool off. Here, as in all simple recipes, the quality of the ingredients is particularly important.

24 large, fresh eggs

Water to cover

6 cups fresh tomato salsa*

Dab of butter or dash of extra virgin olive oil for each serving

Salt or Bragg Liquid Aminos (see resources) and fresh ground pepper to taste

3 tablespoons finely chopped cilantro or chives

SERVES 12

*You may use commercial bottled salsa, but there is little to recommend it other than a lack of ingredients to make fresh salsa.

Coddled eggs have a softer texture than boiled eggs because they are cooked with more gentle heat. If you prefer a firmer texture, use the boiled version and serve them the same way. (If you are not familiar with the difference between a coddled egg and boiled, or are at an unfamiliar altitude, do a preliminary test. The temperatures here are calculated for sea level.) Both versions go well with hot, buttered Sweet Corn Bread (p. 42) or buttered toast and coffee or tea.

Fresh Ripe Tomato Salsa (p. 245) is best when tomatoes are at their seasonal peak — usually sometime in August in the Northern Hemisphere.

For coddled eggs: Place cold eggs in large bowl of extra warm water to bring them to room temperature. As they are warming, set a large pan of water on high heat and bring to a boil. When it reaches a rolling boil take it off the heat. With a large soup ladle gently lower the eggs to the bottom — so they don't crack — and cover with a lid. Start timing the eggs. They will take 6 to 12 minutes. A small, soft-coddled egg takes about 6 minutes; a large, firmly coddled egg about 12. Remove from the hot water and put them in cold water for 30 seconds to cool enough to handle. With your hands quickly remove eggs to a large mixing bowl and serve immediately.

For boiled eggs: Cover cold eggs with cold water by about 2 inches. Place them, uncovered, over medium-high heat. When the first large bubbles start to rise to the surface, lower the heat to low and begin timing. It takes about 4 minutes for soft eggs (whites almost totally congealed), and 10 for hard (which have dry, sulfury yolks and are ruined eggs). Because of the number of eggs being cooked at once, they will probably be stacked and might cook unevenly. To prevent this, with a large spatula, gently move all of the eggs in one direction, or the other, for a few seconds, to distribute the heat. Do this two or three times while they're cooking. This is not necessary with the coddled eggs. If you are cooking at high altitudes make sure to test one or two eggs before cooking a large batch. Use these times as a starting point. The higher the altitude the longer it takes to achieve the same results.

Let the guests remove their own eggs from their shells or do it for them with the help of one or two other guests. In either case, cut the cooking time according to how long the eggs will continue o congeal in their unopened shells. To help make sure the final presentation is warm, while the eggs are cooking, put the salsa in a saucepan and warm it a little over low heat to remove its chill. Don't overheat fresh salsa or it will lose its freshness. Also warm the serving bowls. After putting about a half-cup of warm salsa in the bottom of a warm serving bowl, turn the eggs out on top of the salsa. Put a little butter or olive oil on the eggs, season with salt and pepper and a sprinkle of herbs. Serve immediately.

SPELT PORRIDGE

This is a bone simple, but luxurious dish when prepared correctly. Like all porridges it reaches far back into culinary history. Perhaps because it is such an ancient food it satisfies a deep hunger some people have for breakfast grains. Like all whole grain recipes it's at its best when made with freshly ground grain.

1 cup finely ground spelt

4 cups spring water

Salt to taste
(1/4 to 1/2 teaspoon)

SERVES 4

Thoroughly whisk ground spelt and spring water together until smooth. Place on medium-low heat. Stir continually with a heatproof spatula, so you can keep the bottom and sides of the pan properly scraped. Simmer for 10 to 15 minutes. Season to taste with salt. Pour into bowls and let cool for a few minutes before serving.

Serve with coconut milk, cow's milk or half-and-half. Dribble a little maple syrup or honey over the top of each serving. It may also be cooked with a handful of currants or raisins.

Scatter seasonal fruit or crushed raw nuts over the top if desired.

BEVERAGE RECOMMENDATION

Serve with Chocolate Nut Milk (p. 312).

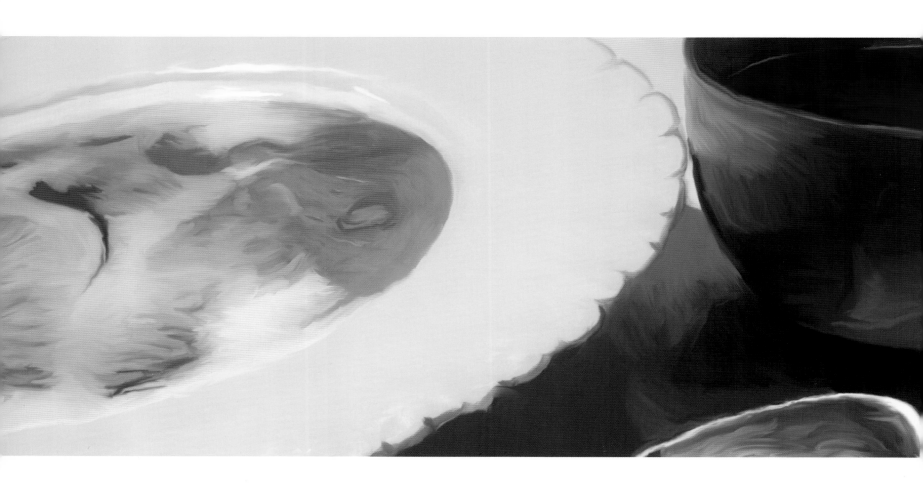

A Bold Experiment

{ SALAD }

A BOLD EXPERIMENT

I will always remember my birthday in April 2005. I was driving our farm tractor alongside a dormant wetland on the family farm. It was dry and solid because of a drought that had been dragging on for years, and it was covered with a layer of dry bull rushes. I had a cultivator attached to the tractor, and on an impulse I decided to see what kind of soil lay under the thick dry thatch on the one-acre-plus area. I drove out over the thick mat and lowered the cultivator, and to my surprise it immediately sank through the thatch and into the soil below with very little resistance. It turned up the richest soil I had ever seen. I was elated and called my mother, the matron of the family farm where she also had grown up. She caught the excitement and gave me permission to go forward with my idea of growing produce on what we had always called "the swamp." The experiment only lasted one season but what a remarkable season it turned out to be. I'm not sure how long that swamp had been there. It could have been hundreds of years. The soil had the consistency of peat moss. It was saturated with organic matter.

Within a few hours I had prepared a remarkably rich seedbed. First I harrowed it. (A harrow is like a big comb.) It very effectively dragged off the thatch, which I deposited around the edge. Then I attached our disc to the tractor. Usually the first step with virgin soil would be to plow and then disc or harrow to break up the lumps. That was unnecessary. The disc dropped into the soil up to the axle, and dark loamy earth poured out of the back end. To see a seedbed of that quality was a rare and exhilarating experience for me.

The next step was to shovel the soil from the two-foot walkways, leaving a five-foot-wide raised bed, tossing the soil from the walkways onto the strips. The seeds were then planted in the rich, spongy beds.

Despite the drought the water table was high enough to nurture the plants once they were established, so irrigation was largely taken care of by nature. Within days plants began germinating and pushing up from the soil. It was quite remarkable. The amount of food we grew from that one acre that year, in addition to the land we regularly farmed, yielded as much produce as I was able to sell. We grew English peas, fava beans, turnips, beets, sweet corn, several varieties of summer squash, cucumbers, several varieties of melons, mixed baby lettuces, arugula, beautiful French breakfast radishes and a stunning array of fingerling potatoes. The soil was so full of organic matter than one day I decided to check on a bed of potatoes to see if they were ready. Rather than digging up a perfectly good plant and possibly finding out it wasn't ready, I slipped my hand down the side of its perimeter. My hand slipped underneath the plant with ease and I could feel the individual potatoes. Some were ready and others were not. I harvested the mature ones and would come back after a few days to check on it again. It was a little like milking a cow. Rather than the usual method of digging up the entire plant, I would harvest the individual plants as they matured. I'd never seen anything like it before.

For two of the three years we farmed, I delivered produce to about 30 restaurants every Thursday. Our first stop was the Sundance Resort in Provo Canyon. They have an excellent fine dining restaurant named "The Tree Room." At the time the chef was Colton Soelberg. Like almost all of the chefs, it was always a pleasure to work with him. He not only purchased a lot of produce but his level of enthusiasm was infectious. Because it was the first delivery

the truck was always loaded to its maximum capacity and it was always a pleasure to see the look on his face when I pulled the coolers from the truck, sat them on the ground and opened their lids. Inside, in two or three inches of ice water was some of the finest produce any chef could possibly hope for and he was always elated. At that time I think we were the only farm that delivered locally grown produce to the restaurants we served. It took years for me to realize how unusual that was. The one thing that was always apparent was the amount of appreciation and respect the chefs lavished on us. It was a deeply satisfying experience for me. One of the great ironies of those farm years was, what with the tight budget we operated on, we were unable to afford to eat in the restaurants to which we delivered produce.

Another image I will never forget is when my mother would drive out from our ranch house across the valley from the farm and set up her lounge chair on the edge of the beds to watch us working. The Thursday morning harvest was her favorite. She was always amazed at the amount of produce that came from that acre. By the end of the season the water table started to rise and by late fall as we harvested the last beds, the water, as if perfectly aware of what we were doing, closed in, and our one-year experiment was over.

PINK POTATO SALAD

I learned the original recipe from *The Good Cook,* a wonderful set of Time-Life Books published in the early 1980s. Richard Olney, the chief series consultant, was, through my early years of learning to cook, my most influential teacher. He is no longer with us but to him I tip my hat.

The amount of pink in the finished salad depends on both the potato and the wine. The question is whether you are going for color or flavor. Give me the latter. This salad admirably accompanies grilled meats or full-flavored chicken dishes such as Coq au Vin.

---

8 medium-sized boiling potatoes such as Yukon Gold

1/2 teaspoon sea salt

1/2 cup good red table wine that should also be served with the meal

2 tablespoons of a combination of minced fresh tarragon, parsley and chervil

1 tablespoon red wine vinegar

1 generous teaspoon Mother Alvey's Mustard (p. 239) or Dijon Mustard (optional)

1/4 cup extra virgin olive oil

Freshly ground pepper to taste

SERVES 4

Peel and slice the potatoes into 1/8-inch slices. Rinse them in cold water to wash off the starch so they won't stick together. Pat them dry. Steam them, until tender, about 15 to 20 minutes.

Dissolve the salt in the wine and set aside. Place the potato slices evenly on a platter in a layer or two while they are hot. Generously sprinkle the seasoned wine over them. Tilt the platter a little and use a spoon to baste the potatoes with the wine that collects at one end of the platter. After the potatoes have been basted and have soaked for about 30 minutes, pour the excess wine into a jar and reserve it for cooking. Taste, and correct the seasoning if necessary. If you want, add a little bacon fat to the salt and wine mixture and baste the potatoes the same way.

Put half of the herbs in a mortar with a generous pinch of salt and crush them with a pestle to bring out their flavor. Add the vinegar and whisk until the salt has dissolved. Whisk in the mustard. Add the olive oil and whisk until it becomes a smooth emulsion. Lightly dress the potatoes turning them gently with your hands so they won't break apart. Correct the seasoning with salt and a few grinds of pepper, sprinkle on the rest of the herbs and serve.

BEVERAGE RECOMMENDATION

Accompany with the same or a similar wine used to marinate the potatoes. For simply seasoned, grilled meat such as lamb chops a good choice would be a fine Petite Syrah such as a nicely aged Fulton from St. Helena, California. For Coq au Vin with the heady combination of onions, mushrooms, red wine, brandy, salt pork, garlic and parsley, pour a simple inexpensive Malbec from Argentina.

A BOLD EXPERIMENT

CRISP ROMAINE WITH ROASTED RED PEPPER DRESSING

This salad is meant to be eaten with your fingers as whole, dressed leaves—even on formal occasions. It makes a crisp, textural contrast when served on a cold plate alongside a smooth soup, such as Smoky Squash, Roasted Red Pepper, Pine Nut, Cilantro Soup (p. 103). Many varieties of heirloom, romaine-type lettuces, such as White Paris Cos or Bath Cos, can be grown in the kitchen garden or found in farmer's markets. They are definitely superior to the commercial romaine you find in most supermarkets, but a respectable version of this salad can be made with the more delicate inner leaves of the commercial variety.

1 red bell pepper

1 clove garlic

Salt to taste

1 tablespoon Bragg Apple Cider Vinegar (see resources)

4 tablespoons extra virgin olive oil

1/4 of one medium-sized sweet, white or mild red onion, chopped fine

1 tablespoon minced Italian flat leaf parsley

1 large head romaine lettuce

Freshly ground pepper to taste

SERVES 2

*Reserve the good outer leaves. Pack them in a buttered, tight-lidded saucepan and cook over low heat until tender. Season with salt and pepper and a dash of red wine vinegar. Serve as a side dish.

Roast the pepper directly over a wood fire or gas flame turning every few minutes until evenly blackened. Put it in a paper bag and crimp the top closed for 20 or 30 minutes. Cut the pepper lengthwise into quarters. Scrape off the black outer skin and the membrane and seeds from the inside. Do not rinse off the pepper as it will diminish the smoky taste. Chop the pepper into 1/8-inch dice.

In a mortar, crush a clove of garlic and pinch of salt to a smooth paste with a pestle. Add a tablespoon of the chopped red pepper and crush to a coarse paste with another pinch of salt. Add the vinegar to the red pepper mixture and whisk together. Add the olive oil and whisk until all are blended into a smooth emulsion. Mix the onion, parsley and the rest of the chopped pepper into the dressing. It will be very thick.

Strip the outer leaves from the romaine until you get to the tender, more flawless inside leaves For the salad, make sure the lettuce is cold, clean, crisp and blotted dry before assembling, taking care not to break the leaves. Lay the romaine leaves all the same direction on a large platter. Pour the dressing mixture over them and gently toss with your hands. Most of the dressing solids will fall out of the leaves so before serving them on individual plates, spoon it back onto the leaves. Dress with a few grinds of pepper and serve.

A BOLD EXPERIMENT

Smoky and Crisp Pepper Salad

FOR THE SALAD

2 each of red, green and yellow bell peppers, seeded, stemmed and cut into matchstick-sized pieces

1 medium-sized sweet onion, chopped fine

1 tablespoon finely chopped fresh cilantro or fresh parsley

1 firm, ripe Hass avocado, pitted, skin removed, cut into 1/4-inch dice

FOR THE DRESSING

1 tablespoon pepitas (Mexican pumpkin seeds), toasted in a dry frying pan until light golden brown (pine nuts or sunflower seeds may be substituted)

Pinch of cumin seed, toasted in a dry frying pan until fragrant

1 small clove garlic

1 mild poblano pepper, roasted, peeled, seeded and chopped fine

Salt and freshly ground black pepper to taste

1 tablespoon fresh squeezed lime juice

4 tablespoons good avocado oil or extra virgin olive oil

4 small squash blossoms for garnish

8 cilantro sprigs for garnish

SERVES 4

This salad combines both the fruity crispness of raw peppers and the soft, smokiness of roasted pepper dressing, giving it a unique, unexpected texture and flavor. It is especially good with grilled meats and fresh pasta dishes.

Gently toss the salad ingredients together in a bowl, taking care not to crush the avocado pieces. Refrigerate while preparing the dressing. Grind the pepitas, cumin seed, garlic and poblano pepper with a little salt to a paste in a mortar and pestle. Whisk in the lime juice followed by the oil until you achieve a smooth emulsion. Correct the seasoning. Dress the salad.

Plate the salads and grind a little black pepper over each if desired. Garnish each plate with a squash blossom and cilantro sprigs.

A BOLD EXPERIMENT

WINTER GREENS

Because greens grown in the winter have no insect or snail damage, they are the year's most pristine and ready at the time they are least expected and consequently are the most appreciated. This method of providing such an exquisite luxury through the cold months has the allure of magic, but it's really quite simple. The system consists of a simple wooden box and a simple system of sun control, using a translucent plastic to protect the tender plants from the winter storms, and shade cloth in the hot months to prevent the plants from growing too quickly and going to seed before they are harvested. After the construction of the box itself, the most important consideration is its location. Ideally it should be placed against a brick, stone or concrete wall (however, it still works quite well without this advantage). These massive surfaces act as solar collectors storing the sun's heat during the day and releasing it into the box's interior through the night. In the winter the sun stays quite low in the sky so the box's top surface should have a slope that captures as much of the sun's rays as possible, and it should be oriented as closely as possible to the north-south axis so the sun floods into the box's interior unimpeded by shadows and for as long as possible during those short days. In the Southern Hemisphere, all of these directions and angles are progressively reversed as you move from one hemisphere to another.

The grow box can be built in place or in a more convenient space such as a shop, and then carried to its final location. All four sides are insulated but its bottom is left open so it can rest directly on the ground, supplying heat from the soil depths to the roots which penetrate to absorb heat as well as moisture and nutrients.

For each new yearly cycle the soil should be replaced or at least rejuvenated with organic materials to replace the nutrients that are withdrawn from the soil with each crop. It should be free of weed seeds and chemicals of any kind. Once the bed is carefully prepared, scatter seeds and rake them into the soil and then gently water with a fine mist and cover with a layer of black plastic. Each day a corner of the plastic should be lifted to monitor the seeds until they sprout. At that point the plastic should be removed, allowing the new crop access to sunlight. Using black plastic for this purpose is a refinement on nature. It traps moisture and keeps the seeds damp as a higher percentage of seeds germinate in darkness. Of course this piece of plastic can be saved and reused for many seasons. A further refinement is to pierce the plastic with hundreds of small slits with a sharp paring knife. This will allow you to water the seeds when necessary from the top, without removing the plastic, until the seeds sprout.

Too much heat can accumulate in the box's tightly constructed, well-insulated interior, so it is important to allow the heat to escape on sunny days even in the winter. I use a small piece of two by four on a small hinge that I can flip up under the lid. Too much heat can encourage the growth of mold in the box's interior, so it must be watched carefully.

Once the box's frame is built, the lid must be covered with plastic both top and bottom. Either 6mm clear plastic from a hardware store or a more rigid and permanent plastic sheet can be used. The lighter plastic must be replaced once a year in the fall. In the early summer both types of plastic must be removed and replaced by shade cloth on the top surface only. The ridged plastic can be stored until fall when the cycle starts over.

Shade cloth comes in different percentages of light to shade ratios. The percentage is best determined by talking to a nursery expert in your area. Light-gauge plastic is installed by first stapling it on the top edge surface along the hinge side of the lid, then drawing it across the top and stapling it to the opposite top edge. It is then drawn over and around the 2 x 4-inch opposite the hinge side and then across the bottom to the edge below and stapled below where it was first stapled. This provides a large air pocket between the top and bottom layers. Wood lathe can be nailed over the staples on the top surface for extra strength.

If you have heavy snow in your area, you may want to consider using the heavier, rigid plastic sheeting. It can be removed and saved each year and used for several years before it wears out. In the spring when the plastic-to-shade-cloth conversion is made, the remaining plants from the winter crop should be removed and the grow box soil tilled and enriched with compost, and the planting procedure repeated. With a little care and attention to detail, using either new or recycled materials and good sun exposure, this system can provide you with high-quality salad greens all year.

Also important to consider, in the fall greens are planted ahead so they get a good start before the temperature drops and growth slows down. Otherwise they have a difficult time establishing themselves in the cold. Depending on your local weather, the lead time should be three to five weeks before the temperature drops below freezing at night. The plants should be an inch to an inch-and-a-half by freezing time so their leaf surface is large enough to collect enough sunlight to drive their growth.

Even though water consumption falls off during winter, a reliable watering system is essential. The beds must be monitored and watered as needed. Depending on the type of plant, approximately once a week should work as an average watering cycle in the winter.

Arugula with Goat Cheese and Black Walnut Dressing

Serve this salad before (American style) or after (European style) a full-bodied entree. Black walnuts are a lot of work to shell but well worth the effort. If your preparation time is limited they can be purchased shelled (see resources). Arugula is easy to grow and homegrown is much better than commercially grown. A leaf about 3 inches tall is what I call baby arugula.

4 cups loosely packed baby arugula leaves plus 8 leaves for the dressing

4 tablespoons shelled black walnuts

A silver of raw garlic

Salt to taste

1/4 teaspoon Dijon mustard or to taste (optional)

2 tablespoons Vilux Cognac vinegar or red wine vinegar

8 tablespoons new crop walnut oil or extra virgin olive oil

4 ounces fresh goat cheese rolled into four equal balls then flattened slightly

Freshly ground pepper to taste

SERVES 4

With a mortar and pestle crush 8 arugula leaves, half of the black walnuts and garlic with a little salt. Add mustard if using. When smooth add the vinegar and whisk together thoroughly. Add the walnut oil and whisk until blended into a smooth emulsion. Correct the seasoning. It is important to get the salt balance right in a salad dressing. It is one of the many small details that separates an average cook from a good cook.

Rinse arugula and spin the leaves in a salad spinner. Toss them with enough dressing to evenly coat the leaves but don't overdress them. Arrange a bed of leaves on each plate and set the goat cheese on top. Drizzle a little dressing over the cheese then sprinkle the rest of the walnuts on top. Grind a little fresh black pepper over each salad.

BEVERAGE RECOMMENDATION

By itself this salad is nicely complemented by a Sauvignon Blanc such as Cakebread Cellars, which creates a delightful combination of layered lemon, grapefruit, pear and melon, flavors which play off the rich black walnuts, nutty arugula and creamy goat cheese.

A Bold Experiment

A FEW WORDS ABOUT SALAD DRESSING

Don't use bottled dressings—they are notoriously bad. Even mediocre salads deserve a handmade dressing. If there is not enough time, drizzle fresh squeezed lemon juice or vinegar and olive oil over all, season with good salt and fresh ground pepper and toss. It is far superior to the stuff that comes out of a bottle. To elevate a salad further one of my favorite things to do is what I call "recursive infusion." Use some of the tender bits of the salad that best represent its flavors. Put them in a mortar with a pinch of good salt and crush to a paste with a pestle. Add an acid such as lemon juice or red wine vinegar and whisk in good olive oil. By coating the salad with some of its own ingredients you reinforce its flavor, and you can always depend on it being in harmony with itself.

Its delectable treasure lies inside a shell as tough as steel, its blackness as deep as its mysterious flavor.

Root Salad with Arugula/Basil Vinaigrette

FOR THE SALAD

1 medium carrot, peeled and grated

1/2 medium red or sweet onion, chopped fine

1/2 medium turnip, peeled and grated

1/2 medium parsnip, peeled and grated

1/2 small celery root, peeled and grated

1/2 medium beet, peeled and grated

Salt to taste

2 tablespoons minced, flat leaf or curly leaf parsley plus a few sprigs for garnish

1/4 cup toasted pine nuts (optional)

FOR THE DRESSING

3 or 4 arugula leaves

3 or 4 basil leaves

Salt to taste

2 tablespoons Bragg Apple Cider Vinegar (see resources)

1 teaspoon grainy or smooth Dijon prepared mustard

6 tablespoons extra virgin olive oil

Fresh ground black pepper to taste

SERVES 6 TO 8

NOTE: Other roots that are also good are daikon radish, jicama, rutabaga and Jerusalem artichoke.

Root salad is as close to the earth as a salad gets. With high-quality ingredients this salad is deeply nourishing as well as aesthetically pleasing. To obtain a supply of fresh roots through the winter months, I cover all of our garden root vegetables with about a foot of leaves in the late fall, drive stakes at both ends of the rows, and dig them up all winter through the snow. Unless you live in extremely cold climates, I'm not sure why people bother with root cellars. As soon as a root is pulled up it begins to wither and die. Roots left in the ground, on the other hand, stay crisp, continue to grow with very little sunlight, and get sweeter as the winter progresses. About a month before the soil is plowed in the spring, I rake the leaves from the remaining roots so the sunlight can stimulate new sprouts to grow from the tops. At this time of year the new sprouts are tender delicacies to be used in salads or briefly steamed. Raw or cooked, their flavors are enhanced with walnut or olive oil vinaigrette.

The idea is to end up with more or less equal amounts of each root. Select the size and amount of roots with this in mind. Grate half the roots with a coarse grater and the other half with a fine grater. This creates a more balanced texture than either an all-coarse or all-fine grate will. Place the grated individual roots into separate small bowls. Mix each with a little of the parsley.

Salting any food is also a matter of balance. Add enough salt so that the grated roots have a similar saltiness. Unfortunately, or not, rarely do two people seem to have the exact taste for anything, including salt. The best you can do is please your own palate. Crush the arugula leaves and the basil leaves with a mortar and pestle and a pinch of salt. Add the cider vinegar and the mustard and whisk together. Add the olive oil and whisk until the mixture becomes a silky emulsion. Divide the dressing between the six bowls and toss each separately. Taste each vegetable mixture and correct the seasoning. Roots absorb a lot of flavor. You may want to make extra dressing.

Place a rounded teaspoon of the onion mixture in the middle of a small individual salad plate and evenly space a rounded teaspoon of the other mixtures around the outside. Garnish each plate with a sprig of flat leaf parsley and a grind or two of pepper.

Assorted Tomatoes with Sweet Marjoram and Marinated Olives

This dish can be as colorful as an impressionist painting. Its dramatic visual effect deserves to be a centerpiece. I like to use a generous oval platter for the presentation and to serve Home Bread (p. 51) alongside to sop up the delicious liquid that remains on the platter. It fits pretty much anywhere in the meal — beginning, middle or end.

8 medium, vine-ripened tomatoes preferably mixed, such as Brandywine, Costaluto, Green Zebra or Olga's Giant

Sea salt to taste

A handful of small garnish tomatoes, such as yellow pear or gold currant

Extra virgin olive oil to taste

1 recipe of Marinated Olives (p. 211)

1 tablespoon fresh sweet marjoram leaves for garnish (or fresh basil leaves)

SERVES 8

Core the stem end of the large tomatoes. Cut them into 1/4-inch slices with a serrated bread knife. Arrange them on a platter and sprinkle with salt to taste. Scatter the garnish tomatoes on top then drizzle lightly over all with olive oil. Arrange the olives and the marjoram leaves over the finished platter, keeping in mind the colorful paintings of the French Impressionists.

Green Pea, Avocado, Golden Pepper and Red Onion Salad

Small, new-crop green peas are among the finest of all produce. Their chilled, raw crispness perfectly complements the buttery flesh of an avocado. This salad is nice on the same plate alongside casual meals such as sandwiches or cold cuts. With hot dinners it's best to serve it on a leaf or two of crisp lettuce on a cold salad plate before, after or alongside the main dish.

Bruise the herbs a little in a mortar and pestle with a pinch of salt and whisk in the vinegar until the salt is dissolved. Whisk in the oil until it turns smooth and silky. Lightly toss salad ingredients in a bowl with the dressing. Correct seasoning. Grind a little black pepper over the salad.

FOR THE DRESSING

2 tablespoons finely minced mixture of fresh chervil, chives, parsley and tarragon

Salt to taste

1 tablespoon Vilux Cognac vinegar or red wine vinegar

3 tablespoons extra virgin olive oil

Freshly ground black pepper to taste

FOR THE SALAD

1 cup freshly shelled baby green peas

2 large ripe avocados, pitted, halved and cut into 1/8-inch slices or 1/4-inch dice

1 golden bell pepper, stemmed, seeded, ribs removed, diced medium

1 red onion, sliced 1/8 inch thick and pulled apart into rings

SERVES 4 TO 8

Slivered Celery, Apple, Celeriac and Sweet Onion

Baby celery is best for this recipe but if none is available use the tender leafy stalks of the celery heart.

FOR THE SALAD

2 or 3 hearts of celery (reserve some of the light green leaves for garnish and dressing)

1 Granny Smith Apple

1/2 sweet onion sliced very thinly across its equator and pulled apart into rings

FOR THE DRESSING

1 or 2 leaves from the celery heart stalks, minced

2 tablespoons grated celeriac (celery root)

2 tablespoons Granny Smith apple peeled, sliced and minced

2 tablespoons minced shallot

Sea salt to taste

2 tablespoons Bragg Apple Cider Vinegar (see resources)

4 tablespoons extra virgin olive oil

Freshly ground mixed green, red and black peppercorns (or black peppercorns)

SERVES 4

In the days before they were picked in late summer and rushed to market, apples would be left hanging on their trees for an extended period. This long, slow ripening process in the late fall cold developed them into one of today's forgotten delights — the "water core apple" — a crisp jewel filled with sweet, perfumed juice at its center.

Working with a sharp knife cut the individual stalks of celery heart into 6-inch tapered pieces, about 1/8 inch at the base.

Peel, core and cut the apple into thin slices.

In a mortar, crush the celery leaf, celeriac, apple, shallot and a pinch of salt with a pestle to a medium paste. Add vinegar and whisk together until the salt is dissolved then whisk in the olive oil until it becomes a smooth emulsion.

Place the salad ingredients in a bowl and toss with the dressing. Divide among 4 cold salad plates. Grind a little pepper over each. Garnish each salad with a celery leaf or two and serve.

A BOLD EXPERIMENT

A BOLD EXPERIMENT

Spring Dandelion with Bacon, Egg, Scallion and Violets

This is an early spring salad. It is best when the dandelions are young and tender and the violets are new. Unlike most salads it is better accompanied with wine. With crusty bread it makes a nice, light lunch or supper.

2 cups loosely packed dandelion greens

2 tablespoons white parts of scallions, slivered

1/2 pound natural smoke-cured bacon

Red wine vinegar to taste (about 2 to 3 tablespoons)

Salt to taste

4 soft boiled eggs for garnish

A handful of loosely curled scallion greens

A handful of fresh, spring violet flowers for garnish

Fresh ground black pepper

SERVES 4

Pick through, wash and trim the stem ends then dry the dandelion greens. Wrap them in a damp cotton cloth and chill them in a salad bowl in the refrigerator for about 1 hour. Wash and cut off the green parts of scallions and reserve the white parts. Finely slice the green parts lengthwise into slightly tapered 2 to 3-inch long slivers. They will usually contract into beautiful little Botticelli curls. If they are not curly enough, pull each piece between your thumb and a paring knife blade. Cut the white parts lengthwise through their centers into 1/16-inch-wide slivers. Pat them dry and set them aside.

Cut the eggs lengthwise into quarters with a sharp, thin-bladed knife dipped in water. Rinse the blade and leave it wet between each cut. The yolks should have a moist center. Sprinkle the sliced eggs with a little salt and put them in a small dish. Cover with plastic wrap and set aside.

Fry the bacon over moderate heat until thoroughly crisp. Take care not to raise the heat too high or the bacon will burn and become bitter. Remove the bacon and drain on paper towels. Cut crosswise into 1/4-inch strips or crumble. Set aside. You should have about 6 tablespoons of bacon fat reserved. Whisk 2 to 3 tablespoons of vinegar into the bacon fat to create a smooth emulsion. Correct the seasoning and allow the dressing to sit for a few minutes until the salt has completely dissolved. Taste. Add more salt or vinegar if necessary. Keep in mind that it will taste less salty and less flavorful when it is tossed over the greens. Brush a little dressing over the yolks to moisten and flavor them.

Remove the dandelion greens from the refrigerator. Warm the dressing a little. It should be just warm enough to be whisked together smoothly. Pour a little over the greens and the white onion slivers. Toss to lightly coat them. Divide the greens onto four large dinner plates. Garnish with bacon, eggs, slivered scallion greens and violets and serve. Grind a little fresh black pepper over each salad if desired.

BEVERAGE RECOMMENDATION

A good white Burgundy such as a Louis Latour Chablis tames the smoky bacon flavors and creates a balance with the bacon dressing and egg.

A BOLD EXPERIMENT

Sweetnin' table linens
The smell of scrubbed cotton sweetened in the open air and sunlight
Takes me back — before I was inducted into Kindergarten
To a warm spring day behind our house where I grew up
Beside the clothesline supported by wooden posts under a cumulus sky
I was lying on the grass
Looking up at my mother hanging wet clothes with wooden pins
I watched a silver airplane — a B29 — a bird of war
Droning its way across the patches of blue
Above and between the white cumulus
And I smelled the faint smell of homemade soap
Not knowing how long I would remember that moment
But somehow feeling it register deep in my soul

COUNTRY SUPPER SALAD

Growing up in the country was an experience of seasonal abundance. The big meal, what we called "dinner" was always based on what was available in the garden or from bottled produce on the shelves in the "fruit room." It may have been an old hen for the pot, a mess of turnip greens, new potatoes, a fresh loaf of bread or a bottle of pickled beets. It was always served around noon. The evening meal was simpler, usually homemade bread, milk, cottage cheese and garden vegetables.

My wife and I still have a similar evening ritual but wine and aged cheese have replaced the milk and cottage cheese. Everything else is much the same.

This country salad, much like it was then, is a combination of what is in season and it is always composed on a platter that is passed around the table. It is more of a light supper than a salad. As we did then, we start by harvesting what is in the garden. In early summer it may include fava beans, radishes and baby lettuces. Later as the garden produces in rising and falling waves, tiny string beans, assorted tomatoes and corn appear. In the autumn it may be cabbages and mustard greens, peppers and new potatoes. For variety we may include pinkeye beans that braise during the day in a broth flavored with garlic and fistfuls of sage or rosemary. Round out the meal with thin slices of country ham or salami and chunks of homemade cheese (refer to Farmer's Cheese p. 26, or Spicy White Cheddar p. 28).

Those evening meals on the farm are the inspiration for this salad. If you don't have a garden, seek out the best available sustainably grown produce preferably from local growers when you have the choice. Farmer's markets are a good place to meet local growers and a chance to support one of the healthiest movements in the U.S.

FOR THE SALAD

2 or 3 handfuls of seasonal greens, such as spinach, immature lettuces, mache, mizuna or arugula

Young beets (red or gold) with their greens, steamed until tender

6 raw new carrots

1 medium sweet onion, such as Vidalia, sliced thinly and pulled apart into rings or a bunch of sliced new scallions

Tiny green beans (haricot verts) blanched until tender, plunged into iced water and drained

Fresh sliced tomatoes

1 or 2 heaping tablespoons Pinkeye Beans per plate (p. 120)

FOR THE DRESSING

1/4 clove garlic

Salt to taste

2 tablespoons red wine vinegar

6 tablespoons extra virgin olive oil

Few grinds black pepper

SERVES 4 TO 6

Arrange salad ingredients on individual plates or on a platter. If prepared ahead cover with plastic wrap to retain moisture and put in the refrigerator to chill. Tomatoes should be sliced and added to the salad just before serving. Crush the garlic and a little salt with a mortar and pestle. In the mortar whisk in the vinegar then the olive oil into a smooth emulsion.

Remove salad from the refrigerator. Add tomatoes and toss salad with enough dressing to evenly coat the vegetables. Grind a little fresh pepper over each serving.

BEVERAGE RECOMMENDATION

Our preference with this meal is usually a simple day-to-day red such as a Woodbridge Zinfandel from Lodi, California.

LONG CANYON

{ SOUPS & STOCKS }

LONG CANYON

In the early seventies I was on a horseback trip with my brothers, nephew and father in a pristine wilderness, a place *National Geographic* magazine called "The last true wilderness in the contiguous United States." Located in Southern Utah, it was just north of what would become Lake Powell. Eight of us were riding single file, trailing several pack horses. We had just come around a perilous cliff-side trail approaching the only entry point of an ancient box canyon, named Long Canyon by the early pioneer settlers. We were face-to-face with a makeshift gate of tightly woven cedar posts. My father was in the lead on his favorite trail horse. He dismounted and pulled the posts out, one at a time from the snarl, and laid them aside by the trail. Then, as we all looked on, he raised his hand in a solemn gesture and said: "Today we are going to double the number of white people who have been in this canyon." It was a moment I will never forget.

He, along with several of his boyhood friends who all had ranches and a common need for good working horses, were the only people who knew where that box canyon was and how to get there on over fifty plus miles of a mostly invisible slick-rock trail. For years they used the approximately ten-mile-long by one-mile-wide canyon for breeding their slick-rock horses. Years earlier they had installed a handsome black thoroughbred stallion in the canyon with a dozen or so mustang mares. They would go into the canyon every year to catch the new crop of two-year-olds and take them back to their respective ranches to train. Because they had grown up in that challenging slick-rock terrain, these horses were well suited to do ranch work in that challenging area, something quite difficult for the average ranch horse.

If this ladle could talk it might share tales of honest soup taken on cold nights with good bread, simple wine and friends.

LONG CANYON

CHICKEN, LEMON & LEEK SOUP WITH YOGURT

This is a hearty soup with a meaty texture imparted by the complementary combination of chicken and leeks. With a large dollop of Pavel's Yogurt (see resources) floated on top and a crusty bread, it makes a nice supper.

For best results, use as fresh and natural a chicken as available. One of my jobs growing up on the farm was killing and cleaning chickens for the kitchen pot. I came to know the smell of a good chicken. Conventional, high-volume chickens don't have that same clean, sweet, slightly sulfurous aroma. A free-range chicken will always yield more flavor and stay fresh longer both before and after it is cooked—a sure sign of production integrity.

---

1 4- to 5-pound roasting chicken, giblets reserved

Spring water to cover

2 medium garlic cloves

3 large leeks split lengthwise, washed carefully and cut (greens and all) crosswise on an angle in 2-inch pieces

2 teaspoons lemon zest

Salt to taste

Freshly squeezed lemon juice, strained (about 2 to 4 tablespoons)

Yogurt for garnish

SERVES 8 TO 12

Wash the chicken and place it in a 20-quart stockpot with the giblets. Cover with spring water. Place the pot on medium-high heat and bring to a simmer. Do not allow the broth to boil or it will make the broth cloudy. Lower the heat to medium low. Skim off the foamy residue that forms on top several times until it subsides. Reduce the heat to very low and simmer about 1 hour more. At this point add the garlic and continue simmering until the meat is about to fall off the bone (15 to 30 minutes or more). Turn off the heat and let the chicken cool slightly. Carefully lift the chicken out of the pot by inserting a wooden spoon into the tail-end cavity and steady it with a spatula or tongs. Place chicken in a large bowl. If the chicken falls apart, remove it in pieces with a large slotted spoon. After it has cooled some, cover the bowl with plastic wrap to prevent the chicken from drying out. Let it cool until it can be handled comfortably.

Carefully separate the meat from the bones, skin and gristle and cover with plastic wrap. Strain the cooking liquid through a sieve to remove any solids. Save any good scraps of meat and all the giblets. Cut the breast meat into 2-inch long crosscuts at a sharp angle, to resemble the leeks. Cut the tough skin from the gizzard and discard. Chop the remaining gizzard. Strip the meat from the neck, chop it and reserve. Discard the neck bones. Chop the liver into small pieces. Chop the heart into 3 or 4 pieces. Add all the chopped giblet meat to the reserved chicken meat and cover.

Bring the strained broth to a simmer in a large stockpot. Add the leeks. Simmer on low, stirring occasionally, and cook until they are barely tender, about 20 minutes. Add the reserved meat. Crush the lemon zest, pinch of salt and a little lemon juice with a mortar and pestle. Add the remainder of the juice to the crushed zest in the mortar. Stir together and add to the soup. Lightly season with salt. Taste the soup and if you want it to be more lemony, add the crushed zest and strained juice of another lemon. If possible, allow the flavors to further develop by placing the cooled soup, covered, in the refrigerator for a few hours or overnight. Gently reheat the soup and serve it quite warm. Adjust the salt if needed.

BEVERAGE RECOMMENDATION

This lemony soup goes well with a Sauvignon Blanc like a New Zealand Villa Maria.

Lima Bean and Roasted Red Pepper Soup

This is one of my favorite comfort foods. During preparation it fills the kitchen with rich fall aromas. On a rainy fall day especially, after the peppers have been harvested and the air is pungent with the promise of winter, I like to prepare and serve this soup with warm crusty Home Bread (p. 51) and Spicy White Cheddar Cheese in Grape Leaves (p. 28). Even if you don't have 6 people to feed, it keeps well and the flavor improves for a day or two. Surprisingly, it is good for breakfast with poached or boiled eggs and buttered toast.

2 cups dried lima beans, picked through and washed

6 cups Wild Mushroom Stock (p. 126), chicken stock or spring water

1 medium yellow onion, chopped

2 green bell peppers, roasted, peeled, seeded and chopped (roasting method on p. 106)

2 cloves garlic, crushed

Bragg Liquid Aminos (see resources) to taste

Few sprigs curly leaf parsley, minced

2 tablespoons extra virgin olive oil

SERVES 6

Put the dry beans, stock, onion, green pepper, 1 clove of garlic, and a little Bragg Aminos in an ovenproof pot on medium heat and bring to a boil. (Adding aromatic ingredients at this first stage increases the flavor of the finished dish considerably). As soon as it reaches a boil turn it off and let it rest on the stove for about an hour.

Bring the beans back to a boil, uncovered, for about 10 minutes. Vigorous boiling at this stage will rid the beans of volatile lectins, a mild toxin found in all dry beans. It will give off a distinctive smell that dissipates after a few minutes. Skim off any foamy impurities and lower the heat to a very low flame.

Cover and simmer slowly on low with the lid ajar until the beans are almost tender (30 to 60 minutes). Delicate simmering keeps the beans from disintegrating. Add the second clove of garlic. Cover and place the pot in a preheated 500° F oven. Immediately turn it down to 350° F. Bake for 15 to 20 minutes then remove and check for doneness. (Finishing them in the oven also helps keep them from breaking apart.) Adjust the seasoning with Bragg Aminos, add the parsley and stir. Allow the soup to cool, and the flavors to mature and blend, in the covered pot for several hours or overnight in the refrigerator. Just before serving, reheat the soup and add the olive oil to the pot, or drizzle a little on top of each serving.

BEVERAGE RECOMMENDATION

Serve with a medium-weight, well-balanced Cabernet Sauvignon such as Geyser Peak from Sonoma.

LONG CANYON

With the versatile squash family you can make dumplings, pastas, puddings, pies, cakes, breads and soups. You can serve squash steamed, sautéed, deep fried, pureed, baked, braised, microwaved or boiled. Their preparation can be as simple as a baby summer squash steamed with nothing but a dash of olive oil a little sea salt and a grind or two of black pepper added at the end of the cooking process. You can deep fry their blossoms plain or with a light batter or chop them raw to toss into soups or salads. You can also eat certain squash seeds raw or cooked, plain or seasoned, straight or as garnishes.

LONG CANYON

Smoky Squash, Roasted Red Pepper, Pine Nut, Cilantro Soup

I came up with this recipe on New Year's Eve when I was cooking for friends. They have a "Vita-Mix," an industrial-strength blender. After completely cooking the squash whole in the microwave oven, I discarded the stem, then blended the rest of it — seeds, skin and all — with chicken stock. It turned into an incredibly smooth, intensely flavored puree that hardly required any straining.

This soup is good with the onion version of Flatbread (p. 45) or tortillas. Both are good topped with Mexican cheese such as Añejo or Chihuahua, grated on top of the soup and run under the broiler until it melts.

1 medium butternut or similar squash, stem removed

1 red bell pepper

1/2 cup fresh pine nuts

1 quart of chicken stock, cooked and reduced to 1 pint

1/4 teaspoon smoked chipotle pepper or to taste

1/2 cup cilantro leaves, stems reserved

Cream or half-and-half to taste

2 tablespoons white wine (same as served with the meal)

Salt to taste

SERVES 4 TO 6

Steam the whole squash, or cook it in a covered glass dish in a microwave oven until very soft.

Put the pepper on the stove or a moderate gas flame (or wood fire). Turn it a few times until it is evenly blackened. Remove the pepper from the heat and place it in a paper bag. Roll the top of the bag closed. Let it rest until the flesh has softened and the skin is loosened (about 20 minutes). Remove the charred skin, seed and chop. Set aside.

Roast the pine nuts over medium-low heat in a dry skillet, gently shaking the pan and tossing or stirring the nuts until they are golden brown.

Remove the seeds and pith of the squash, then scoop out the flesh and purée it in a blender with some of the chicken stock until smooth. Add more of the stock until it reaches the consistency of cream. Blend the mixture with one third of the roasted red pepper, all of the chipotle pepper, one fourth of the toasted pine nuts and a few chopped cilantro stems until it is smooth. Add the cream and wine. Blend a little more and correct the seasoning with salt. If you're not using a blender, you'll need to push the cooked mixture through a medium-mesh strainer with a wooden spoon. Strain through a finer strainer until velvety smooth — the consistency of heavy whipping cream.

Divide the soup into bowls and garnish each serving with a few toasted pine nuts, bits of roasted red pepper and a few whole cilantro leaves.

BEVERAGE RECOMMENDATION

A good match for this spicy, smoky soup is a Beringer Gewurztraminer which has just the right amount of residual sugar, tropical spice and hints of apricot.

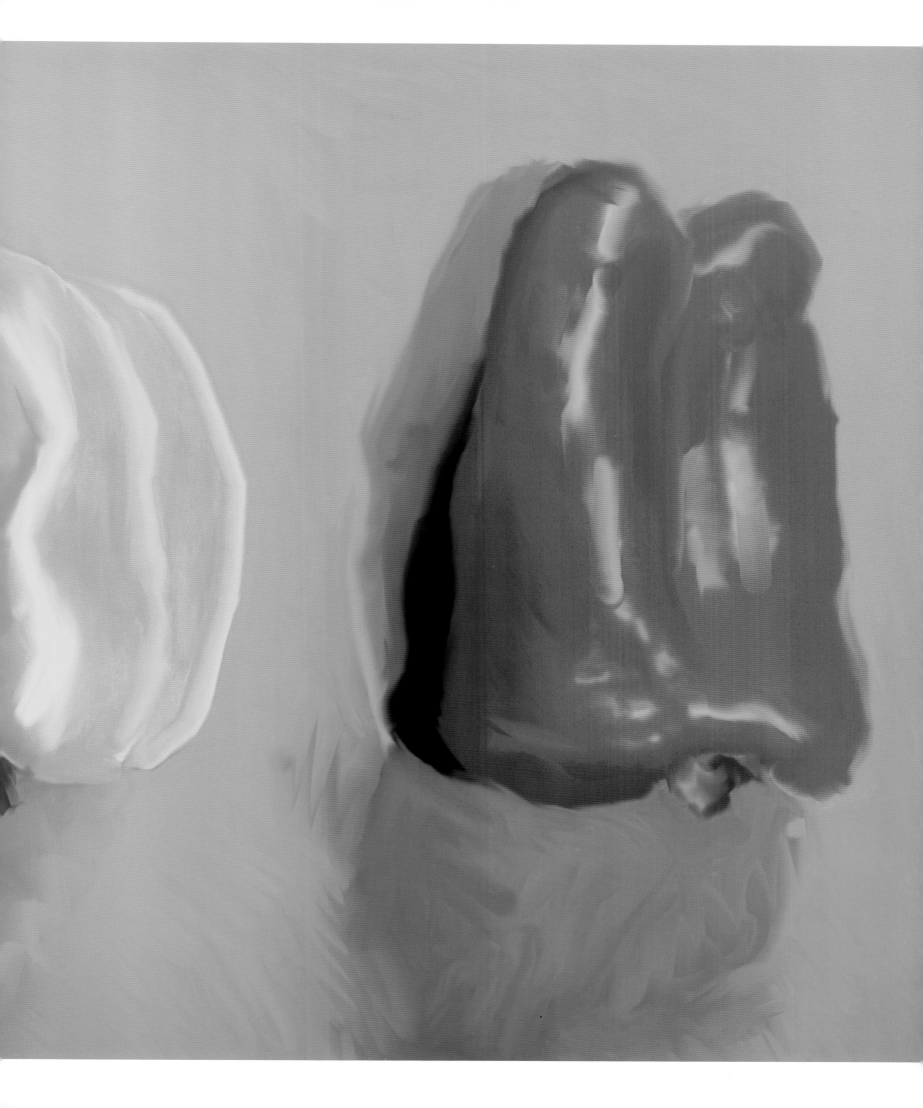

Corn Soup with Three Pepper Salsa

FOR THE SALSA

1 each green, yellow and red bell pepper

Strained lime juice to taste

Salt to taste

FOR THE SOUP

6 ears sweet corn

1/4 cup clarified Sour Cream Butter (p. 20) or half butter and half corn oil

1 quart spring water (or 2 quarts chicken stock reduced to 1 quart)

2 cups coconut milk or cream, or half of each

1 tablespoon lime juice, strained

Salt to taste

Cornstarch to thicken (optional)

SERVES 6

This is a delightful summer soup best served at room temperature. As a first course, it suits a trout or salmon dinner nicely.

In my kitchen, its life began as an Alice Water's recipe from the mid-1980s. She used butter instead of a corn oil and butter mixture and she dressed her soup with a tomato, basil and whole-corn kernel salsa. In my version, I use three different roasted peppers for the salsa.

I also altered her method for extracting the corn flavor, preferring to cook it less and processing it a little in a blender, but not enough to break down the cellulose, which reduces the delicate flavor of the corn. This method imparts a very fresh corn flavor. I also like to use reduced chicken stock instead of water and to include coconut milk mixed with cream instead of simply using cream. My Indonesian-born wife introduced me to the combination of corn and coconut milk — a favorite in that country.

Put the peppers on the stove over a moderate gas flame (or wood fire). Turn them a few times until they are evenly blackened. Remove the peppers from the heat and place them in a paper bag. Roll the top of the bag closed. Let them rest until the flesh has softened and the skin is loosened (about 20 minutes).

Scrape the charred skin from the flesh with a paring knife taking care to remove all traces of it. Quarter the peppers lengthwise. Remove the stem, membranes and seeds from the interior and discard. Keep each color separate and chop the peppers into confetti-sized pieces. Season to taste with salt and lime juice. Set aside.

Cut the corn from the cobs into a large bowl or pan. Using a knife, scrape additional milk from the cobs into a bowl.

Put the corn, corn milk and butter in a large saucepan over medium heat. Stir and scrape the pan continually with a heatproof spatula to prevent scorching. After the corn has softened a bit and started to release its rich aroma, add the water or stock. Scrape any bits from the bottom of the pan and bring it to a simmer for about 10 minutes, stirring and scraping frequently.

Remove the broth from the heat and let it cool for 5 to 10 minutes. Put it in a blender or food processor and blend to a smooth consistency. Push the mixture through a medium sieve with a wooden spoon. Discard any cellulose left behind. Stir in the coconut cream and lime juice. Pour through a finer strainer or a chinois if desired. Lightly season to taste with a little salt. If you use corn oil instead of butter, it will be slightly thinner, so you may want to thicken the soup with a teaspoon of cornstarch mixed well with some stock. Whisk the mixture into the soup and bring it back to a simmer, stirring until it thickens (about 2 minutes).

Float a small spoonful of each of the three peppers separately on the top of each bowl of soup and serve.

BEVERAGE RECOMMENDATION

A good match is a 2005 Elyse, a delicious white wine from the L'Ingénue winery in the Sierra Foothills of California. It is usually paired with fish or fowl so either would be a good accompaniment if you wish to continue with the same wine.

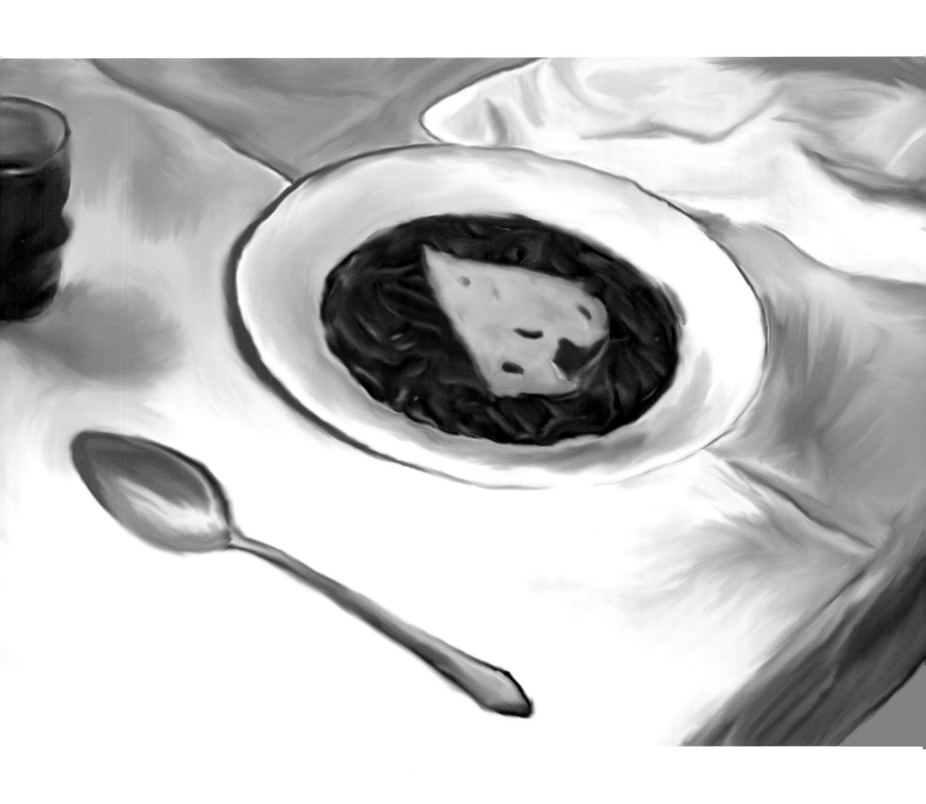

LONG CANYON

CARAMELIZED ONION SOUP WITH ROSEMARY-GARLIC BREAD

This is a simple, heart-warming soup, good for a light supper. The heartier version has a few gratings of cheese on top and is finished in a hot oven or under a broiler. The rich flavor of the soup is obtained by slowly cooking the onions, caramelizing their sugars until they turn a rich mahogany color.

FOR THE SOUP

4 medium yellow onions

6 tablespoons extra virgin olive oil

3 tablespoons butter

4 cups beef stock, chicken stock, or spring water

Dry white wine or dry sherry for deglazing pan

Salt or Bragg Liquid Aminos (see resources) to taste

3 or 4 tablespoons minced flat leaf parsley

FOR THE BREAD

1/2 cup Rosemary Garlic Oil (p. 239)

3 tablespoons extra virgin olive oil

4 large or 8 small slices good crusty bread

SERVES 4

Remove the core from the tough end of the onions and cut in half lengthwise. Peel the outer layer and discard. Slice lengthwise into a medium-fine julienne. A sharp serrated bread knife works well. Put 2 tablespoons olive oil and the butter in a heavy, nonreactive stock pot with a tight lid. Add the onions and sauté, covered, over low heat, stirring as needed to prevent scorching, until they become a rich mahogany color, about 45 minutes. Add a splash of white wine or water if the onions begin to stick to the pot.

Add more wine as needed, scrape the pan drippings to loosen and add the stock. Bring the mixture to a simmer, scraping any bits from the bottom of the pan. Season to taste with salt or Bragg Aminos and add the parsley.

Preheat oven to 450° F and make Rosemary Garlic Oil ahead of time.

Brush the oil liberally on both sides of the bread. Place a slice or two on top of the soup in individual bowls. Place under the broiler or in the preheated oven, until the bread is golden brown.

For the heartier version: Place a slice of toasted rosemary garlic bread in the bottom of the soup bowls and cover with soup. Or place bread on top of the soup, grate cheese such as Spicy White Cheddar Cheese in Grape Leaves (p. 28) or sharp cheddar over the bread and place the bowls under a hot broiler (watching carefully) or in a preheated 450° F oven until the cheese turns bubbly and the bread is golden brown. Remove from the oven with care and serve immediately.

BEVERAGE RECOMMENDATION

With the lighter no-cheese version made with water or chicken stock serve a full-flavored Chardonnay such as a J. Lohr, Monterey. With the hearty beef stock and cheese version serve a rich, red Zinfandel like Ridge from Geyserville.

MEXICAN SOUP

This soup has been evolving in my kitchen since the 1960s. It is best when made with fresh produce, but if necessary it can be made quite successfully with frozen lima beans, frozen corn and canned tomatoes. With a sprinkle of grated cheese, cilantro leaves and diced avocado, it makes a colorful, satisfying everyday soup. Serve with tortillas or Flatbread (p. 45).

In a large sauté pan, cook the onion and garlic in 3 tablespoons of olive oil over a low flame until transparent (about 5 minutes). Add the peppers and continue cooking for 5 more minutes. Add all the other ingredients (except the garnishes) Gently simmer until the potatoes are tender (about 20 minutes). Correct the seasoning, remove the pan from the heat and let it rest for an hour or more before serving. Leaving it covered overnight in the refrigerator will bring out the best flavors.

To serve, gently warm the soup through. Add the rest of the olive oil and lime juice. Gently stir into the soup and ladle into soup bowls. Garnish the individual bowls with the cheese, diced avocado and a few cilantro leaves.

BEVERAGE RECOMMENDATION

Best with a mild, low-hopped Mexican beer such as Dos Equis or Tecate, Limeade with Lime Zest and Honey (p. 318).

FOR THE SOUP

1/2 large yellow onion, chopped medium

2 cloves garlic, crushed

3 tablespoons extra virgin olive oil

1 medium red bell pepper, chopped

1 medium green bell pepper, chopped

3 ripe tomatoes, seeded and diced or one 14-ounce can crushed tomatoes

1/2 cup shelled fresh, immature beans such as limas or favas

1/2 cup yellow sweet corn kernels

3 cups peeled and cut potatoes, 1/2-inch dice

3 quarts chicken stock, chicken broth or spring water

1/4 teaspoon ground cumin or 1/4 teaspoon cumin seeds, lightly toasted in a dry skillet and crushed with a mortar and pestle

Smoked, dry or paste chipotle pepper to taste

Salt to taste

FOR THE GARNISH

3 tablespoons olive oil

Juice of 1 lime

Grated queso Añejo or Romano cheese

1 or 2 large ripe avocados, cut into 1/4-inch dice

1 tablespoon whole cilantro leaves

SERVES 8

LONG CANYON

LONG CANYON

Fresh Pea and Watermint Soup

Peas are one of the most pleasurable bounties from the garden and pair beautifully with garden fresh mint. Though you can make this soup from mature peas, young, delicate ones work best. If you have young peas leave some whole and put them in the pureed soup for a minute or so at the end of cooking.

The addition of Amaretto is an idea borrowed from my friend Mikel Covey. It adds a distinctive little tone like a miniature bell.

3 tablespoons Sour Cream Butter (p. 20) or clarified unsalted butter

3 tablespoons finely chopped shallots

1 small clove garlic, minced

1 bay leaf, fresh or dried

2 cups freshly shelled peas or petite, premium frozen peas

4 cups good chicken stock boiled and reduced to 2 cups

3 tablespoons chopped fresh mint plus whole leaves for garnish

Salt to taste

1/2 cup cream or half-and-half

1 or 2 gratings fresh nutmeg

1 teaspoon Amaretto, or to taste

SERVES 2 TO 4

Melt the butter in a frying pan over low heat and sauté the shallots and garlic until transparent (about 5 minutes). Add the bay leaf and 1 1/2 cups of the peas. Cover and continue to sauté over medium-low heat for another 5 minutes, gently stirring every minute or so. Add the chicken stock and simmer on low until the peas are barely tender (about 5 minutes).

Remove the bay leaf. Add the mint, pour the mixture into a blender or food processor and puree until smooth. Pour the mixture through a fine-meshed strainer, and using a wooden spoon, push the contents through it into a clean saucepan and return it to the stove. Bring to a low simmer. Add the remaining peas and cook the mixture for a minute or two, depending on the pea size, freshness, and how soft you want them to be. Correct the seasoning with salt. Add the cream, nutmeg and Amaretto. Remove the pan from the heat and allow the mixture to mellow and the flavors to meld for about an hour. Warm gently before serving and garnish each serving with a fresh mint leaf. Serve with toast triangles and Sour Cream Butter.

BEVERAGE RECOMMENDATION

Serve with a lightly chilled, sophisticated Champagne like a Perrier-Jouët.

Potato-Horseradish Dumplings in Broth

These are nice as a first course for a meal of game. They also make a good light lunch or supper when accompanied by a green salad.

2 tablespoons minced shallots or red onion

2 tablespoons mild walnut or olive oil

1 large potato

1 tablespoon Prepared Horseradish (p. 249)

Salt and freshly ground pepper to taste

1 egg plus 1 yolk beaten together

Few gratings nutmeg

2 tablespoons finely chopped fresh herbs such as tarragon and parsley or chervil and parsley

2 to 6 tablespoons all-purpose flour (depending on moisture content of mixture)

5 cups reduced stock of choice

SERVES 4

NOTE: Several stocks can be used for this recipe. Their flavor should first be concentrated to taste by simmering to about half of their original volume. Try Chicken Stock, Root Vegetable Stock (p. 122) or Wild Mushroom Stock (p. 126). Meat Stock (p. 124) made from game, such as venison, elk or lamb, is ideal.

In a large pot, bring the potato and water to a boil. Reduce the heat to a simmer and cook until the potato is tender when pierced with a small knife. Put it through a potato ricer with the skin on. Remove the skin from the ricer. A second method is to peel, cook and mash the potato with a potato masher until it is smooth and fluffy. Set aside.

In a medium sauté pan, cook the shallots in oil over a low flame until transparent (about 5 minutes). Add the mashed potato and other ingredients except for 1 tablespoon of the chopped herbs and the flour. Mix well.

Turn the mixture out on a surface sprinkled with flour. Roll the mixture into a ball, coat the surface with flour and knead, incorporating flour into the mixture until the dough stiffens to the consistency of bread dough. Refrigerate for 30 minutes to further firm the mixture so it can be formed into balls.

Make 2 or 3 1/2-inch dumplings by rolling them lightly between the lightly oiled palms of your hands. Put them on a plate. Transfer them to a floured surface and lightly coat them so that they won't stick together. In a 2- or 3-quart saucepan, heat the broth to a bare tremble and poach the dumpling in 3 or 4 groups.

Remove the first one that rises to the surface and taste. Depending on the consistency they are usually cooked as soon as they rise; if not, allow them to simmer a little more then taste again. Ladle the dumplings into soup bowls with some of the broth. Serve with a grating of fresh nutmeg and a delicate sprinkling of herbs.

The Chambers FIRELESS Gas Range
COOKS WITH THE GAS TURNED OFF!

In 1963 for $8—the price of a good meal including tip in those days—we purchased an unusually fine old kitchen stove, in a thrift store. It was in excellent condition and has been working quite admirably ever since.

LONG CANYON

SIMPLE TOMATO SOUP

This is a very simple soup and one of the best. It completely depends on using excellent tomatoes. It is good with nothing more than a drizzle of olive oil. For extra flavor garnish it with a little minced fresh sweet marjoram.

2 or 3 vine-ripened heirloom tomatoes such as Brandywine or Black Krim, chopped

Sugar to taste

Salt to taste

Extra virgin olive oil

Minced sweet marjoram

SERVES 4

Put the tomatoes in a small saucepan, cover and simmer for a few minutes. Gently mash with a potato masher, cover and continue to simmer for another minute or two. Push through a medium strainer until the remaining pulp is quite dry. Discard pulp. Place tomato liquid back in the pan and correct with sugar and salt. Allow a minute for both to dissolve and retaste. Divide into serving dishes and drizzle the soup with a little olive oil. Garnish with sweet marjoram.

BEVERAGE RECOMMENDATION

A young fruity Zinfandel or a chilled sparkling wine.

My dad grew pinkeye beans (see resources) in his garden as did his dad and as far back as we can remember. It's the best kidney bean I have ever cooked. If Italian cooks got their hands on this bean I think it could conceivably replace the venerable cannellini in their cooking. After long slow simmering it turns into a large buttery jewel of the highest quality.

LONG CANYON

Pinkeye Beans with Rosemary and Garlic

This is my favorite kidney bean. It's an old Utah bean, probably brought here by the first settlers from New England by way of Missouri. My father always grew them in his garden at our farm as did both of my grandfathers. With all due respect, the legendary pinkeye bean, in my opinion, is quite superior to the venerable cannellini bean.

This is a simple dish exploiting the ability of the bean to absorb flavor. When dry beans are presoaked in water for 10 to 12 hours, the usual method, they become saturated with water and subsequently resist absorbing flavors from their cooking broth. Start dry beans in their full-flavored broth minus salt and when finished cooking they will have much more flavor. Adding the salt at the end ensures that they will soften to their ideal condition. Otherwise it will be difficult for them to do so.

Serve as soup, or as a side dish by simply lifting them out of the liquid with a slotted spoon and serving alongside the main course. The beans are excellent in combination with Whole Roasted Deer Liver (p. 136) and quite delicious with any full-flavored meat or fowl. Mashed, they are excellent as an appetizer mounded on toasted bread, drizzled with fruity olive oil and freshly ground black pepper. For a smoother version push them through a strainer with the back of a spoon to separate them from their skins.

LONG CANYON

1 pound (2 cups) dry Pinkeye (see resources), Cannellini or Great Northern beans

2 quarts chicken stock

3 or 4 sprigs fresh rosemary or sage

3 cloves garlic, minced

8 tablespoons extra virgin olive oil

Salt to taste

Fresh grated white or black pepper to taste

SERVES 4 TO 8

Sort through beans and discard any dirt or pebbles. Cover them with tap water and after a minute or two discard any beans that float to the top. This indicates that they have an air pocket that may harbor dirt or mold. Rinse the remaining beans well and drain.

Reduce chicken stock over medium heat by half and set aside. Cover the drained beans with the stock. Add 1 sprig of rosemary and 1 clove of garlic. Put the pot over medium-high heat until stock begins to boil. Turn off the heat and set aside to cool and let beans absorb the liquid for about an hour.

Bring the beans to a medium-rolling boil and cook uncovered for 10 minutes to force the lectins to escape. Skim off any foam that rises to the surface. During this time they will need to be watched to make sure the liquid stays above the top of the beans. Add additional stock as needed to keep them covered. Lower the heat to a very low simmer, add 4 tablespoons olive oil then cover. From this point it is important that they cook very slowly so they will not break apart during their lengthy cooking time.

After an hour or two add another sprig of rosemary and another clove of garlic. Every 30 minutes or so remove one of the beans and check it for doneness. This will give you an idea of how fast they are cooking. They should be cooked until they are creamy soft (2 to 5 hours) but not to the point where they begin shedding their skins and falling apart. When the beans are getting tender, add the rest of the herbs and the remaining clove of garlic. Correct the seasoning with salt.

After beans are cooked remove them from the heat. If you prefer to thicken the liquid, purée 2 cups of beans with some broth in a food processor or blender until smooth and stir it back in with the beans. Stir in 2 tablespoons olive oil and let them rest for an hour or two before serving. Reheat before serving and drizzle extra virgin olive oil and a grind of pepper over each serving.

BEVERAGE RECOMMENDATION

Well-chilled Prosecco.

ROOT VEGETABLE STOCK

This stock is sweet, earthy and adds depth of flavor to various dishes. Experiment with the addition of wild roots such as burdock, sunchoke and wild garlic. Wild roots and vegetables have incomparably rich flavors that resonate beautifully with wild game.

1 cup peeled and chopped parsnips

2 cups peeled and chopped carrots

2 cups peeled and chopped turnips

2 yellow onions, peeled and chopped

1/4 cup coarsely chopped celery root

2 cups coarsely chopped Jerusalem artichokes or red potatoes

3 cloves unpeeled garlic

1 to 2 cloves

4 tablespoons extra virgin olive oil

1 cup all-purpose flour

1 herb bundle: 1 sprig each of thyme, parsley and marjoram and a bay leaf tied with cotton string

1 gallon spring water

Salt to taste (add only after stock is finished or reduced)

MAKES 2 QUARTS

Preheat oven to 400° F.

Put all of the vegetables in a roasting pan and drizzle the olive oil over them. Toss them with your hands until they are evenly coated. Sprinkle with the flour and toss with your hands until the oil and flour have combined to evenly coat the vegetables. Roast in the preheated oven until the mixture turns a rich dark brown (about 1 hour), stirring and turning every 10 minutes or so as they brown.

Put all the roasted vegetables in a large stockpot and deglaze the roasting pan with a little water. Scrape up any bits of residue that are left behind. Pour the deglazed liquid from the roasting pan into the stockpot along with the spring water. Bring to a boil, reduce the heat at once and simmer gently, with the lid slightly ajar, for at least one hour. Skim the surface every 10 minutes or so and discard the foam. Continue skimming until the foam residue stops forming on the surface. At the end of the cooking time allow it to cool so it can be handled comfortably.

Carefully pour the entire contents of the pot into a big cheesecloth-lined strainer that has been placed over a second medium-sized pot. Discard the solids left behind in the strainer. Don't try to press more liquid from the vegetables or it will make the stock cloudy.

Transfer the strained stock to the smaller pot. Add the herb bundle then reduce the stock to about 2 quarts. Remove the herbs, cool the stock and freeze it in 1-pint containers with tight-fitting lids. Alternatively, put the reduced stock in a sealed container. Refrigerate and use it within 1 week.

For most braises and poaches I like to tie up two bundles of herbs before I begin the process. Along with garlic the first bundle is added at the start. This gives the meat a deep penetration of flavor. About 20 minutes before the finish I add more garlic and the second bundle, giving it more intensity of perfume.

MEAT STOCK

Just as going to the garden or market to plan a dish or an entire meal around seasonal produce, meat scraps and bones can determine what kind of stock to make. If pork is available you may wish to make a stock for a white bean soup. Beef stock might suggest braised beef. A leftover chicken carcass can add sweetness to beef stock. Lamb scraps and bones lend complexity and a distinctive herb-scented sweetness to a stock that is excellent when used to moisten a venison or rabbit braise.

Using stock to deglaze pan drippings after the fat has been poured off is one of the best uses for stock. By combining stock with pan drippings the finished sauce has more intensity than it would if the pan was deglazed with water. This combination complements the meat it was made from better than a sauce made from stock alone.

For those daunted by the stock-making process I offer a few words of encouragement. Don't be intimidated. Stock is simple and forgiving to make—it just requires quite a lot of time. Plan to make it at least a day ahead of use. Besides a basic kitchen infrastructure all you need is a 12- to 20-quart stockpot, time and patience, and you're most of the way there. Make it on a day when you can stay fairly close to the kitchen so you can keep an eye on it.

Stockpots are available at any good restaurant supply store. A pot with a heat-distributing copper or aluminum disk on the bottom is best to prevent scorching if you also plan to use it for soup or stew.

LONG CANYON

5 pounds beef, lamb, chicken or pork scraps and bones such as: knuckles, ribs, neck bones, tail bones and hambones

1 cup all-purpose flour

Spring water to cover ingredients (4 to 5 quarts)

1 herb bundle: 2 or 3 sprigs thyme, 2 or 3 sprigs parsley, and 2 or 3 bay leaves tied together with cotton string

2 or 3 yellow onions cut in quarters

1 or 2 cloves stuck in 2 of the onion quarters

2 medium carrots, coarsely chopped

2 or 3 stalks celery or a slice of celery root, coarsely chopped

2 or 3 cloves garlic with skin left on (so it won't dissolve and cloud the liquid)

Salt to taste (add only after stock is reduced)

2 QUARTS REDUCED STOCK OR NEARLY 4 QUARTS UNREDUCED

Preheat oven to 400° F.

Using a hammer, crack the bones a little, on a solid surface. Put the bones and scraps in a large, uncovered roasting pan, sprinkle with flour and place in preheated oven. Stir and turn them every 10 minutes until evenly browned (30 to 40 minutes). Transfer the browned mixture to a large stockpot. Add a little water to the roasting pan, deglaze it and scrape all of the bits that stick to the bottom of the pan. Add the deglazed mixture to the stockpot, and add the rest of the water.

Cover the stockpot with the lid slightly ajar. Heat the stock to a simmer. Remove the lid or it may heat to a boil and cloud the stock. Do not stir the pot as this too will disturb the ingredients and cloud the stock. Heat the stock slowly. Skim off the surface residue. After the residue reduces to a small amount of white foam, add the herbs and vegetables and bring the heat back up to a low simmer.

Simmer on low for 4 or 5 hours skimming often to free it from the residue that will continue to rise. Stock that has been carefully skimmed is more clear with a cleaner, more focused taste. Don't allow the liquid to drop below the level of the meat and bones. To avoid stirring up the stock and making it cloudy, gently pour boiling spring water down the inside surface of the pot, to top off the surface level as needed. The level of the solid ingredients will drop as they cook down and so the overall amount of stock will diminish as it cooks.

When the cooking is finished, gently pour the stock through a colander lined with a double layer of dampened cheesecloth into a smaller pot. Take care not to disturb the liquid any more than necessary when pouring it to retain the stock's clarity. Don't squeeze liquid out of the solids or it will also cloud the stock. Discard the spent solids.

Bring the stock to a simmer over medium-high heat and reduce the liquid to 2 quarts. Cool to room temperature then chill the reduced liquid overnight in the refrigerator. Remove any solidified fat from its surface. Warm the pot on low to liquefy the contents then ladle the warm stock into 1-pint, tightly covered containers. Cool the containers to room temperature. Store them in the refrigerator or freezer for later use. Frozen stock keeps for up to 6 months. Refrigerated stock should be used within 2 weeks.

WILD MUSHROOM STOCK

It is vitally important for anyone hunting wild mushrooms to take every precaution to identify poisonous varieties. If possible, take a class on the subject or go into the field with an expert. In any case always carry a concise field guide. Collect only the mushrooms you know. Don't pick, or even touch, mushrooms in the wild you are not familiar with.

Most mountainous regions in the world have wild mushrooms at higher altitudes in the fall and at lower elevations in the spring and summer. This recipe is a good way to use an over-supply. They can also be dried and used for making stock as needed. Mushroom stock adds a sumptuous touch to soups, stews, braises, sauces, grains, pulses and pasta.

---

8 cups fresh wild mushrooms, such as chanterelles, boletus, shaggy manes or meadow mushrooms, coarsely chopped

Safflower oil to coat mushrooms

1 cup all-purpose flour

1 yellow onion, peeled, cored and quartered

2 cloves

1 carrot, coarsely chopped

1 small herb bundle: a small leafy stalk of celery; a green onion split lengthwise; a sprig each of thyme, parsley, marjoram; and a bay leaf; tied together with cotton string

1 gallon spring water

Salt to taste (add only after stock is reduced)

2 QUARTS REDUCED STOCK OR
NEARLY 4 QUARTS UNREDUCED

Preheat oven to 400° F.

Thoroughly toss the mushrooms with oil so the flour will stick to them and place them in a large roasting pan. Sprinkle with the flour, stirring to coat evenly. Roast mushrooms uncovered in the preheated oven, occasionally stirring and turning them, until they turn a rich, dark brown (about 30 to 40 minutes).

Transfer the mushrooms to a large stockpot and add all the other ingredients. Deglaze the roasting pan with a little water and scrape up all the bits of mushroom and flour. Pour it into the stockpot with the other ingredients. Cover and bring the mixture to a low simmer. As soon as it begins to simmer, remove the lid and continue to simmer slowly for at least one hour. Every 10 minutes or so, skim off any residue that forms on the top surface. Do not allow the liquid to boil, or its turbulence will cause it to turn cloudy. After about an hour the flavors will be adequately extracted and the mixture will have reduced and concentrated somewhat.

Transfer the stock to a smaller pot and reduce to about 2 quarts. Cool the stock to room temperature. Store in 1-pint containers with tight-fitting lids in the freezer or refrigerator. If frozen it can be safely stored for up to 6 months. If refrigerated it should be used within 2 weeks.

LONG CANYON

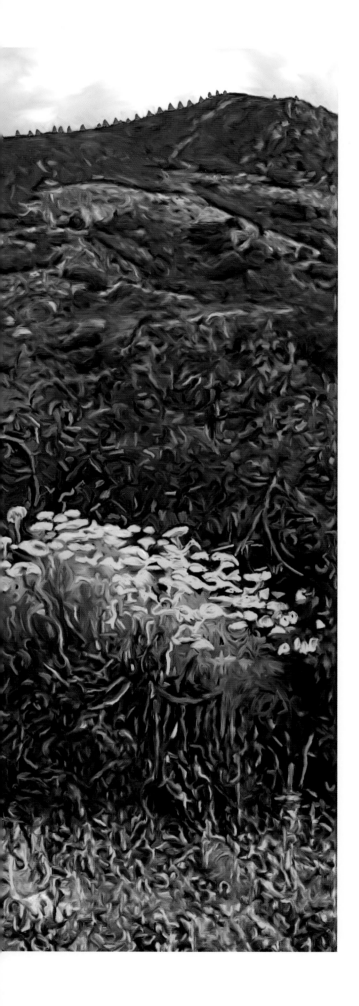

THE VENISON HUNT

{ MAIN DISHES }

THE VENISON HUNT

There was always plenty to eat on our farm and ranch but hunting was considered to be a practical matter of thrift and a way to introduce variety to our diet. Having domestic meat on a regular basis, our family always considered high-quality wild game to be a seasonal treat. Both venison and elk, two of our favorite game animals, are clean, rich, herbaceous meats that reflect the environment the animal lives in. Both are beautiful, noble animals that we were taught to respect. Nothing encourages respect for the game animal as much as hunting, killing and experiencing its suffering. I don't think of hunting as sport. Taking the life of an animal as sensitive as an elk or deer should not be taken lightly. I feel the same about all game including game fish. Catch-and-release fishing is another example of a carefully crafted excuse for pleasure at the game animal's expense. In my mind the only thing that justifies making an animal suffer is to use it for food, and catching a fish definitely makes it suffer whether it's released or killed and used in the kitchen.

Whether an animal is domestic or wild, it must always be put to good use. In the case of both deer and elk, the animal is usable from its antlers to its tail and everything in between. We were taught that after tagging, field dressing and transporting the animal back home and carefully removing its skin, its hide should be sent to the tannery and turned into leather. Buckskin is much more delicate than elk hide but both are very useful. In times past a resourceful wife considered buckskin a very superior material for making clothing—some still do. Few things are as nice as a pair of handmade buckskin gloves. Elk hide,

on the other hand, is a tough, resilient material that can be used in endless ways such as covering a chair or making a jacket. The antlers can also be used for making buttons, knife handles and such. In ancient times before metallurgy, antlers were even more useful, and people made many other things with them such as digging tools, spear tips and daggers.

There is an honesty about hunting game—a primal transaction with the forces of nature. Although I don't hunt anymore I consider my years of practicing that ancient art to be my foundation for handling and cooking game.

The most visceral hunting experience I ever had was on the mountain above our ranch in Spring Lake. It will always be in my mind when I prepare venison. It was late fall and my father wanted to take his sons hunting for the camaraderie that a father and his sons share in the hunt. I was in college and needed provisions for the winter so hunting was a good way to help fill the larder. We checked our rifles, caught and saddled our horses and headed up the mountain. I was riding Socks, a palomino mare, all heart and soul as horses go. About halfway up the mountain I decided to stay behind in a bunch of pine and quakies. The others continued on up the mountain. It was a tactic I was partial to, based on the mule deer's habit of silently circling around any oncoming predator then heading in the opposite direction. This was an obvious survival technique that usually served the animal well. Deer are highly sensitive, especially in their sense of sound. Folklore claims they are so sensitive they can hear a plant grow.

I'm not sure that's true but I get the point, and waiting for them to come to you is by far the quietest method.

I tied Socks to a tree 20 feet or so off the trail and sat down a few feet from the trail's edge with my loaded, ancient British .303, a solid, bolt-action military rifle that the British Empire and Commonwealth started using in 1895. Less than a half-hour had passed when I heard a loud, crashing, rapidly approaching wave of chaos. Within seconds a large doe accompanied by two of the most magnificent bucks I had ever seen came up over a small rise on the trail, trotting very rapidly—foam trailing from their lips. They were exhausted and obviously fleeing danger. By the time they were in range I was on my feet and ready. I flipped the safety off before they reached where I was. My plan was to take both bucks with a high neck shot to avoid damaging the meat—one shot, reload, wheel and take the second. The doe bounded away as soon as she heard the first shot. The first buck fell as I flipped out the spent cartridge and whirled and shot the second. Both shots hit with deadly accuracy. On the hoof both deer weighed well over 300 pounds. When we tagged then loaded them on the horses, Socks, a big-boned, stout mare, groaned as we tied one of the animals to her saddle. Even with a mare of her size and strength it was a full load and meant I would have to lead her home. But first there was the matter of "cleaning" both animals.

I was nineteen years old and had been taught the important process of field-dressing a freshly killed animal. It can make all the difference in the quality of the meat that reaches the table. With the adrenal rush that comes with killing an animal it is important to stay calm and work with care and attention to detail. Avoiding a self-inflicted cut is most important. First

the animal must be rolled onto its back and straddled between the hunter's knees to hold it steady. A very sharp knife is a must, and I learned proper sharpening early on. First a slit is cut from the testicles straight up to the sternum. It is important to cut very carefully—just deep enough to get through the outer layers of skin and fascia but not enough to cut into the entrails. Next the connective tissue that holds the entrails in place must be removed. Once this is done the deer is rolled back on its side and the entrails are allowed to spill out onto the earth—left for any carnivores that happen to be in the vicinity.

For me it is an almost overwhelming experience to dress a freshly killed elk or deer. The sulfurous pungency of entrails and fresh blood with its warm, sticky sweetness thick with mineral, earth and herbaceous aromas borders on the extreme. Except in the lean, cold months, deer live on a diet of chlorophyll-rich plants—green leaves, forbs, various grasses and succulents. They are also fond of grape and berry vines, mushrooms, ferns, juniper and mountain mahogany, all rich in aromatic nutrients.

After it is removed from the animal, the liver, which is a true delicacy, is placed in a special sack and tied to the saddle to keep it clean and undamaged. It is traditionally the first thing consumed and is always best when fresh as possible. Hunting is a primal experience—a connection to an ancient past—incorporating the joy of the great outdoors, the excitement of the hunt as well as the suffering of the hunted animal. When I cook game I do it with reverence and respect. Wasting food of any kind shows a lack of both but I think it's especially true with meat and even more so with game. Healthy game is the cleanest and most flavorful of all meat and I feel honored to prepare it whenever it is available.

THE VENISON HUNT

I LOOK ACROSS THIS ONCE WELL TENDED FARM VALLEY, WHERE I GREW UP, WITH A MIXTURE OF PLEASANT MEMORIES AND PAIN. IT IS ON AN IRREVERSIBLE PATH AWAY FROM THE OPEN LAND, WITH ITS RICH, UNPREDICTABLE TREASURES AS IT RAPIDLY BECOMES ONE BIG SPRAWLING BEDROOM COMMUNITY OF CONCRETE, BLACKTOP AND STERILE SUBDIVISIONS DEVOID OF TREES AND CHARACTER — A PLACE TO ORDER-IN AND NUMB STARVING MINDS WITH JUNK FOOD, COMMERCIAL TELEVISION PRESCRIPTION DRUGS AND ANXIOUS SLEEP. SADLY IT REMINDS ME OF A LINE FROM JONI MITCHELL'S "BIG YELLOW TAXI" — YOU TAKE PARADISE AND PUT UP A PARKING LOT.

THE VENISON HUNT

Venison Medallions with Brown Sauce and 3-Corn Cakes

FOR THE CORN CAKES
(24–30, 3 inches IN DIAMETER)

1 1/2 cups fresh ground red, yellow or blue corn flour (see resources)

1 teaspoon baking powder

1/2 teaspoon salt

1 1/2 cups spring water

2 tablespoons unfiltered sunflower oil

Grapeseed oil as needed on griddle

4 tablespoons sour cream or unsalted butter to top the cakes (optional)

FOR THE MEDALLIONS

Safflower oil as needed for griddle

Salt

3 pounds venison or lamb tenderloin, fat and silver skin carefully trimmed

3 tablespoons Sour Cream Butter (p. 20) or unsalted butter

4 tablespoons shallots, finely minced

1 teaspoon fresh thyme leaves, minced, plus 6 to 8 sprigs for garnish

3 tablespoons good Cabernet Sauvignon wine

1 1/2 cups Brown Sauce (p. 260)

Finely ground fresh black pepper

SERVES 6 TO 8

NOTE: If you have all three colors of corn, make three separate batches, one for each color. Cut the dry ingredients to 1/3 their volume, specified above, which yields about 8 cakes per color.

Both the meat and the cakes are excellent with Brown Sauce (p. 260). A good side dish to serve with these medallions is Honey Glazed Carrots with Tarragon (p. 196).

Mix the dry ingredients together. Add water and oil. Stir well. The batter(s) should be thin enough so that the cakes come out just a little thicker than crepes. Thin the batter as necessary with a little extra water. To get an idea how long they should cook start with one tester cake and note the amount of time and the way it looks and tastes. Lightly oil a hot griddle or nonstick frying pan and cook the rest of the cakes. Put a small pat of butter on top of each cake after you turn them. Keep them warm in the oven. Keep in mind it's best to prepare these at the last possible moment so that they are fresh when you serve them.

Cut tenderloin into 1/2-inch-thick slices on a slight angle, across the grain. Sprinkle with a little salt. Give it a few minutes to dissolve and absorb into the meat. Heat some of the safflower oil in a frying pan over medium-high heat until it begins to smoke. Place the medallions in the pan 1/2 inch or more apart. If the medallions are placed too close together they will trap their own steam and it will toughen the meat.

Sauté them in batches, giving them one to two minutes per side. Scrape and wipe the pan if necessary and add more oil for each batch. The best way to tell if they are done is by poking them with the tip of your finger after they are turned. The approximate feel can be duplicated by closing one hand into a fist, gripping with medium pressure then pressing the muscle between the thumb and index finger with the index finger of your other hand. The medallions should be a bit underdone as they will continue to cook while being held on a warm plate in a warm oven for the few minutes while you make the sauce.

Melt 3 tablespoons butter in a frying pan. Add the shallots and thyme and sauté over low heat for a few minutes until translucent. Add the red wine and scrape all the bits from the sides and bottom of the pan. Simmer and reduce to about half the original volume. Add the Brown Sauce and bring to a simmer. Taste and correct the seasoning if necessary. Add a grind or two of black pepper and strain the sauce. Puddle the sauce on warmed plates and slightly overlap a few of the medallions. Place the cakes alongside and spoon a little sauce over them. Add carrots, if desired, and garnish each plate with a sprig of fresh thyme.

BEVERAGE RECOMMENDATION

This is an excellent meal to showcase a special Cabernet Sauvignon. Here are a couple of fantastic wines if you should be so lucky: the legendary 1975 Lafite Rothschild or John Daniel's 1941 Cabernet Sauvignon from Inglenook made during their glory days which ended in 1964. According to James Laube this is Daniel's masterpiece, and still was a 100 point wine with decades of life left in it when he tasted it in 2000—amazing.

WHOLE ROASTED DEER LIVER WITH GARLIC AND SAGE

Deer liver is at its best when it is very fresh, so traditionally it is the first meal to come from a venison kill. You can use calves liver but the flavor will be milder. Both are a delicacy that must be cooked with care so they will be pink at the center. Overcooking causes liver to become bitter.

The flavor from the marinade will be greatest on the outside. It will taper off as it progresses to the more delicate interior. It is good with Blue Collar Polenta with Mixed Herbs (p. 197) and mushrooms sautéed in butter or Braised Turnips (p. 208).

1 venison liver (2 to 3 pounds) outer membrane removed

Salt

6 cloves garlic

2 tablespoons fresh sage leaves, finely chopped

Few grinds fresh nutmeg

1 cup plus 3 tablespoons good red wine

3 tablespoons walnut oil or extra virgin olive oil

Freshly ground black pepper to taste

Olive oil to brush on surface

1 large sprig of sage for garnish

SERVES 4 TO 8

Preheat oven to 450° F.

Salt the liver and allow it to rest for 30 minutes to penetrate the meat. Crush the garlic, chopped sage, nutmeg and a pinch of salt to a paste with a mortar and pestle. Add 3 tablespoons red wine and 3 tablespoons oil and stir together. Place the liver with the garlic-sage mixture in a plastic zip bag for 1 or 2 hours at room temperature or overnight in the refrigerator. If refrigerated it must be brought back to room temperature for one hour before placing it in the oven.

Remove the liver from the marinade and blot it dry with paper towels. Brush it liberally with olive oil. Roast in a preheated 450° F oven for 10 minutes to sear it. Dip the branch of sage in the marinade to keep it from drying out and place it in the roasting pan alongside the liver. Reduce the heat to 250° F and continue roasting until the liver almost reaches desired doneness (depending the size of the liver, 10 to 20 minutes or more for a pink interior). A quick read thermometer inserted into the center of the liver should read 135° F to 140° F. Pull the sage branch out of the oven when it is light brown. Turn off the oven and open the oven door a little to keep the liver warm. Allow it to rest for 5 minutes in the oven. It will continue to cook so have everything ready. It is important that the liver remain moist and pink inside.

While the liver is resting, strain the marinade into a saucepan and add a cup of red wine. Bring to a simmer and cook until reduced by half, stirring occasionally. Slice the liver on a diagonal about 1/4 inch thick and serve on warmed plates. Since most liver purists will probably not want to distract from the delicate flavor, offer the sauce on the side. Garnish each serving with lightly roasted edible sage leaves and a thin slice of lemon. Place a shaker of sea salt and a pepper grinder on the table.

BEVERAGE RECOMMENDATION

An excellent wine with this meal is a well-aged Chateau Beychevelle from the Medoc region or a Napa Petit Sirah such as a David Fulton 2001.

Barley Risotto-Stuffed Poultry with Pine Nuts and Plum Sauce

This is an elegant dish that makes good use of poultry, wild or domestic. It takes care and 3 or 4 hours to prepare. Unless you are a proficient cook you should prepare it once or twice before making it for guests. With the exception of the wing and leg bones the bird is completely boned, yielding a large cavity for the stuffing, redolent of toasted pine nuts, goat cheese, herbs and caramelized plums.

The bones and trimmings obtained from boning are used to make a rich sauce, which is further enhanced by the addition of Wild Plum Jam (p. 246). After boning, the bird yields 6 servings instead of the usual 2 or 3.

FOR THE BIRD

1 3- to 4-pound bird such as pheasant, chicken or duck

2 tablespoons olive oil

1/2 cup chicken stock

12 small carrots, blanched

3 parsnips cut into 12 finger-size chunks, blanched

Splash of vermouth or white wine

FOR THE SAUCE

Bones and trimmings from the deboned bird, coarsely chopped

1 quart chicken stock

1 herb bundle: a sprig or two each of fresh sage, thyme, rosemary, parsley; 1 small leafy celery stalk; 1/2 leek; and 2 bay leaves

1 medium carrot, coarsely chopped

1/2 yellow onion, peeled and split lengthwise

1 clove stuck in the onion half

2 cloves garlic

Peelings from the prepared carrots and parsnips, coarsely chopped

Spring water to cover

Pinch of cinnamon

1/4 cup Wild Plum Jam (p. 246) or to taste

1 tablespoon cornstarch mixed into a little water

Salt to taste

FOR THE STUFFING

1/2 yellow onion, finely chopped

1 medium carrot, finely chopped

1 stick of leafy celery, finely chopped

2 tablespoons olive oil

1 tablespoon minced fresh herbs (parsley, rosemary, thyme, sage, etc.)

1/4 cup pine nuts, toasted golden brown in a dry frying pan

1/2 cup halved and pitted plums, cooked in the 1/4 cup apple juice or Tawny Port, in an uncovered pan until liquid is reduced by half; add both plums and liquid

1/4 cup fresh goat cheese (optional)

2 eggs, slightly beaten

1/2 recipe Barley-Miso Risotto (p. 216)

Prepare to debone the poultry by resting the bird upright, on its tail. Loosen the skin around the neck and gently pull it down and away from the upper shoulders. Do this so that you can better see where to begin.

With a small, sharp paring knife begin cutting the flesh away from the neck area using frequent, light scraping motions as opposed to larger continuous cuts. Begin removing the bones. Start with the wishbone disconnecting it from the shoulder bones. Take care not to cut through the flesh during the boning process. (The skin and flesh remain together creating a sack for the stuffing. The bones are removed from the inside of this sack.)

Disconnect both wing bones from the shoulder bone sockets, severing them at the joint. Leave the bones in the wings. Disconnect the collarbones from the breast. Pull the flesh away from the bones gently with your fingers as you work carefully, cutting when necessary. Break the cartilage that connects the shoulder and breastbone and remove. Remove both collarbones and shoulder blades. Gently pull the flesh away from the rib cage again, cutting when necessary. Disconnect the leg joints from the hip sockets severing the cartilage that connects them. Remove the thigh bone, leaving only the drumstick bone in each leg. (Leaving the drumstick bones in retains just enough of the bird's shape.) Carefully remove the rib cage. Cut out any other bones that remain; chop them coarsely with a cleaver to add to the simmering sauce.

For the sauce, put the chicken stock, bones and the rest of the sauce ingredients, with the exception of the cinnamon, plum jam, cornstarch and salt, in a large pot over low heat. Add additional stock or water. Simmer the sauce gently as the bird roasts in the oven.

For the stuffing, gently cook the minced onion, carrot and celery in olive oil until soft and translucent. Add the mixed chopped herbs and stir for an additional minute or two.

Fold the vegetable/herb mixture together with the pine nuts, cooked plums and their syrup, goat cheese and eggs into the prepared risotto and mix together gently but thoroughly. Just before stuffing the bird, warm the risotto mixture in a covered pan over medium-low heat stirring a few times. This will raise the heat of the stuffing and help ensure that the egg in the stuffing sets up by the time the bird is done.

Preheat oven to 450° F.

With a trussing needle and cotton string carefully sew up the tail opening of the bird. At this point the bird will resemble a sack with wings and legs. Put the stuffing into the neck cavity. Don't overstuff the cavity, however, as it will expand a little while cooking. Make sure there are no openings from which the stuffing can escape. Lay the stuffed bird on its back, tie the wings together then the legs. If the bird is large you may need to tie the leg and wing twine together. Carefully insert a 10-inch metal spike (See resources) through the center of the stuffing from the tail to the front of cavity. It should stick out the back a few inches. The metal spike conducts the heat into the stuffing while it roasts, helping it set up so that when you remove the spike and slice the bird, you will get firm, clean slices.

Rub the outside of the stuffed bird with a little olive oil and put it in an uncovered roasting pan. Place in the preheated oven for 15 minutes to brown. After it is nicely browned add 1/2 cup chicken stock, and the blanched carrots and parsnips to the pan. Cover the pan and turn the heat down to 350° F. Roast until the internal temperature reaches 170° F. Monitor the temperature by inserting either a meat thermometer or a quick read thermometer into the thickest part of the thigh. It should reach this temperature in about one hour. Baste every 10 minutes or so with the stock and juices that accumulate on the bottom of the pan.

When the bird is finished roasting, remove it from the oven. Remove the spike and tent the bird with foil or cover with a large mixing bowl to keep it warm while it rests for a few minutes. At this point the roasting liquid will have mostly evaporated so it may be necessary to deglaze the roasting pan with a splash of vermouth, white wine or 2 or 3 tablespoons of the sauce liquid and scrape the bits from the sides and bottom of the pan. Pour the liquid back into the sauce.

While the bird rests strain the sauce and discard solids. Boil the strained sauce to reduce it. Thicken the sauce with cornstarch and simmer for a minute or two. Add a pinch of cinnamon. Mix in the jam. Correct the seasoning, cover and set aside.

Warm the plates. To serve, carve the bird crosswise into one-inch-hick individual servings. Cut the slices that contain the wings and legs in half, vertically, so that each of the two slices has a leg or wing. Puddle some sauce on each plate and top with a serving of poultry.

Serve with the blanched and roasted carrots and parsnips along with some steamed chard doused with a little red wine vinegar, seasoned with salt and served with a dollop of good mayonnaise.

BEVERAGE RECOMMENDATION

Two Spanish wines work well with this dish: Artazuri Garnacha (100 percent Garnacha) or Mas Donis, a delicious combination of Garnacha and Syrah.

SHEEP HAVE THE ABILITY
TO TURN EVEN THE
POOREST PASTURE INTO
THE SWEETEST, MOST
AROMATIC MEAT OF ALL
DOMESTICATED ANIMALS

BONED LEG OF LAMB WITH BASIL-INFUSED PEANUT SAUCE

This is a moderately spicy dish that goes well with risotto, steamed long beans or asparagus dressed with a simple vinaigrette.

3- to 6-pound boneless leg of spring lamb (4 to 8 months old)

1 large head of garlic

1 cup loosely packed, fresh, stemmed Thai basil or other fresh basil leaves plus more for garnish

1 cup canned coconut milk

1 cup creamy natural peanut butter

Chile oil or chile paste to taste

Bragg Liquid Aminos (see resources) to taste

1/2 cup Wild Mushroom Stock (p. 126) or Meat Stock (p. 124)

SERVES 6 TO 12

NOTE: Keep in mind that some people are violently allergic to peanuts as well as other foods, so always check with your guests about their food sensitivities before deciding a menu.

Ask your butcher to debone the lamb when you buy it —they're usually happy to do this. Otherwise use a sharp boning knife and working from the large end of the leg, carefully remove all of the bones. Trim off any excess fat. Pound the thickest parts of the meat with a heavy mallet or the flat side of a cleaver, to achieve a more even thickness so that the meat will cook uniformly. (The butterflied leg will not be perfectly even.)

If you have an open fire, wrap a whole bulb of garlic, bury it in the hot ashes and roast until soft (30 to 60 minutes). Otherwise, wrap a bulb of garlic in aluminum foil and bake it in a preheated 375° F oven for about an hour. Squeeze the garlic out of the cloves and place them in a mortar or food processor with the basil leaves and work into a smooth paste thinning with a little coconut milk as needed. Stir or process together with the peanut butter, remaining coconut milk, chile oil and Bragg Liquid Aminos until it is a consistent, thin paste. Set aside.

Place the meat in a gallon plastic zip bag with the peanut mixture. Squeeze the air out of the bag to make sure the marinade contacts all surfaces of the meat. Marinate the meat in the bag, in the refrigerator, for 2 or 3 hours or overnight. One hour before grilling, remove the lamb from the refrigerator and from the bag and allow it to reach room temperature. Scrape any excess marinade back into the bag. Seal the bag and set it aside for later to make the sauce.

Cook the lamb on a hot charcoal grill to desired doneness (15 to 25 minutes per side for medium rare). Move to a cooler part of the grill if it begins to burn or take it off the grill until the fire burns down a little more. Watch closely — don't overcook. Keep in mind that lamb is traditionally served pink in the middle. Remove the meat to a cutting board and allow it to rest for 10 minutes before carving. Resting the freshly cooked leg will allow the juices to redistribute and allow the meat to relax and soften. It will continue to cook slightly while it is resting.

As the lamb is grilling, pour the marinade from the bag in a small saucepan. Place over medium heat, add the stock and simmer for 2 or 3 minutes. Remove it from the heat. Cover and set aside. It should have the consistency of heavy cream. If it is too thick, thin it with a little more stock. If it is too thin, let it reduce more, whichever is needed. Taste the sauce and correct the seasoning. Before carving the lamb, warm the plates, strain and reheat the sauce.

Carve the lamb, cutting across the grain of the muscles as much as possible. Cut off any tough or stringy sinew from the meat. Have the plates warm. Puddle sauce on plate and place freshly carved lamb slices on top. Garnish with fresh Thai basil or small leaves of regular sweet basil.

BEVERAGE RECOMMENDATION

Any good Alsatian Gewürztraminer is very complementary to this dish. The characteristic flavors and spiciness both complement and counterpoint this dish. If you prefer red, serve a good California Zinfandel.

THE VENISON HUNT

THE ANNUAL RANCH PARTY

Our family ranch was like a movie set except more real—no matte paintings, no cameras, no scripts. In its heyday it was a vibrant, working ranch with a herd of Hereford cattle, sheep and a band of working horses. It was, as dad preferred, a self-contained operation, meaning we did everything ourselves. We raised a garden, grew wheat and milled our own flour, overhauled our own tractors, poured our own concrete, did our own welding, broke our own horses, bred our own animals, grew our own feed and built our own houses. It was a place of active dreams where a lot of hard work and personal growth took place.

"The Annual Ranch Party" always took place in the autumn on Labor Day weekend. The main course was a pit-roasted lamb prepared the same way our ancestors had for generations. The pit was first filled with fire wood, lit and fed through the entire night. In the morning the lamb was cut into manageable pieces, wrapped in wet burlap, placed in the tin-covered bottom of the pit, covered with another layer of tin, then a foot or so of hot coals, then earth. By dinner time it was cooked in the rancher's favorite way with the meat falling from the bone. We served it with Extra Classic Mint Sauce (p. 241) and a Brown Sauce (p. 260) made from stock based on the local wild porcini and the bones and trimmings from our meat processing house. Buttered corn on the cob and sliced tomatoes were served with homemade bread and butter, country-style potatoes, pickles of various kinds and an array of beverages including soft drinks for the youngsters and beer and red wine for the adults. Dessert starred local seasonal fruit—usually peaches and red raspberries. The peaches were peeled, cut, sliced and macerated in sugar; the berries were left plain so as not to lose their shape and color. Then both would be scattered over homemade ice cream. Fantastic Almond Shortbread cookies (p. 290) were offered along with an assortment of cobblers and pies.

Braised Elk with Noodles, Braising Sauce and Thyme

Because elk are carefully protected by law and difficult to hunt, elk meat is a special treat for the table. Its scarceness and rich flavor make it one of the most prized game meats. If you are not fortunate enough to have elk for this recipe, you can substitute venison or beef.

FOR THE MEAT

1 6-pound elk shoulder

Salt

Freshly ground black pepper

3 tablespoons extra virgin olive oil

1 or 2 tablespoons safflower oil for browning the meat

FOR THE MARINADE

4 whole cloves

2 bay leaves

6 whole peppercorns

1 cup good red wine

1 yellow onion, sliced and pulled apart into rings

1 carrot, coarsely chopped

1 tablespoon finely minced fresh thyme

2 whole cloves garlic with skins removed

12 unpitted Kalamata olives

1 tablespoon Wild Plum Jam (p. 246) or apricot jam

SERVES 8

FOR THE STUFFING

1 yellow onion, coarsely grated

1 carrot, coarsely grated

2 cloves garlic, crushed

1 tablespoon finely chopped fresh thyme

1/2 cup breadcrumbs

2 or 3 heaping tablespoons finely chopped elk bone marrow (optional)

2 tablespoons extra virgin olive oil

1/2 teaspoon salt

FOR THE NOODLES

2 cups all-purpose flour or mix 1 cup each all-purpose flour and whole-wheat pastry flour

2 large eggs

1/2 teaspoon salt

2 tablespoons extra virgin olive oil

2 tablespoons minced, fresh thyme

2 tablespoons red wine (same as served with the meal) or water, or more as needed

8 sprigs thyme for garnish

THE VENISON HUNT

Carefully bone the shoulder with a knife and place the meat in a 1-gallon plastic zip bag. Mix the marinade ingredients together and pour over the meat. Squeeze the air out of the bag, seal and manipulate the bag to distribute the marinade around the meat, making sure it covers all surfaces. Let rest in the refrigerator for 3 or 4 hours or overnight.

Remove the shoulder from the bag and pat it dry with paper towels. Season with salt and pepper. Let the salt dissolve and penetrate the meat for a half hour or so. Rub 3 tablespoons olive oil all over the meat. Heat the safflower oil in a large, heavy roasting pot over medium-high heat, watching it carefully. When the oil is shimmering, add the shoulder, then immediately turn the heat down to medium and brown the meat on all sides.

Mix all of the stuffing ingredients together in a medium-sized bowl. Put the browned meat on a work surface with the interior, boned surface facing up. If its thickness is overly irregular, use a meat mallet or the flat side of a cleaver to flatten any extra thick areas. Be careful not to overwork it or it will make the meat too soft, even mushy. Spread the stuffing on the meat to within 1 inch of the edges. Roll it and tie it carefully with cotton string. Place the tied shoulder in a heavy copper pot with a tight lid and add the marinade from the zip bag. (If you don't have a copper pot, use a heavy roasting pot with a lid.)

Cover the pan and place over very low heat. Cook until very tender (3 to 6 hours). Baste with pan juices and turn about once an hour. A slow braise of this type cannot be rushed. It should be meltingly tender when finished.

Add a little spring water or more wine if necessary, to maintain the braising liquid. Roast the meat in a 300° F oven. Follow the instructions for stove top cooking, above.

An hour or two before the roast is done cooking, make the noodles from the Herb Noodle recipe (p. 174). Use the same method as the noodle recipe but some slightly different ingredients listed above.

Remove the meat from the pan, tent it with foil to keep it warm and set aside to rest. Skim any excess fat from the braising liquid. Pour the liquid through a large strainer and press the flavorful juices from the solids with a wooden spoon. Discard the solids. You should have about one cup of liquid, if not, add more wine or spring water. Put the liquid back in the pot and scrape any bits from the sides and bottom of the pot. Correct the seasoning if necessary with salt and pepper.

Add the noodles to the braising liquid and gently toss them to coat. Bring the mixture to a simmer, cover and turn off the heat. Carve the roast into 1/2-inch slices. Arrange the meat on each plate with a portion of noodles. Pour a little of the braising liquid over all. Garnish each serving with a sprig of thyme and serve.

BEVERAGE RECOMMENDATION

Valley View Merlot from the Rogue River Valley has gamey overtones and ripe blackberry flavors that admirably complement this meal. Another good Rogue River Valley wine choice would be Griffin Creek Cabernet Sauvignon.

THE VENISON HUNT

FOR THE BEANS

1 cup pinkeye (see resources), great northern or cannellini beans

6 cups chicken stock or spring water

1 herb bundle: a sprig or two each of fresh sage, thyme, rosemary, parsley; 1 small leafy celery stalk; 1/2 leek; and 2 bay leaves

2 cloves garlic

3 tablespoons extra virgin olive oil

FOR THE RABBIT AND VEGETABLES

1/2 cup all-purpose flour for dredging

Salt and pepper

3- to 4-pound young, fresh rabbit cut into 8 pieces (2 front legs, 2 hind legs, the breast separated, the back split lengthwise, then cut crosswise across the middle)

Safflower oil

1 yellow onion, chopped medium

2 cloves garlic, crushed

1 large bay leaf

6 cups Meat Stock (p. 124), Wild Mushroom Stock (p. 126) or water

8 small, red new potatoes, unpeeled

1 turnip, peeled and quartered

1 carrot, peeled and cut into 1/2-inch rounds

2 tablespoons all-purpose flour thinned with a little spring water

2 cups good red wine that will be served with the meal

Dash of cayenne pepper

1 tablespoon tarragon

Few gratings fresh nutmeg

3 tablespoons parsley, finely chopped

2 tablespoons extra virgin olive oil

SERVES 4 TO 6

Rabbit Stewed in Red Wine with Pinkeye Beans

This dish is quite hearty and best served hot during cool weather. It takes about 3 hours to prepare and should rest and mellow another 3 or 4 before serving. Follow the stew with a green salad, a good blue cheese like Stilton and a glass of the same wine used in cooking. If you have a sweet tooth, serve a glass of port with the blue cheese instead of the wine. Add a few walnuts or pecans.

Preheat oven to 200° F.

Pick through the beans for bits of dirt and pebbles. Rinse them well with tap water; drain. In a large 4-quart pot cover the beans with chicken stock, and add herb bundle, garlic cloves and olive oil. Bring to a rolling boil. After about 10 minutes, lower the heat to a simmer. Cover with a lid and simmer until the beans are slightly soft when squeezed between the thumb and index finger (1 to 2 hours). Add water or stock as needed to keep the beans covered. Put the covered pot in a 200° F oven to finish cooking. Depending on the beans this should take 1 to 3 hours more. It will yield a consistent, soft, creamy bean with a minimum amount of disintegration. Season to taste with salt. For a smoky version, put the pot of beans uncovered inside a prepared barbecue grill. Use wood chips for flavoring and cook for the same amount of time.

While the beans are cooking, mix 1/2 cup of flour with salt and pepper. Dredge the rabbit pieces in the flour mixture. Heat safflower oil in a large skillet to medium-high. Add the rabbit and brown the pieces evenly. Set the browned meat aside and turn the heat to low. Wipe out the skillet. Add a little more oil, the onions and garlic. Gently cook them until they are translucent (about 5 minutes). In a large pot add the meat/onion mixture, bay leaf and stock. Cover with a lid and gently simmer until the rabbit is almost tender (about 1 hour).

Add the potatoes, turnip, carrot, and flour and water mixture and stir together. Gently simmer until the potatoes are tender (20 to 30 minutes). Add the beans with their liquid, wine, tarragon, cayenne and a few gratings of nutmeg. Bring to a low simmer for a few minutes. Remove from heat. Taste and correct the seasoning. It is important to let this dish rest for 3 or 4 hours or more before serving. This gives the flavors a chance to cross-penetrate, blend and mellow. To develop an even deeper flavor, cool the beans and meat mixture to room temperature. Put in the refrigerator covered, overnight.

When you're ready to serve, bring the stew to a gentle simmer and cook for about 5 minutes more (longer if the beans have been refrigerated overnight). Remove and discard the herb bundle, sprinkle with minced parsley and turn off the heat. Add a couple tablespoons of fruity olive oil to finish. Serve a ladle or two of the stew in warmed soup bowls. Accompany with good crusty bread (p. 51).

BEVERAGE RECOMMENDATION

A Bogle Petit Sirah or a good California Cabernet such as a BV. Preferably the wine should be the same as used in the stew.

NAKED MILLER'S TROUT

This is a simple, luxurious dish that combines skinless fillets with butter and herbs. It is good with steamed or blanched new vegetables such as baby squash. I call it "Naked Miller's Trout" because no flour is used as in the classic sole meunière. It should be sautéed very gently to preserve the delicate flavors and texture of the fish's flesh.

4 medium-sized (4-ounce) fresh, skinless trout fillets

Salt

8 tablespoons unsalted butter

2 tablespoons freshly squeezed and strained lemon or lime juice (about 1/2 large lemon or lime)

1/2 teaspoon each minced parsley, chervil and tarragon

SERVES 2 TO 4

Clean trout fillets under running water and pat them semi-dry with paper towels. Lightly season with salt. In a 14-inch skillet melt 6 tablespoons of butter until it foams. Add trout fillets and gently cook on low until the flesh turns a light pink. Gently turn the fish and cook until barely done, about 2 minutes. Remove fillets from the pan to a warm serving platter. Tent with foil or place the plate in a warm oven.

Clean the skillet. Working quickly, melt the remaining 2 tablespoons butter over medium heat until it foams. Remove from heat. Add lemon or lime juice and tilt the pan. Whisk the juice rapidly into the butter until it turns into a creamy emulsion. Stir in minced herbs. Taste and add salt if necessary. Pour butter sauce over trout and serve immediately.

BEVERAGE RECOMMENDATION

As usual I encourage people to seek out wines from their own area. Local wines can make uniquely appropriate matches with foods also made with local ingredients. If local Chardonnay is not available a good choice is a Napa Valley Cuvée Sauvage Chardonnay, an opulent wine made with uncompromising standards. A number of white Burgundies would match this recipe nicely. One that I recommend is Dominique Cornin Domaine de Lalande.

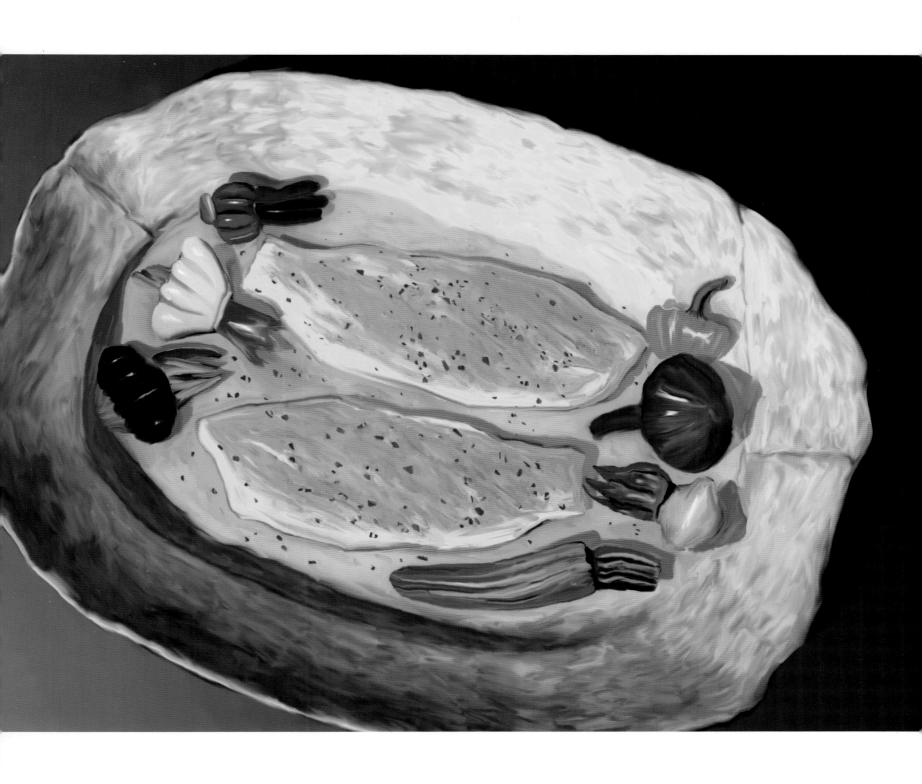

THE VENISON HUNT

LAKE BASS WITH BRAISED FENNEL

FOR THE MARINADE

1/2 teaspoon lime zest

2 tablespoons lime juice

1 cup dry white wine
(preferably the same type as
will be served with the meal)

1 clove crushed garlic

1 whole roasted red bell pepper,
skinned, and seeded (half minced
for the marinade, the other
half diced and reserved for
the side dish with fennel)

FOR THE FISH

4 8-ounce fresh water bass fillets
(or other freshwater fish such as
pike or trout)

2 tablespoons grapeseed oil

FOR THE FENNEL

2 tablespoons grapeseed oil

4 medium fennel bulbs trimmed
and quartered (reserve 4 sprigs
fennel leaves for garnish)

1/2 cup dry white wine

1/2 cup spring water

1 clove garlic, crushed

1/2 roasted red bell pepper
cut into 1/4-inch dice

Salt to taste

SERVES 4

This is a bright and colorful dish with a mellow side. The roasted red pepper gives it a blush of color and a soft, smoky flavor that harmonizes nicely with the citrus flavors. Serve with good crusty bread to mop up the juices.

Stir the marinade ingredients together in a small bowl. Put the fish in a plastic zip bag and add the marinade. Squeeze the air out of the bag and seal it. Gently massage the marinade around the fish so it contacts all surfaces. Set aside for one hour at room temperature.

Add 1 tablespoon grapeseed oil into a large nonreactive frying pan with a tight-fitting lid, over medium heat. When hot, lightly brown the fennel on all sides turning as needed (about 3 minutes per side). In a small bowl, mix together the wine, spring water, garlic and the diced half of the roasted pepper. Add to the pan. Scrape the bottom of the pan to loosen any bits. Cover the pan with the lid and lower heat to medium-low. Simmer until the fennel is tender (20 to 30 minutes). Occasionally scrape the pan and add more spring water, if necessary, to keep the fennel moist. Add salt to taste. When the fennel softens, put the fennel and the braising mixture in an ovenproof saucepan in a warm oven. Clean and dry the frying pan.

Remove the fish from the marinade and pat it dry with paper towels. Reseal the marinade in the bag and set it aside. Add 1 tablespoon grapeseed oil to the frying pan and place it over medium heat. With a spatula distribute the oil evenly around the pan. When the pan is medium-hot add the fish fillets, skin side down, and sear them until they turn a light brown (about 1 minute). Salt to taste each side before turning them. Turn the fillets gently taking care not to break them apart. If they stick, lower the heat a little and let them continue to cook until they release easily. Pour the marinade from the bag into the pan. Cover the pan with the lid and cook the fillets until barely done (about 4 minutes more).

Divide the warm fennel mixture among 4 large soup plates and place 1 fish fillet on top of each. Scrape and deglaze each pan with a splash of white wine and pour it equally over each serving. Garnish with fennel sprigs.

BEVERAGE RECOMMENDATION

A dry white wine with notes of citrus such as a Treanna Marsanne Viognier. Now, wouldn't that make a marvelous local wine?

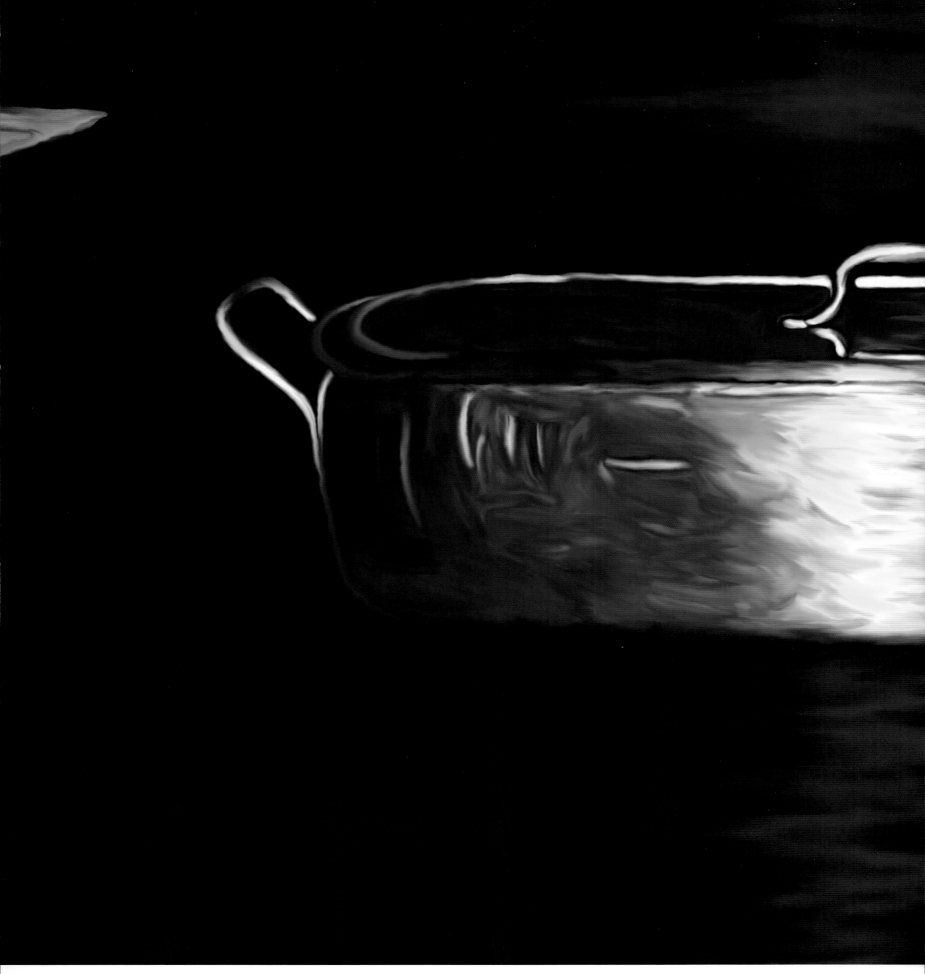

INSIDE THIS SPECIAL PAN
A MAGNIFICENT FISH HAS GIVEN UP ITS LIFE
TO SWIM ONE LAST TIME IN COURT BOUILLON

THE VENISON HUNT

CELEBRATORY BACON-ROASTED CAPON

A capon is a castrated rooster that can be special-ordered from most good butchers and typically weighs from 5 to 9 pounds. It is as large as a small turkey and can generously serve 6 to 8 adults. It is an unusual bird because it has an added layer of fat beneath the skin, which helps keep it moist during dry roasting.

To enhance the moistness and add a rich smoky flavor, carefully wrap bacon around the torso of the bird before roasting. Of course there are a number of other ways to create a variation on the basic theme such as rubbing the skin and inner cavity of the capon with raw garlic, or stuffing the interior with risotto or bread stuffing. I like to use a garlic rub and stuff the cavity abundantly with sage. Making a rich sauce with the pan juices is another delicious addition to a special meal. The bird is very good served with whipped potatoes topped with a warm pool of melted butter.

FOR THE BIRD

1 9-pound capon or 7-pound chicken if you can't find capon

2 or 3 cloves garlic, crushed

1/2 to 1 pound natural thick-sliced bacon

2 or 3 large bunches of fresh sage

Salt and pepper to taste

FOR THE SAUCE

1/4 cup dry white wine

2 or 3 tablespoons good Sour Cream Butter (p. 20) or unsalted butter

1 tablespoon finely minced parsley

1/4 cup heavy cream

SERVES 6 TO 8

Preheat the oven to 400° F.

Allow the capon to rest at room temperature for one hour before roasting. Rub the entire bird with crushed garlic inside and out. Carefully wrap the bacon around the torso, legs and wings. Stuff the sage into the cavity of the bird.

Place the capon in a roasting pan and place in the oven. Reduce the temperature to 350° F. Roast until the juices run clear when the large leg joint is pierced from the side (about 1 1/2 half hours). Remove the bird from the roasting pan. Reserve any excess oil for other uses such as frying potatoes. Tent the bird with foil and set aside.

Over medium-low heat deglaze the pan with the wine and bring wine to a simmer. Add the butter and parsley and stir with a whisk until the butter is melted and the parsley incorporated. Add the cream and bring it to a simmer. Reduce the sauce until it has thickened. Pour into a gravy pitcher. Carve the bird. Include some of the crunchy bacon with each piece. Pass the sauce to nap over the meat.

BEVERAGE RECOMMENDATION

A sturdy old vine Zinfandel from California, such as Bogle or Renwood.

FRESHWATER FISH CAKES WITH SHALLOTS AND CILANTRO

FOR THE STRAW POTATOES

2 medium-sized russet potatoes

3 or 4 cups peanut oil
or grapeseed oil

Salt to taste

FOR THE FISH

Enough trout, bass, perch or pike
to yield 2 cups of meat (roughly
two medium trout should do it)

1 lemon or lime, sliced crosswise
into thin slices

1 tablespoon Old Bay Seasoning

Spring water to cover fish

FOR THE FISH CAKES

2 cups crumbled fish meat

4 tablespoons finely
chopped cilantro

1/2 cup breadcrumbs
or mashed potatoes

4 tablespoons minced shallots
or red onion

2 teaspoons grated horseradish

Chile oil, chile paste or cayenne
to taste (optional)

Salt to taste

Juice and zest from
1 lemon or lime

1 teaspoon salt

2 eggs, well beaten

2 tablespoons safflower oil
or butter for frying

SERVES 4

I don't use fresh crab in Utah because it is expensive, hard to find in good condition and puts added pressure on the world's ocean. Canned crab is a failed substitute. The obvious replacement for making these cakes is local freshwater fish. They make a nice lunch or casual supper. Serve with lime wedges, Special Tartar Sauce (p. 237) and straw potatoes. (For hearty appetites you may want to double the recipe.)

Peel and coarsely grate the potatoes from end-to-end creating the longest shreds possible. Rinse them well with water to remove excess starch. Pat them dry with a clean cotton dish towel. Heat the oil in a deep fryer, wok or slightly less than half-filled saucepan to 375° F. If you don't have a deep fry thermometer, test the hot oil with an individual strand of potato. Lower it into the fat. If it sizzles and browns within a minute the oil is hot enough. Take care not to overfill the pan with oil or plunge a large mass of raw potato into the hot oil all at once or it may boil over, creating a fire hazard.

Fry the potatoes in three or four small batches until they are golden brown. Use caution whether you have a frying basket or are adding the potatoes by hand so that the oil does not splash. Remove potatoes with a slotted spoon. (Any pieces left behind between batches will burn and taste bitter so remove them all.) Place the finished batches on a plate covered with a paper towel to absorb any excess oil, sprinkle them with salt to taste and set them aside. (Shoestring potatoes can be made ahead and allowed to cool to room temperature.)

Wash the whole, dressed fish. Measure their thickness (measured at its thickest point) and place them into a pot along with the lemon, Old Bay Seasoning and spring water. The liquid should completely cover the fish. Bring it to a bare simmer over medium-high heat then turn the heat to very low. Poach for 10 minutes per inch of the body thickness of the fish. Start timing when you lower the heat and add the fish. Carefully remove the fish from the poaching liquid. Let them cool enough to allow handling then separate the meat from the skin and bones, reserving the meat and discarding the rest. Crumble the meat a little so it has a fairly consistent texture. In a mixing bowl blend all the ingredients for the fish cakes except the eggs. Add more chile, horseradish, juice, zest, cilantro or chopped onion if needed. Season with good salt. (Season lightly to begin, so that a small piece can be fried as a test after all the ingredients are mixed in. If necessary add more salt and repeat the test.) Mix in eggs, and depending on the size and number of patties you want to serve each guest, divide the mixture into 4, 6 or 8 portions. Mold each into half-inch-thick, round disks (the diameter can vary but not the thickness). Fry them on a medium-hot, lightly oiled griddle for 4 to 5 minutes on each side or until golden brown (the smaller cakes will need slightly less time to brown).

BEVERAGE RECOMMENDATION

A good beverage match with the citrus and spice of this meal is Hefeweizen — a delicate sweet beer made with wheat. A good wine would be a chilled Gewürztraminer like a Washington Hills grown in the Columbia Valley in Washington.

Pork Tenderloin with Rosemary, Garlic & Bacon

This recipe makes a nice dinner for a reasonable price. The bacon protects the tenderloin from the heat of the oven, bastes it, and keeps it moist while it roasts. The result is a rich, smoky flavor that pairs well with the garlic and rosemary.

Good side dishes for this meal are Pinkeye Beans with Rosemary (p. 120) and Honey Glazed Carrots with Tarragon (p. 196). Mashed potatoes are also a good choice. If you choose the mashed potatoes, double the sauce recipe and spoon some of it over the potatoes.

FOR BASTING

2 or 3 peeled cloves garlic

Leaves from 2 or 3 sprigs of fresh rosemary, plus 6 whole sprigs for garnish

1/2 cup extra virgin olive oil

1/2 cup Cabernet Franc

Salt

FOR THE MEAT

2 1-pound pork tenderloins

Salt

2 slices thick-cut bacon

FOR THE SAUCE

4 tablespoons butter

1/3 cup all-purpose flour

1 cup Meat Stock (p. 124) or Wild Mushroom Stock (p. 126)

2 or 3 tablespoons liquid from the Pinkeye Beans if you include them as a side dish, or stock if you don't

SERVES 6

Preheat oven to 400° F.

Place the garlic, rosemary leaves, olive oil and wine in a blender or food processor. Process until quite smooth. Season the tenderloins with salt and place in a gallon plastic zip bag. Pour the garlic mixture into the bag and squeeze the air out. Make sure the tenderloins are evenly coated. Allow the meat to rest overnight in the refrigerator (or at room temperature for an hour).

Remove the tenderloins from the bag and put them in a roasting pan. Cover each one with a strip of bacon and pour basting liquid around meat. Insert a meat thermometer on a diagonal angle into the center of the largest part of one of the tenderloin. Baste the tenderloin every 10 minutes with the liquid in the bottom of the roasting pan. Roast until the internal temperature reaches 150° F. (Start checking the temperature after about 20 minutes.) Remove from oven. The internal temperature will increase to about 155° F as they rest. They should be a rich, gold color. Remove from the roasting pan and place on a cutting board for 10 minutes while you make the sauce.

With a dinner fork work the butter and flour together thoroughly. Divide into 3 or 4 balls by rolling them between the palms of your hands. Set aside.

To make the sauce, pour and skim off most of the fat leaving the juices in the pan. Place the pan on a stove top burner. Deglaze pan with the stock and bring it to a simmer, scraping the residual bits from the bottom and sides of the pan. If you serve the beans add two or three tablespoons of the bean liquid into the sauce. If you don't serve the beans use an additional two or three tablespoons of stock.

Warm the serving plates. Carve the tenderloins into 1/2-inch slices. Whisk the flour and butter balls, one at a time, into the simmering liquid until it reaches the thickness of cream. It should only take a minute or two to thicken. Divide the sauce evenly among the plates. Lay the sliced pork on top of each puddle of sauce. If you choose to serve the Pinkeye Beans and the Honey Glazed Carrots, be sure to use a slotted spoon to lift them out of the liquid to drain them before plating.

BEVERAGE RECOMMENDATION

A good wine to serve is a Cabernet Franc, such as Land and Reed, a fruity, lighter cousin of Cabernet Sauvignon. If keeping within a budget serve a Chilean version from the Maipo or Maule Valleys. These are honest wines at reasonable prices.

Meatloaf Stuffed with Marrow, Black Walnuts and Capers

This is an elegant variation on an old American favorite. It is served with either lovage or parsley potatoes and brown sauce. Depending on how well-done you choose to bake it, the marrow will dissolve, giving the center a meltingly luxurious texture. Medium-rare will leave a little marrow texture, medium to well-done will completely melt it. One hour in a 375° F oven will yield medium.

FOR THE STUFFING	FOR THE MEAT	FOR THE POTATOES
1/2 cup fresh bone marrow	1 pound ground elk chuck or round (beef may be substituted)	16 small red organic potatoes
1 cup fresh breadcrumbs	1 cup breadcrumbs	2 tablespoons minced fresh lovage or parsley
2 tablespoons minced onion	2 cloves garlic, crushed	1 teaspoon minced fresh lovage for dressing the cooked potatoes
1 teaspoon salt or 1 tablespoon Bragg Liquid Aminos (see resources)	1 tablespoon Prepared Horseradish Sauce (p. 249)	3 tablespoons extra virgin olive oil
1 tablespoon crushed, black walnuts	1 teaspoon Tabasco Sauce	Salt to taste
1 tablespoon small capers, drained	3/4 teaspoon salt or 2 teaspoons Bragg Liquid Aminos	Fresh lovage sprigs or parsley sprigs for garnish
1 tablespoon minced fresh thyme	2 tablespoons crushed black walnut meats	2 or 3 cups Brown Sauce (p. 260)
Freshly ground black pepper	2 tablespoons capers, drained	
	1/2 teaspoon cayenne pepper	
	Freshly ground black pepper	

SERVES 4

Marrowbones are available at most butchers. They should be large leg bones, sawed into 3- or 4-inch lengths by the butcher. Because the amount of marrow can vary considerably in marrowbones, it is wise to buy at least 3 pounds from which to obtain the 1/2 cup needed for this recipe; 4 pounds is even better. After the marrow is removed, reserve the bones to make stock for the Brown Sauce. If there is excessive marrow add it to the sauce.

Preheat oven to 400° F.

Compared to commercial beef, elk is very lean. By itself it will usually yield dry meatloaf. So if using elk, you'll want to add ground marrow or suet, or mix the ground elk with some ground beef to make about 1 pound. When you're ready to make the meatloaf, blanch the marrowbones in lightly salted, boiling water for a minute or two. Remove the marrow from the bones with a chopstick or skewer. Chop the marrow into wheat-berry sized pieces and thoroughly mix it with all of the stuffing ingredients and set aside.

Thoroughly mix all of the ingredients for the meat together and spread it into a 3/4-inch layer on a piece of plastic wrap. Shape the stuffing into a tube. Place it lengthwise on the meat layer and roll it away from you. The object is to make sure there is marrow in all 4 servings and that it is in the center of the loaf. Smooth and seal the ends. Roll the meat loaf out of the plastic wrap and into an oiled loaf pan. Because the meatloaf will shrink a little, use a 9 x 4-inch loaf pan.

While you are preparing the meat, place a pan containing one quart of hot water on the bottom rack of the oven and preheat the oven to 400° F. The water may need to be replenished with more boiling water during the time the meatloaf is in the oven. It should be conveniently positioned so it doesn't have to be removed from the oven. (The boiling water maintains high humidity in the oven giving the loaf a softer, moister texture.) Lower the heat to 375° F and place the meatloaf on the rack above the pan of hot water and bake for approximately 1 hour.

While the meatloaf is baking, wash and trim any flaws from the potatoes and gently simmer them in salted water with the chopped lovage until they are just tender. Drain the cooked potatoes and toss them in a little olive oil with the remaining lovage. If you are using parsley, cook the potatoes by themselves. Toss the parsley and the olive oil with the potatoes after they are cooked.

Warm the Brown Sauce and the plates before assembling and time everything so it will be hot when the meatloaf comes out of the oven. Puddle the Brown Sauce on the plates. Divide the meatloaf into portions and place each, cut side up, to reveal the interior. Arrange the potatoes on the plates and garnish with fresh lovage leaves or parsley sprigs.

BEVERAGE RECOMMENDATION

A wine from the Saint-Julien appellation of the Bordeaux region, such as Chateau Beychevelle, is a special treat with this dish.

Rocky Mountain Oysters

Ranch women usually draw the line somewhere on the other side of preparing this dish — so the preparation falls to the men in a kind of ancient ritual of tribal, two-fisted virility. At the end of a hard day of branding and castrating calves on our ranch we would send someone off for a case of cold beer while we fried the "oysters" in a big, cast-iron skillet over the branding fire. Like ocean oysters, land oysters are reputed to be an aphrodisiac, but only seem to work when accompanied by several cans of beer.

1 pound of good bacon

2 or 3 dozen fresh calves testicles (code name "oysters")

Salt to taste

Few grinds black pepper

SERVES 8

Heat a large, cast-iron skillet over a branding fire and fry the bacon until nicely brown and crisp taking care not to burn it. Set it aside on a plate. Pour off most of the hot grease from the frying pan into an old hubcap to cool for the dogs.

Rinse the oysters thoroughly with water and pat them dry with paper towels. Season them with a little salt. Let the salt dissolve and penetrate the oysters for a few minutes. Fry them in the bacon drippings in batches so they are not crowded. Turn them until they are cooked through and golden brown (about 5 minutes). Season the oysters with a few grinds of black pepper then put the bacon back in the pan with the oysters to warm. Serve directly from the pan.

BEVERAGE RECOMMENDATION

Accompany with ice-cold American 3.2 percent see-through beer such as Pabst Blue Ribbon.

GARDEN SNAILS

FOR THE SNAILS

7 cups yellow cornmeal

Water

160 to 200 snails

1/2 cup salt

1/2 cup red wine vinegar

FOR THE STOCK

2 cups chicken stock

Herb bundle consisting of a sprig of thyme and parsley, small stalk of celery, a strip of leek or green onion and a bay leaf securely wrapped together with cotton string

1 cup dry white wine

FOR THE BUTTER

1/2 pound Sour Cream Butter (p. 20) or unsalted butter for stuffing

4 cloves finely minced garlic

4 tablespoons finely minced parsley

4 tablespoons finely minced shallots

1 teaspoon salt

EQUIPMENT

1 5-gallon bucket and 1 smaller bucket

Mesh screen large enough to cover the 5-gallon bucket

A brick or rock to weigh down the screen

SERVES 4

Few people in the United States realize that you can eat garden snails. They mistakenly think of them as pests. Many people around the world, with more adventuresome palates, however, consider the small garden snail to be one of the best culinary varieties. Far from thinking of them as a pest, I consider them a food crop and a delicacy . . . but, never use snails that have been in an environment with snail bait. Even organically grown snails must be carefully cleansed for a week before they are ready for consumption.

Snails used as a main course make a sumptuous meal and are best appreciated when served with no preceding appetizers. I also think they are at their best with nothing more than good crusty bread and a robust red wine that stands up to the garlicky flavors.

After it rains the snails head for the vegetable garden so I always try to gather them then, or carry them away from the garden where I release them to be gathered later when their numbers increase. I consider this task to be a small price to pay to protect the garden without the use of deadly chemicals and to be blessed with this delicacy. The garden snail is usually quite small (the shell, in a mature garden snail, is only 1 to 1 1/2 inches in diameter), so it will take about 40 for an adult serving.

Before cooking, gather 160 to 200 snails and put them in a 5-gallon plastic bucket. Cover the bucket with a rigid fine mesh wire screen. The screen must be fine enough to prevent the snails from getting out. Place a weight on the screen and set the bucket in a cool, shady place.

Before you feed the snails, remove the screen and lay the bucket on its side. Wash the snails daily by spraying them in the bucket with a garden hose. Immediately pour off any excess water. Handle them gently and be careful not to drown them. Discard any that expire. Put the snails in the other bucket while you clean the interior surfaces of the larger bucket. You must do this each time you wash the snails. This gives them a clean environment to live in. Pour one cup of yellow cornmeal in the bucket. Repeat this ritual daily for a week. It is essential to give the snails one thorough, final rinse to completely clean them before cooking.

Put a 4-quart pot on the stove and bring to a simmer. While the water is heating, place the freshly washed snails in a large mixing bowl and cover them with water. Add 1/2 cup salt and 1/2 cup vinegar. This purges them of any waste materials. Wearing rubber gloves, stir them with your hand for a few seconds until the water thickens. Discard the water. Repeat the process until they are fully purged and the water is no longer viscous.

Heat a pot of water large enough to just cover the snails. Bring to a simmer. Rinse the snails in a colander with cold water. Put them in the simmering water for 3 or 4 minutes. Pour off the water and remove the meat from their shells with a nut pick or crab fork. Set the delicate shells aside, being careful not to damage them. Place the meat in a saucepan with the stock and herbs and bring to a low simmer.

Cover with a tight lid. Cook the snails in the stock until they are almost tender (about 45 minutes). Add the wine and continue to cook until they are tender. For small garden snails this should take about another hour. If you are squeamish about it, remove the small dark vein at the thin end of the snail. This is optional since the snails have been internally cleansed with cornmeal.

As the snail meat is simmering, carefully wash the shells and cover them in water in a saucepan and bring to a gentle simmer for 5 minutes to sterilize them. Drain them and set them aside to dry. Preheat the oven to 425° F.

With a wooden spoon or butter paddle soften the butter and mix in the garlic, parsley, shallots and salt. Stuff some of this mixture into a shell, then insert a cooked snail. Seal it over with more of the butter mixture. Only the butter mixture should show. Repeat with all of the snails. Place the stuffed and buttered snails on a large baking sheet with their openings facing up. Crowding them together will help hold them upright. Place them in the hot oven for about 5 minutes until the butter is bubbling hot and serve immediately.

Present the snails on a large platter in the middle of the table. Let your guests serve themselves. Pass warm, crusty bread around the table so your guests can sop up the juices and melted butter from their plates. You should set a few empty bowls on the table for the discarded shells.

Follow this main course with a green salad dressed with vinaigrette. For the final course, serve good cheese such as Edam, Brie, fresh Chèvre or Farmer's Cheese (p. 26).

BEVERAGE RECOMMENDATION

An excellent wine for this meal is a Beringer Cabernet Sauvignon from Knight's Valley in Napa. This full-bodied Cabernet has just the right amount of oak and nicely layered fruit to complement the snails.

When my brother Fred and I were young boys on the farm one of our favorite games was hypnotizing chickens. What makes this partly possible is the natural fascination birds have with shiny objects. With our pockets full of marbles we would go into the chicken coop, catch a hen and take her outside. One of us would set her down in front of a straight furrow we had drawn in the dirt and the other would place a marble in the end of the furrow away from the chicken and then move the marble slowly back and forth. In a short time the chicken would fall into a hypnotic trance. While we left her lying flat with her head and beak at the end of the furrow staring motionless at the marble we would rush back in to get the next chicken. The object of this game was to see how many chickens we could hypnotize before they started waking up wondering where they were. I think our record went into the twenties. It was good clean entertainment that would probably get us in trouble these days.

PAN-FRIED POULTRY WITH MASHED POTATOES AND GRAVY

FOR THE POULTRY

1 3- to 4-pound pheasant or free-range chicken

Salt to taste

1 cup all-purpose flour for dredging the pheasant

Fresh, finely ground black pepper to taste

1 cup light cooking oil such as safflower or grapeseed

FOR THE MASHED POTATOES

2 pounds Pontiac Red or Yellow Finn potatoes

1 1/2 cups warm cream, half-and-half, or whole milk

10 tablespoons soft Sour Cream Butter (p. 20) or unsalted butter

Salt to taste

FOR THE SAUCE

3 tablespoons butter at room temperature

3 tablespoons all-purpose flour

1/4 cup dry white wine

2 cups milk or half-and-half

Salt to taste

Pepper to taste

1 tablespoon finely minced fresh tarragon leaves

SERVES 2 TO 4

When we were young, my brothers and I were given the job of cutting alfalfa for our farm animals with the tractor and mowing machine. For me the most painful part of the job was the difficulty of avoiding the hen pheasants in the uncut alfalfa as they were lingering on their nests to protect their eggs. The dubious reward was a pheasant lunch as only my mother could prepare it. To this day, regardless of price or setting, I've never eaten pheasant a fraction as good as those were.

She prepared pheasant simply and without fuss, as she would fried chicken. The rich flavors of fresh, wild pheasant made it very special. This version is much the same as hers. Instead of making cream gravy with the drippings, the pan is deglazed with white wine and thickened at the last minute with beurre manié.

Finish this meal with a green salad such as young dandelion greens with sweet raw onion rings and chervil dressed with a simple vinaigrette. Serve the salad separately on a chilled plate.

Cut the poultry into 8 pieces. Detach the legs, thighs and wings from the body at the joints. Separate the breast from the back by splitting the bird vertically between the ribs and back on both sides, forcing the breast and back apart with your hands. Finish the separation with a sharp knife, a cleaver or poultry scissors. Carefully cut the breast lengthwise down the middle to the bone. Cut through the breast bone to yield two symmetrical pieces. Cut the back crosswise in the middle. Trim any loose skin and fat edges from the pieces.

Carefully wash the pieces under warm running water then dry them a little with paper towels. While they are still quite damp, sprinkle lightly and evenly with salt and let them rest for a few minutes to absorb the salt. Dredge the pieces in flour seasoned with pepper.

Heat the oil in a large skillet until it just begins to smoke. Brown the pieces on both sides over medium-high heat then lower the heat to medium-low. Cover and cook until the juices no longer are pink when the bird is pierced at the upper leg joint (usually 10 to 15 minutes per side after browning). Don't crowd the pieces together or they will trap steam inside the pan and lose their crisp coating. For 8 pieces it will take two medium-sized frying pans or two batches in one pan. The breast halves will take about 10 minutes less to cook than the other pieces, so start them later or remove them as soon as they feel springy to the touch. When cooked properly the meat should be moist but not pink inside. As the pieces cook, set them aside on paper towels on a warm plate.

While the pheasant is cooking, gently simmer unpeeled potatoes in water until soft (about 30 minutes). If you peel them before boiling they will absorb excess water causing them to lose some of their flavor. After they are cooked, drain them then let them dry in the warm pan for a couple of minutes over low heat.

Peel them or put them through a potato ricer, one at a time, with their peelings on. A potato ricer will trap the peeling so it can be easily removed between each potato. If you peel them first they can be mashed with a potato masher or electric mixer (take care not to overmix if using an electric mixer or potatoes will turn gummy). If there are still lumps, push them through a strainer.

Place the peeled potatoes back in the warm pan over low heat. Stir in a little salt, wait a minute or two for it to dissolve then taste. Add more as needed. Keep the potatoes hot over low heat. Add cream and butter a little at a time, stirring vigorously until each batch is completely absorbed. Taste and correct the salt if necessary. Put the finished potatoes in a warm oven. (Good olive oil and a little of the water that the potatoes were cooked in can replace both the cream and butter if preferred. In either case add the ingredients incrementally, incorporate them, taste and repeat until the desired results are achieved.)

Before preparing the sauce, work the butter and flour together thoroughly with a fork. Divide into 3 or 4 balls by rolling them between the palms of your hands. Set aside. Pour off all the oil from the frying pan. Deglaze it with the wine stirring and scraping for a few minutes on medium-low heat. Add the milk and vigorously whisk it in. Bring to a simmer. If desired strain our any lumps at this point and put the strained sauce back in the pan. Taste and correct the seasoning. Vigorously whisk in the balls of flour and butter until desired consistency, then stir in the tarragon. The sauce will thicken within a minute. Immediately remove it from the heat. Serve immediately.

BEVERAGE RECOMMENDATION

Serve a chilled Chandon Blanc de Noir Sparkling Wine. It matches well with all fowl — especially pheasant.

Chicken Soup with Herbed Noodles and Garlic Mashed Potatoes

FOR THE CHICKEN AND BROTH

1 large (5- to 6-pound) roasting chicken

Spring water to cover

1 teaspoon salt

2 cloves garlic, crushed

FOR THE NOODLES

2 cups all-purpose flour, or for a richer flavor but slightly thicker noodle, mix 1 cup each all-purpose flour and whole-wheat pastry flour

2 large eggs

1/2 teaspoon salt

2 tablespoons extra virgin olive oil

4 tablespoons finely minced, fresh herbs in combination, such as tarragon with parsley, thyme with flat-leaf parsley or chervil with curly leaf parsley

2 tablespoons white wine (same as served with the meal) or water

FOR THE MASHED POTATOES

8 to 12 medium-sized waxy boiling potatoes

Water to cover the potatoes

1 tablespoon salt

1 head of garlic (about 20 cloves)

1 teaspoon vanilla extract (optional)

Extra virgin olive oil to taste

Freshly ground pepper to taste

SERVES 6

As a boy I was fascinated by the way my mother and her sisters made pasta. With a few simple ingredients they created a thin, elastic dough you could see your hand through. It was — and still is — a labor of love and one of my favorite forms of kitchen alchemy.

Noodles and mashed potatoes served together make a hearty and comforting meal. Most people today would balk at serving two starches in one dish, but the combination is unusual and delicious, even to a jaded palate.

In post-war rural Utah, where appetites were as real as the foods that satisfied them, this dish was served at noonday to the threshing and haying crews. In my version I add garlic to the potatoes and fresh herbs to the noodles for more definition between the flavors of the two starches. I like to follow this dish with a green salad.

Preheat oven to 375° F.

In a large stock pot, cover the chicken and its giblets with spring water and add salt. Simmer on very low heat. After you put the chicken on to cook wrap a bulb of garlic in aluminum foil and place it in a 375° F oven. The chicken and garlic will finish at about the same time. When the chicken is almost tender enough to separate from the bone (1 to 1 1/2 hours) carefully lift the whole chicken from the broth and set it aside to cool in a large bowl. Cover it so it won't dry out. Remove the garlic from the oven and set it aside to cool.

Pour the flour into a pile on a clean counter. Make a well in the center about the size of a cupped hand. Lightly beat the eggs in a bowl with the salt, olive oil, 2 tablespoons of the mixed herbs and the wine and pour it into the well in the flour. From the lower edge of the mound start drawing up a little flour and work it into the liquid. Continue working until it's all mixed together. Add more wine or water if necessary, to incorporate all of the flour. Begin kneading the dough until it becomes silky and stretchy (about 10 minutes). Set aside in a bowl to rest, covered, for at least 30 minutes to develop additional gluten.

(recipe continued on page 176)

When the chicken is cool enough to handle remove the skin and bones and discard. Reserve the meat and cover.

In a large pot, bring potatoes and water to a boil. Reduce the heat to a simmer and cook until the potatoes are tender when pierced with a small knife. Put them through a potato ricer with their skins on. Remove skins from the ricer. A second method is to peel, cook and mash them with a potato masher until they are smooth and fluffy. Season with salt to taste.

Squeeze the baked cloves of garlic from their skins into a mortar. Mash them to a paste then thoroughly stir in 2 or 3 tablespoons olive oil. Pour this mixture into the mashed potatoes and thoroughly stir together. An alternative method is to put the peeled cooked garlic and oil in a food processor and process on low until smooth, then add the mixture to the potatoes and thoroughly stir together.

Mashed potatoes can absorb a surprising amount of olive oil and salt. This amount of mashed potatoes will easily absorb a full cup of oil. But the amount should be determined by taste. If you choose to continue adding oil, put the pan over low heat to keep the potatoes warm as you stir in the oil. This will help the oil absorb more easily. Working with a large wooden spoon, incorporate the oil into the potatoes 2 or 3 tablespoons at a time. As you work, slowly correct the seasoning with salt, stir it in and allow it to dissolve before adding more. Add vanilla, if using, and freshly ground pepper to taste.

If the mixture seems too dry stir in a little chicken stock. Set aside in an ovenproof, covered container in a warm oven until ready to serve.

After the noodle dough has rested, cut it into 2 or 3 equal pieces and roll them out on a lightly floured surface. Using a rolling pin in concert with your hands, roll and stretch the dough into a circle. With care, you should be able to roll the dough very thin. As you become more experienced you will be able to get it thinner and thinner. Good noodles, when cooked, should not be over 1/16-inch; 1/32-inch is better. Because they become thicker when cooked, they need to be rolled thin. This is perhaps the most important detail of the preparation and success of this dish.

Dust the noodle dough generously with flour so it won't stick together when it is rolled up. Roll the finished circle of dough into a long cigar shape (imagine folding a tight cinnamon roll). With a sharp knife, cut the roll straight across into 1/4-inch strips. Unroll them and drape them across a large platter or hang them across a line of cotton twine to dry for 10 minutes).

An alternative method is to use a roller pasta machine according to the manufacturer's instructions. Unless you're an experienced cook and noodle maker, the machine will probably give you the best results.

Bring the chicken broth to a simmer and cook the noodles in 2 or 3 batches until they are barely soft (5 to 10 minutes). Drain them and put them in a covered pan. As each batch finishes add them together and drizzle a little olive oil over the accumulating pile. Gently toss to evenly coat them so they won't stick together. Put the noodles in a bowl, cover them and place in a warm oven.

Put the reserved meat and noodles back in the broth and bring to a gentle simmer. When they are nicely warmed, add the remaining tablespoon of chopped herbs and turn off the heat. Taste and correct the seasoning.

Stir the potatoes vigorously for a few seconds. Scoop a generous helping of potatoes into a soup bowl. Ladle the soup mixture over the potatoes. Include equal portions of chicken in the bowls. Drizzle a little olive oil over each bowl, add some freshly ground black pepper and serve.

BEVERAGE RECOMMENDATION

A wine that achieves a nice balance with this rich meal is a white Pinot such as a Trimbach Pinot Blanc.

FLATTENED CHICKEN BREASTS WITH MUSTARD, CORIANDER & CILANTRO

This is a quick and simple little supper. It is especially good with sweet corn on the cob or Blue Collar Polenta with Mixed Herbs (p. 197) and a simple green salad dressed with an Asian vinaigrette. Make the vinaigrette with a lower ratio of vinegar to oil (5 parts oil to 1 part vinegar) so it can be served with the chicken. The low acidity of the vinaigrette makes the salad more compatible with wine.

Salad is usually not eaten with an entrée, but rules are made to be broken. The cold crispness of the red cabbage makes an interesting counterpoint to the soft, rich polenta and mildly spicy chicken breasts.

FOR THE CHICKEN

2 whole boneless, fryer breasts, cut down the center into two pieces

Salt and pepper

4 heaping tablespoons all-purpose flour

1/2 cup vegetable oil

FOR THE MARINADE

1 tablespoon finely minced shallot or red onion

1 tablespoon extra virgin olive oil

1 tablespoon Dijon mustard

2 teaspoons ground coriander

Salt to taste

1 cup white wine

1 teaspoon finely minced cilantro

1/2 cup heavy cream for the sauce

SERVES 4 TO 6

NOTE: Prepare whatever side dishes you plan to serve before preparing the chicken, which should be served as soon as the sauce is finished.

Using a meat mallet or the flat side of a large cleaver, place two chicken breasts inside a half-gallon plastic zip bag. Pound and flatten the breasts to about 1/4 inch thickness. Repeat with the other two breasts. Trim any ragged edges. Pounding tenderizes the flesh and creates a uniform thickness, which helps the chicken cook evenly. The chicken will cook quickly so it is important not to overcook it or it will dry out. For chicken breasts, the ideal point of doneness is exactly when its pinkness is almost gone — but no further. They will continue to cook while they rest. Mix the marinade ingredients together except the cream. Pour them into the plastic zip bag over the chicken breasts. Let them rest at room temperature for an hour or overnight in the refrigerator.

Remove the breasts from the marinade. Scrape the excess marinade back into the plastic bag. Lightly season the breasts with salt and pepper, dredge them in flour and set aside. After a few minutes repeat the dredging process so they have a generous, even coating of flour. Gently shake off any excess and set aside.

Heat 1/4 cup of oil in each of two large frying pans. Raise the heat to medium-high. When the oil begins to smoke, add the chicken. Cook quickly for about one minute on each side. Remove the breasts from the pans and set them aside on a prewarmed platter in a warm oven.

Wipe the pan with a paper towel. Add the marinade and stir in the cream. Bring the mixture to a simmer and reduce it by about half. Taste and adjust the seasoning. Place one chicken breast on each warmed plate. Pour sauce over each breast and garnish with a sprig of cilantro. Serve immediately with the polenta and salad.

BEVERAGE RECOMMENDATION

Ste. Chapelle Chardonnay fits this meal quite nicely.

THE VENISON HUNT

POT ROAST AND CABBAGE BRAISED IN RED WINE

In this braise, the roast and cabbage absorb flavor and meld into a delicious little symphony when cooked with the other ingredients for 3 to 5 hours. This is an easy but slow weekend meal. It pairs well when served over ribbon noodles or Blue Collar Polenta with Mixed Herbs (p. 197), either of which can be prepared in less than 30 minutes as the roast finishes.

3 to 4 pounds boneless beef chuck or blade roast

3 tablespoons safflower oil

1 yellow onion, chopped medium

2 cups beef stock

1 cup dry red wine (wine that is similar to the one served with dinner)

2 bundles of herbs: each containing 1 bay leaf, 2 sprigs fresh thyme and 2 sprigs parsley tied together with cotton string

1 medium head of red cabbage, cored, quartered and shredded

4 to 6 cloves garlic, peeled

1 cup dry red wine (for cabbage)

Spring water to replenish braising liquid

Salt and pepper to taste

A few gratings of fresh nutmeg

2 tablespoons finely minced curly leaf parsley

Fresh thyme sprigs for garnish

SERVES 4 TO 6

Pat the beef with paper towels to remove any excess moisture. Pour the safflower oil into a roasting pan, place it over medium-high heat and add the beef. Brown it on both sides. If it sticks, lower the heat a little and let it continue searing until it releases easily. Remove it from the pan and set aside. Add the onion and lower the heat. Cook until translucent (about 5 minutes). Add the stock, wine and one bundle of herbs. Lay the roast on top of the mixture. Bring to a simmer, lower the heat and cover with a tight fitting lid. Turn the roast over every 30 minutes until it becomes fork tender. When it reaches this point, discontinue turning the roast and simply baste it every 30 minutes for an hour or so.

After three hours of roasting, remove the meat and set aside. Put the cabbage, garlic, another cup of wine and the second bundle of herbs into the roasting pan and stir them into the braising mixture. Set the meat on top of the mixture. Return the pan to the oven. After about 30 minutes the cabbage and meat will sink down into the liquid. Continue to simmer on low. Add spring water as needed to maintain the liquid level. Lightly season the meat with a little salt at this point. After 30 minutes more it should come apart easily with a fork. If it doesn't, allow it to continue cooking until it does.

Remove the meat from the pan and strain the juices into a small, uncovered saucepan. Bring to a simmer. Reduce the liquid to about a cup and a half, taste and season with salt and pepper. If you are serving noodles, add the cooked, drained noodles to the reduced braising liquid to warm them. Carve the roast and serve it with the cabbage mixture and any reserved juices. Divide among the plates and include one clove of cooked garlic with each serving. Garnish each plate with little minced parsley and a sprig of thyme.

BEVERAGE RECOMMENDATION

A nice wine choice is Ricasolli Chianti.

Parsnip-Stuffed Lamb Shoulder

1 boneless lamb shoulder,
2 to 4 pounds

Salt and pepper

Olive oil

Safflower oil for browning

FOR THE STUFFING

1/2 cup coarsely grated parsnips

1/2 cup breadcrumbs

3 cloves garlic, crushed

1/2 cup finely chopped
yellow onion

1/4 cup extra virgin olive oil

2 tablespoons flat leaf parsley,
finely minced plus a sprig
to garnish each serving

1/2 level teaspoon salt and a
few grinds of black pepper

2 tablespoons cognac

1/8 to 1/2 teaspoon
cayenne pepper

1 cup red wine for basting

1 cup Meat Stock (p. 124) or
Wild Mushroom Stock (p. 126)

SERVES 4 TO 8

A lamb shoulder dinner is usually less formal than one featuring a leg of lamb. The shoulder meat is more flavorful. Because it must be cooked slowly to break down its connective tissue and release the natural gelatin, it has time to absorb even more flavor from the braising liquid and stuffing ingredients.

This version is a hearty braise which takes 30 minutes to prep and 3 to 6 hours to cook. The parsnips impart a uniquely sweet perfume to the meat. Potatoes Sofia (p. 212) and a vegetable such as braised lettuces or steamed baby beets with their greens attached, dressed with a light vinaigrette, are good choices to serve alongside.

Preheat oven to 300° F.

Season the meat with salt and pepper and rub it with olive oil. Heat a roasting pan over medium-high heat, add the safflower oil and brown the inner and outer surfaces. Remove the shoulder from the pan and let it cool a little so that you can handle it comfortably. Wipe the excess fat out of the roasting pan.

As the lamb cools mix all the stuffing ingredients together except red wine and stock. Lay the shoulder on a flat surface with the inside, boned surface up. Even out the thickness with a basher or mallet. I use a small clawless hammer that hangs next to my chopping block to tenderize and even any thick areas. Spread all of the stuffing on surface, leaving an inch of meat showing along the edges. Carefully roll the shoulder around the stuffing and tie it securely with strong cotton twine.

Place it in the roasting pan. Add a cup of red wine and a cup of stock or water. If you choose to cook it on the stovetop, raise the heat to medium until the liquid begins to simmer then turn the heat down very low and cover. If you have a copper roaster you can cook the lamb on the stovetop over very low heat. It makes it easier to baste the meat and observe its progress. For stovetop braising, copper is ideal because it conducts heat up the sides and across the lid very efficiently surrounding the meat, cooking it gently and evenly.

Another good method is to cook it in the oven at 300° F in a heavy, enameled cast-iron pot with a lid. Set the oven rack low enough so that it will be easy to remove the lid for basting. Brush the braising liquid over the roast every 15 minutes or so as it cooks. Add more wine or stock as needed. Either way, to melt the connective tissue it will require 3 to 5 hours of cooking. This step cannot be rushed. Cooking too long is better than not long enough. Remove the meat from the pan and let it rest for about 10 minutes before carving it.

Spoon off the excess oil and fat and deglaze the pan by adding a little red wine or stock to the liquid that is left in the bottom of the braising pan. Bring it to a simmer on top of the stove. Taste and correct the seasoning. If you prefer the sauce to be thicker, simmer it a little longer. Remove the string and cut the lamb into 1/2-inch slices and serve with the pan juices.

BEVERAGE RECOMMENDATION

A Rosso Del Conte, made from the Sicilian grape varietal Nero d'Avola.

LAMB BURGERS WITH GARLIC AND MINT

This burger is full-flavored and delicious if prepared carefully and finished with the right garnishes. For best results, use fresh ground lamb with around 20 percent fat and don't overcook it.

Garnish with Dijon mustard and Minted Mayonnaise (p. 263). Add a thin slice of sweet onion, a generous slice of vine-ripened tomato and a few leaves of arugula. Serve with a Mama Beth's Dill Pickle (p. 228), a handful of potato chips and a few Marinated Olives (p. 211).

---

1 clove garlic, crushed

2 heaping tablespoons minced fresh mint

1/2 teaspoon salt

1/4 to 1/2 teaspoon chile oil (p. 250) or chile paste (available in most Asian food stores) to taste

1 pound ground lamb

Freshly ground black pepper to taste

2 tablespoons butter

4 whole-grain hamburger buns or kaiser rolls

SERVES 4

Crush the garlic, mint and a little of the salt in a mortar and pestle. Add chile oil or paste and mix together well. Season the meat with salt and pepper and mix in the garlic/mint mixture. Place the seasoned meat in a plastic bag or covered bowl in the refrigerator overnight or at room temperature for about an hour before using for the flavors to absorb.

Divide the meat mixture into four equal portions and shape them into round patties a little less than 1 inch thick. Cook them on a grill over mesquite or hardwood charcoal, under a broiler or in a hot frying pan to desired doneness; 2 to 3 minutes on each side for rare, 3 to 4 minutes for medium should prevent the lamb from drying out. Brushing a little melted butter on the meat as it cooks also helps. Warm the buns on the grill or over the patties during the last minute or so of cooking.

BEVERAGE RECOMMENDATION

Two appropriate wines for this meal are Bogle Shiraz or Woodbridge Zinfandel from California.

I HAVE ONLY ONE BIG BROTHER AND
HERE HE IS AN ARCHETYPE OF HIS
GENERATION — RETRIEVING BURLAP-
WRAPPED CUTS OF LAMB FROM AN
ANCIENT FIRE PIT.

A METHOD HANDED DOWN THROUGH
GENERATIONS OF OTHER COWBOY
ARCHETYPES BACK TO SOME
PRIMEVAL PAST LONG LOST IN THE
MISTS OF HISTORY.

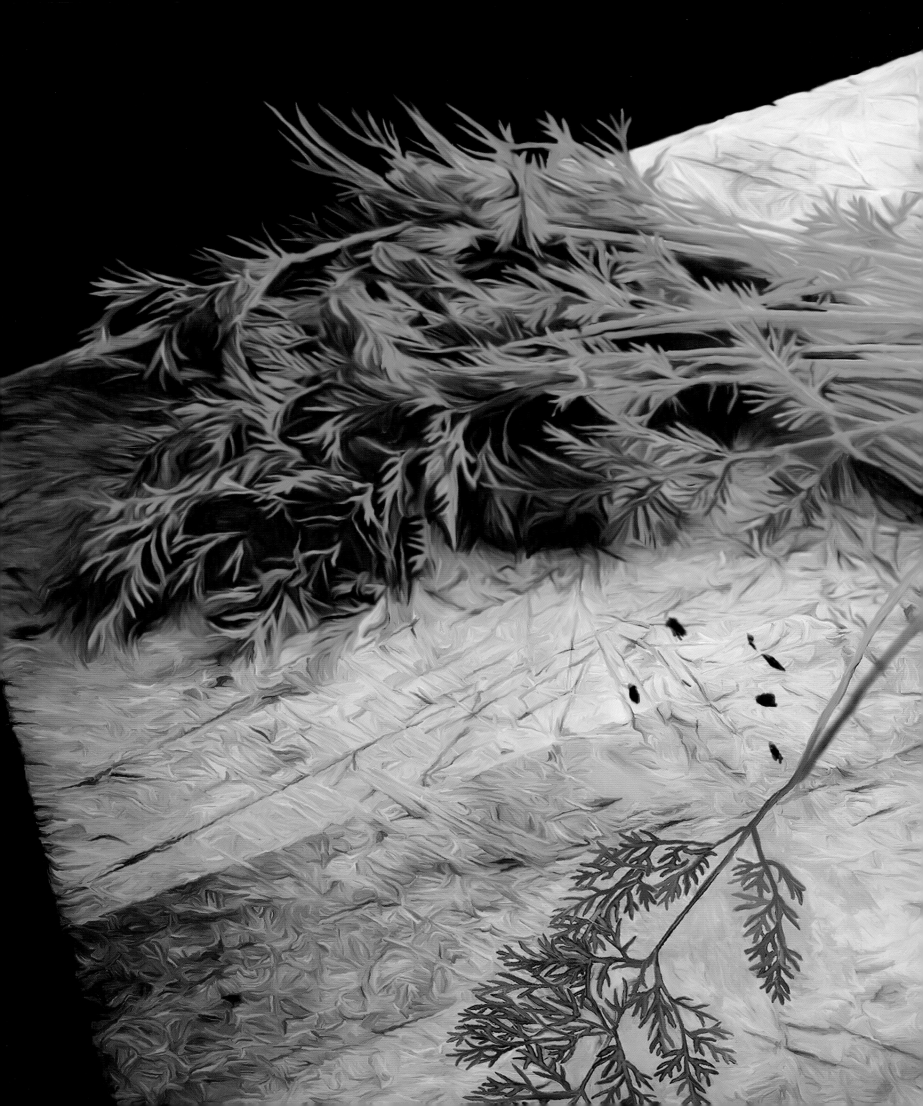

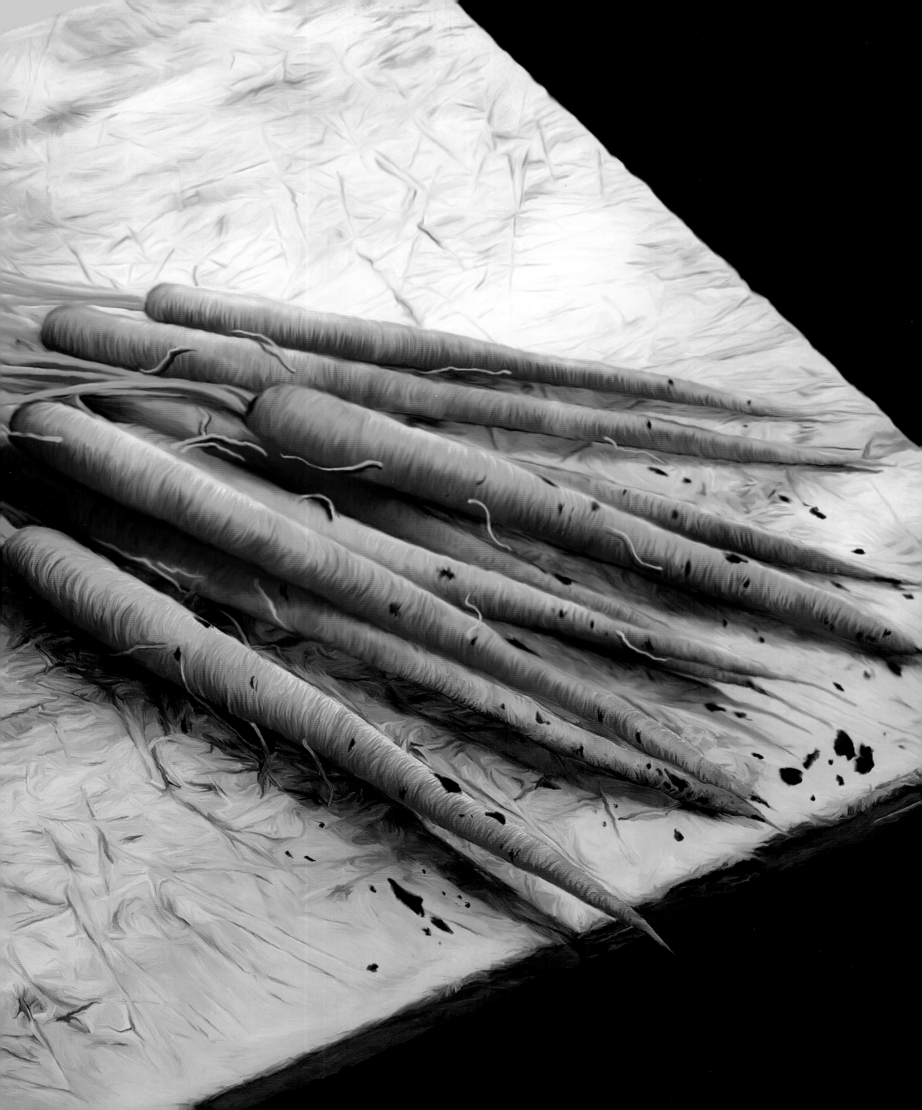

Picnics To Live For

{ SIDE DISHES }

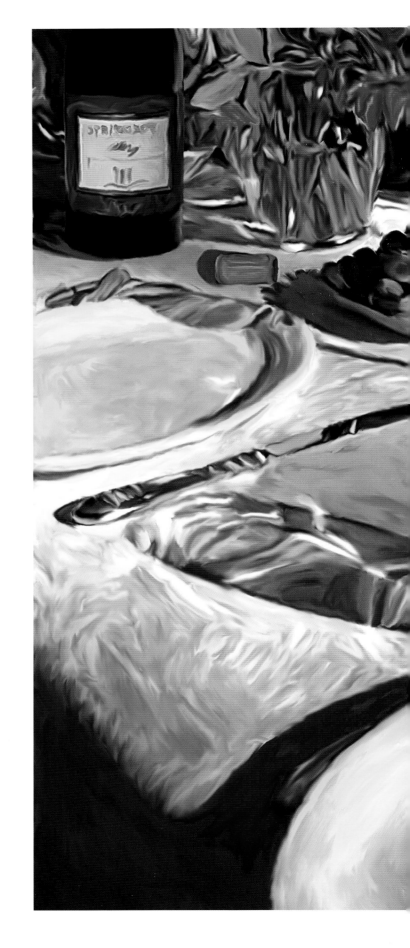

PICNICS TO LIVE FOR

Picnics for us are exciting events. Depending on the guests they range from simple and casual to elaborate and formal. The formal version is an event as special as a fine dinner at home—maybe even more so. We take along table linen, china, silverware and wine glasses. Sofia and I often drive our '59 Mercedes 220S. It has a gracious patina of old world elegance with old teak and leather and the faint scent of good cigars.

The picnic starts with champagne, prosecco or sparkling wine and one or two cheeses, mixed or marinated olives, a crusty loaf of our Home Bread (p. 51) and good butter. Depending on what's going on in our garden or farm, we bring the best produce available to us, such as a plate of French-Breakfast Radishes and young fava beans accompanied by our local salt (see resources) or just-picked, immature carrots sweet with flavor and the lingering smell of good soil.

Our friends always bring an abundance of culinary pleasures. What always stands out is one friend's soup. Mikel Covey is a master of the soup course. Like Thomas Keller, his soup is about essences. He identifies the starring ingredient, which may be green tomato, corn or other seasonal delicacy, then proceeds to create the most concentrated liquid essence

I've ever tasted in a soup plate. Sometimes we change wine at this point but most often we just continue with sparkling wine.

The main course is usually cold. It may be a trout or salmon in aspic on a bed of freshly picked seasonal greens accompanied by a starch such as a Pink Potato Salad (p. 72) or slices of cold polenta infused with roasted pepper and drizzled with a little walnut or olive oil. Scattered over the plate may be more cooked or raw baby fava beans freshly picked only hours earlier. We normally have edible flowers including blue bachelor buttons, orange calendula, rose petals or tiny white arugula blossoms. This course is usually accompanied by a red wine, such as an old-vine Zinfandel from the west slopes of the Sierra's with leg of lamb or grilled game birds. An Oregon Pinot Noir is another favorite with poached fish. Then comes dessert that ranges from a rustic fruit tart made with local seasonal fruit, served with made-from-scratch ice cream, to ripe local fruits and fine cheeses.

Those picnics, held in the spectacular canyons that surround our valley, define the good life for us as nothing else can. The combination of friends, fine food, good wine and the splendors of nature match or exceed any fine dining I've ever experienced around the world.

JADE AND PEARLS

This is an earthy, simple dish I first learned to make in the sixties. It is a satisfying source of complete protein and a good main dish for a vegetarian meal. Even though it is not a recipe I created, I gave it its fanciful name in 1988 when I prepared it for the composer John Cage. He had practiced macrobiotics faithfully for years at that time. He recounted how Yoko Ono had convinced him to eat macrobiotically in an attempt to cure his arthritis, which had become so severe he could no longer play the piano. He said within a short time after beginning the diet he was able to play again.

Unless you want to adhere to the strictly macrobiotic diet, serve each portion with a dollop of good, plain yogurt such as Pavel's Original Russian Yogurt (see resources) and steamed beets and their greens, dressed with a simple vinaigrette. Serve it with crusty bread and a plate of extra virgin olive oil for dipping.

1/2 cup mung beans

1/2 cup short or long grain brown rice

3 cups spring water

1 clove garlic, crushed

Bragg Liquid Aminos to taste (see resources)

2 tablespoons extra virgin olive oil

SERVES 4

Pick through the beans and make sure there are no pebbles. Put the rice and beans in a pot with the spring water. Cover, bring to a simmer and cook on low until the beans are almost tender. Add the garlic. Cook very gently until barely tender — but not too soft — and the cooking liquid is absorbed (about 40 minutes). Toward the end of the cooking process lower the heat and watch closely so as not to scorch the mixture. Remove from the heat and add Bragg Liquid Aminos to taste. Stir in the olive oil gently, so you don't break up the delicate mixture. If done correctly it should look somewhat like my illustration.

BEVERAGE RECOMMENDATION

Excellent with a solid red such as a Petite Syrah or an Italian red such as a Taurino Notarpanaro.

This dish's humble origins lie in the counterculture of the sixties when a generation's idealism signaled a retreat from the slick packaged products of science kitchens.

194

PICNICS TO LIVE FOR

Wood-Roasted Roots with Walnut Oil Vinaigrette

This is a flavorful side dish, good with roast lamb, beef or game such as elk, venison or birds. Roasting root vegetables over wood coals imparts a rich flavor. In this recipe that flavor is further enhanced with a dressing made from roasted shallots.

4 medium-sized beets with skins on

4 medium-sized turnips with skins on

4 medium-sized parsnips with skins on

FOR THE DRESSING

4 large shallots skinned and flattened a bit

1 teaspoon fresh thyme leaves

4 tablespoons Vilux Cognac vinegar or good red wine vinegar

1 cup fragrant, new crop walnut oil or extra virgin olive oil

Salt and pepper to taste

SERVES 8 TO 10

Scrub the beets, turnips and parsnips. Grill them along with the shallots over lump charcoal or a wood fire that has mostly burned down. They will be a rich brown color (about 20 minutes). Remove from the fire and steam the beets, turnips and parsnips until a sharp knife can quite easily penetrate to their centers (about 30 minutes). They should have enough firmness that they can be cleanly cut.

An alternative method is to roast the vegetables in a 400° F oven until they are browned to a deep mahogany color (about 40 to 50 minutes). Within reason, the deeper the brown the richer their flavor will be, but be careful not to let them burn and turn black or they will become too bitter. Turn them as needed and remove them as they finish.

As the other roots roast or steam, chop the shallots fine, caramelized skin and all. Grind the chopped mixture with a pinch or two of salt and the thyme to a paste with a mortar and pestle. Add the vinegar and stir it into the paste. Whisk the walnut oil into the vinegar mixture until you achieve a silky emulsion. Alternatively, blend the chopped shallots with the other ingredients in a blender or food processor until smooth. Correct the seasoning.

When the vegetables are steamed or roasted to the tender stage, plunge them into cold water for a minute or two so you can handle them comfortably. Remove their skins by slipping them off with your hands. Discard the skins. The underlying flesh will be less discolored indicating rich flavor.

Cut the beets, turnips and parsnips into matchstick-sized pieces. Keep the vegetables separate so the beets don't stain the others. Season them all with salt and pepper. Toss each separately with a portion of the dressing and let stand covered at room temperature to absorb the flavor of the dressing for 30 minutes or more. Toss vegetables occasionally to distribute the dressing and once again just before serving.

BEVERAGE RECOMMENDATION

Wood-roasting invariably creates some bitterness that doesn't match well with a very tannic red wine. An affordable red that does complement roasted meats or fowl and roasted roots is a Marietta Old Vine Red — a soft, Mediterranean-style wine from Sonoma.

Honey Glazed Carrots with Tarragon

A richly perfumed side dish with a sweetness that complements seafood, sausages, steaks and chops.

6 medium carrots

1 tablespoon unsalted butter

3 or 4 tablespoons spring water

2 tablespoons clover honey

1 tablespoon finely chopped, fresh tarragon (or 1 teaspoon dried tarragon can be used)

Salt to taste

SERVES 6

Cut the carrots into irregular tapered chunks about the length of your index finger. Steam or parboil the carrots to soften them a little. Blot dry with a paper towel. Melt the butter over low heat in a heavy saucepan fitted with a tight lid. Add carrots and cook them for a minute or two. Stir to coat them with butter. Add a dash of spring water, the honey and tarragon and season with a little salt. Stir to coat carrots with the rich, melted sauce. Cover with a tight lid and simmer on low for a few minutes to desired doneness and to release the aromatics of the ingredients. Add a little spring water as needed to keep them from scorching.

As the carrots finish, the pan juices will reduce to a buttery residue. Depending on the size of the carrots, it may be necessary to remove them from the sauce to keep them from getting too soft before sauce reaches the desired consistency. Serve warm with their sauce drizzled over them.

Red Lentils with Mustard

This is a good dish for those times you feel like indulging in simplicity. An excellent complement to these lentils is a platter of heirloom tomatoes with Marinated Olives (p. 211) scattered over them. Serve with whole grain crusty bread to dip into the mustard-flavored lentils and the richly infused juices from the tomato platter.

1 yellow onion, chopped medium

5 tablespoons extra virgin olive oil

2 cups red lentils

4 cups stock or spring water

Bragg Liquid Aminos to taste (see resources)

1 to 4 tablespoons Dijon style or Mother Alvey's Mustard (p. 239)

SERVES 6 TO 8

Sauté the onion in 2 or 3 tablespoons olive oil over medium-low heat for several minutes, stirring occasionally until it softens and caramelizes slightly. Add the dry lentils and stir until the lentils are coated. Add 2 cups of stock and cover with a lid. Raise the heat a little until the liquid begins to simmer, then turn down to medium-low. Stir occasionally and gently, with a heatproof spatula, scraping the bottom of the pan with each stirring. Add more stock as needed. Cook until the lentils are soft but not mushy (about 15 minutes). They should absorb all of the stock.

Remove from heat. Season with Bragg Liquid Aminos to taste. Gently stir in the mustard and dress with the rest of the olive oil. Allow lentils to rest for a while to absorb flavors. Serve warm.

BEVERAGE RECOMMENDATION

The slightly acidic flavors of this meal pair well with a dry Fetzer Chardonnay.

Blue Collar Polenta with Mixed Herbs

Traditional polenta is usually made thick enough to hold an inserted spoon upright when it is finished and still hot. Thick polenta works well for making leftover polenta cakes. I prefer it thinner so that, as it cools, it doesn't become solid on the plate.

This irreverent version is made with instant cornmeal. It is made with spring water, or with stock for additional flavor, and is redolent with olive oil. It is especially good when the oil has been marinated with roasted peppers or roasted garlic. It is a versatile side dish that goes well with game birds, chicken, a variety of sausages or beef medallions.

1 cup yellow quick-cooking cornmeal such as Albers

3 cups stock or spring water

Salt to taste

1 tablespoon fresh minced herbs such as a mixture of parsley, thyme, rosemary, tarragon or marjoram

3 tablespoons plain extra virgin olive oil or olive oil flavored with roasted red bell peppers or garlic (let the oil and flavoring mingle for a few days before using)

SERVES 4

Whisk the cornmeal and cold liquid together. Place it over medium heat and bring it to a simmer while stirring using a wooden spoon. Turn the heat to low, stirring often until the cornmeal is thoroughly cooked with no taste of rawness (5 to 10 minutes depending on the cornmeal). If the mixture becomes too thick, add more liquid.

Season to taste with salt. Stir in the herbs and olive oil. Cover the top of the finished polenta with a little olive oil to prevent a crust from forming. Serve it hot.

Salt:
The Most Important Seasoning

Besides its basic raw ingredients only a healthy appetite can contribute more to the enjoyment of a prepared dish than good salt. For me it is, hands down, the most important seasoning in the cook's repertory and the most challenging to learn to use correctly. A good cook should always seek out the finest salt available. Here in Utah we are blessed with one of the world's great culinary salts. It is sold under the brand name "Real Salt" (see resources)—which it certainly is. It is ancient, prepollution sea salt with none of today's industrial chemicals. It has a clean rounded taste that is equal or superior to any salt available on the world market.

I admit a certain prejudice. I have a personal history with it. It was the first salt I loved. I first became aware of it when I was about four years old on the ranch where my father was a herder, in Strawberry, Utah. We had a pile of red lump salt behind the enclosure around our cabin where the animals couldn't get at it. In those days most Americans used the bitter, snow-white processed salt available in the grocery stores in their cooking and on the table, including us. My young palette was so sensitive I thought it was nasty and avoided it as much as possible. However, I was drawn to the lump salt outside in the yard. I would go through the pile,

find a small piece and carry it in my pocket so I could pull it out and enjoy it as a savory lollipop.

One of our basic responsibilities on the ranch was to distribute salt to the salt licks around the vast open range where the cattle grazed at their discretion. After saddling the riding horses, dad would saddle a couple of horses with pack saddles and attach two large leather bags to each. These were filled to bulging with lump salt to be carried by the pack horses. Without adequate salt, cattle do not gain weight as efficiently as they do with, so this was a critical task that was an ongoing part of ranch life. I would have the privilege of riding with Dad every other day on a round trip that could be up to thirty miles. For a young boy it was a long day in the saddle. My brother Fred (three years older) and I alternated, one day on and one day off. During those tender years I was usually exhausted by the time we reached the last salt lick of the day, and after the bags were emptied, Dad would put me into one of the leather bags where I experienced my afternoon nap to the sweet rocking rhythm of the packhorse's hooves. It's a pleasure I still carry in my memory.

In the sixties after my own young family had moved to our Avenues Cottage we would go to the mine in Redmond where we were given permission to go through the yard and select a year's supply of the whiter lumps which had less red sand. They charged us the same rate as they would for cattle salt which was $17 a ton at that time. We would take it back home and grind it as needed in the oldest of two cast-iron wheat grinders that we kept exclusively for grinding salt. It is such a superior salt that after a few years we were spoiled and would not have known what to do without it. At about the same time I (and apparently others) made repeated suggestions to the owners that they market the salt for human consumption. Within a few years of that time the first packages appeared in our local natural foods store. That was the early seventies and we have purchased it from the natural food store ever since. Now it's available in supermarkets around the world.

Hunger is the most effective seasoning—then salt.

FRIED RED TOMATOES

1 or 2 tablespoons
extra virgin olive oil

1 large garlic clove, crushed

1 medium, vine-ripened
slicing tomato, cored and
sliced 3/8 inch thick

Salt to taste

2 or 3 fresh basil leaves

SERVES 2

In this blissfully simple side dish, "fried" is a misnomer. To achieve the best results, gently cook these tomatoes on low so they will absorb the essence of the olive oil, garlic and basil and soften just a little. Use the best tomato possible, preferably an organic, vine-ripened heirloom slicing tomato such as Brandywine. This method, however, can give a surprising amount of flavor to a tomato with a lesser pedigree. This dish pairs splendidly with bacon and Eggs in Ramekins with Herb and Buttered Crumbs (p. 64).

In a frying pan over low heat add the olive oil and stir in the crushed garlic. Season the tomato slices on both sides with salt and lay them in the pan. Heat them on the one side for a minute or two then carefully turn them over. Tear the basil and add it to the tomatoes. Cover the pan with a lid to trap the flavors (about 4 more minutes).

Straight-Up Guacamole

For me, this is the simplest and most classic of all guacamoles. The quality of avocados is crucial. Buy them a few days ahead, handle them carefully and allow to ripen.

2 large ripe avocados, preferably Hass

1 clove garlic

2 tablespoons lime juice (about 1 large juicy lime) or to taste

Salt to taste

Corn tortilla chips

SERVES 2 TO 4

When the avocados are ripe and have slightly softened, split them in half from end to end, remove their pits and scoop out the flesh with a spoon into a mixing bowl. Mash the pulp with a fork leaving as much texture as you desire.

Finely crush the garlic and a pinch of salt with a mortar and pestle. Squeeze a little lime juice into the garlic mixture. Squeeze the rest of the lime juice into the mashed avocado. Add the garlic mixture from the mortar. Stir together well and taste. Season with salt and lime juice to taste. Because there are only a few ingredients in this dish, balancing them carefully is the key to its success. Serve immediately with corn tortilla chips.

BEVERAGE RECOMMENDATION

Match with Pink Lymanitas (p. 317).

MAHOGANY ONIONS

2 large yellow onions

2 tablespoons extra virgin olive oil

1 cup Meat Stock (p. 124) or Bragg Liquid Aminos to taste (see resources)

1/2 cup spring water, plus more as needed

1 tablespoon herbs such as parsley, sage, rosemary and thyme or a mixture

Salt and pepper to taste

SERVES 4

These onions are earthy, assertive and slightly sweet. They are at their best with full-flavored entrées especially game, beef or lamb.

Strip one or two of the tough outer layers from the onions. Core and cut the onions in half horizontally, through their equators. Pour the olive oil into a large nonreactive frying pan and place the onions, flat side down. Cover with a tight fitting lid. Turn the heat to medium and brown the bottoms a little. Turn to low. Add stock or Bragg Liquid Aminos and the spring water. Put the lid on the pan and simmer for 20 minutes or more until the onions are soft and caramelized. Toward the end of the cooking process, as the onions soften, add the herbs. After a few more minutes remove the lid and watch closely. Allow the liquid to reduce to a few tablespoons, turning dark and rich. Pour it over the warm onions on a serving plate.

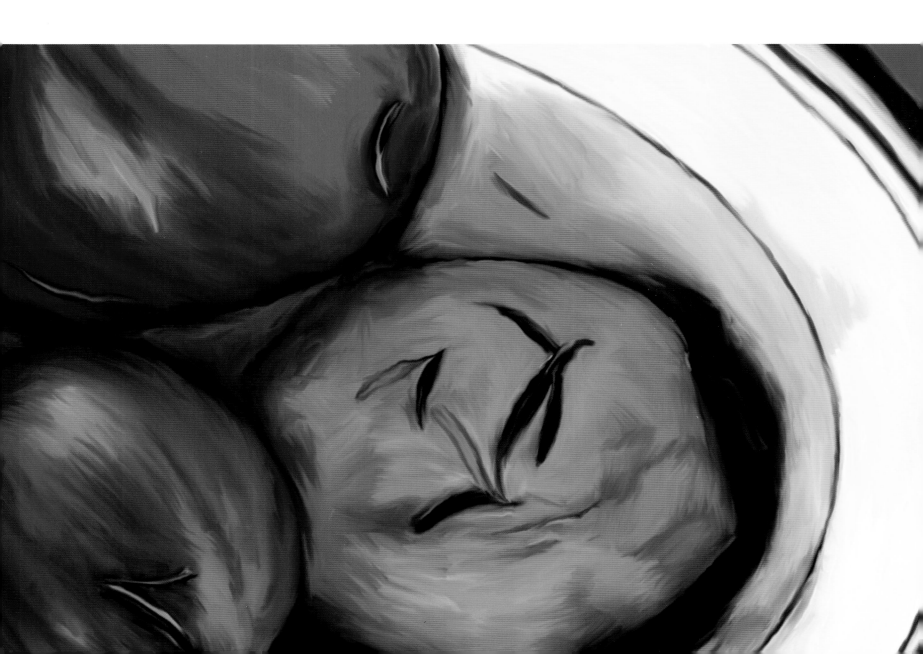

Spicy Potato Cakes

This is my variation on the classic German Potato Cake. These are lighter since there is no need for eggs or milk to hold them together. Instead, the cakes hold together by the starch brought out by cooking the shredded potato mixture in the microwave oven before frying. If you don't have a microwave oven, steam the shredded potatoes. Steaming doesn't work quite as well, however, because the steam washes some of the starch from the potato surfaces, making them slightly less sticky.

They are good as a side dish for various entrees when served with deglazed pan juices or Brown Sauce (p. 260), by omitting the chile oil they are good with butter and maple syrup or Fresh Fruited Syrup (p. 245) for breakfast.

2 or 3 medium-sized starchy potatoes (such as russets), coarsely shredded

1 medium-sized yellow onion, coarsely shredded

1 tablespoon chile oil or to taste

1 tablespoon Bragg Liquid Aminos (resources)

SERVES 4

Mix all the ingredients together into a microwave-compatible bowl. Cover with plastic wrap to trap the steam. Cook for 2 to 3 minutes on high (depending on the power of your microwave) to bring some of the starch out of the potatoes. They should still be undercooked but sticky enough to hold together.

Place 1 or 2 heaping tablespoons of the mixture on a lightly oiled hot griddle and flatten into a cake with a spatula. Cook on medium-high heat until golden brown; turn over and repeat on the other side.

STEAMED PARSNIP PUDDING

This is not the usual sweet steamed pudding, but a savory side dish intended to accompany various entrées. Its pairs especially well with roast beef served with a rich, smooth Brown Sauce (p. 260) and Prepared Horseradish (p. 249), nicely complementing the pudding's luxurious textures and flavors.

2 tablespoons finely minced rosemary

6 cloves garlic

1 teaspoon salt

1/2 cup whole-wheat pastry flour

1 cup all-purpose flour

1 cup beef suet, cold and finely grated, ground or chopped

1 cup finely grated parsnip

1 cup finely grated potato

1 cup coarsely grated onion

1/4 cup finely grated celery root

1 tablespoon finely grated horseradish or prepared horseradish

1/4 cup finely crushed hazelnuts

1/4 cup good Tennessee whiskey such as George Dickel

2 large eggs

Butter for greasing the pudding bowl

SERVES 6 TO 8

Crush the chopped rosemary, garlic and a pinch of salt with a mortar and pestle. Rub the flour and suet together taking care not to overwork the mixture. Don't work it to the degree you would a pie crust, and keep your hands cool by dipping them in ice water and dry them before you work with the suet. (Water will make the flour too sticky). Overworking and warm hands will cause the suet to soften and coat some of the flour, increasing the density of the finished product. Suet is the best way to obtain a light and finely textured steamed pudding. It works by not melting until the starch begins to set, creating millions of tiny holes in the pudding. Order suet from your butcher fresh. Unless you trust your butcher, prepackaged suet is unsuitable as it may be old or mixed with other fat. Suet is the fat that surrounds beef kidneys — nothing else. If you can't find it in your grocery store call a wholesale meat distributor and inquire if you can purchase it directly from them. (You may have to agree to buy 10 pounds or more to get them to sell it to you. If that's the case, freeze the excess or give it to friends who bake.)

In a second large mixing bowl, combine all the other ingredients down to the whiskey. Add the flour and suet mixture. Scrape rosemary mixture from the mortar into the other mixtures and mix everything together with cool dry hands, again, taking care not to overwork it. Pour whiskey into the mortar and rinse out the rosemary residue. Pour into a mixing bowl. Add eggs and whisk together. Lightly fold this egg mixture into the suet mixture. Generously grease a ceramic mixing bowl with the butter and fill it with the mixture to within an inch or two of the top. (To determine the right size of bowl to use for this recipe, test it with 7 cups water. It should fill only to two-thirds maximum; in this case, to within about 2 inches of the top so the pudding can expand. The bowl I use for this recipe is 8 1/2 inches inside across the top and 5 inches tall.) Place it over a trivet or inverted pie tin in the bottom of a large pot (the trivet keeps the bottom of the pudding from cooking too quickly).

Add water half to two-thirds of the way up the bowl. The best way to do this is to carefully pour boiling water down the inside wall of a large pot after the trivet and bowl are placed in the pot and after the bowl is covered with foil then covered with an inverted plate so it will seal. Bring the water to a medium simmer. Check the pudding every hour for the three hours or so it takes to cook and replenish boiling water when needed. When pudding is done it will be firm in the center. Left in the water, it will stay warm for two or three hours after the pot is removed from the heat. This is a good way to hold it if it is kept covered.

To serve, carefully slide a long, flexible knife such as a cake knife down the side between the bowl and the pudding and slide around its perimeter. Invert and carefully coax the pudding from the bowl. Slice it into 1/2-inch-thick slices with a serrated knife and serve it warm.

BEVERAGE RECOMMENDATION

A Pinot Noir with ripe plum and cherry flavors is a good choice. Again, I would encourage you to seek out local producers whenever possible.

Beauty on the plate is very important to me but
I am not a "drizzler" or faux-Abstract Expressionist.
I have been a painter long enough to know that
those techniques work best on canvas.
As the years pass the squeeze bottle paintings
around food on a plate are starting to look
like misplaced clichés. I think food should look
like food, not Action Painting.

GOAT CHEESE CUSTARD WITH GARLIC AND HERBS

FOR THE CUSTARD

1 small clove garlic

Salt to taste

4 teaspoons minced herbs: chervil, tarragon chives and/or sweet marjoram

Butter for custard cups

1 cup milk

1 (5-ounce) package fresh goat cheese

2 tablespoons Gorgonzola or Stilton cheese

Cayenne pepper to taste

2 whole eggs

6 egg yolks

FOR THE SAUCE

1 tablespoon lemon zest

1 tablespoon minced herbs: chervil, tarragon chives and/or sweet marjoram

Pinch of salt

1 tablespoon lemon juice

4 tablespoons extra virgin olive oil

Chives, tarragon and violet flowers for garnish

SERVES 4

These individual custards are elegant and light with a velvet texture and rich flavor. They are especially good with delicately flavored entrées such as freshwater bass sautéed in butter or crayfish poached and lightly sautéed in butter. Another nice pairing is thinly sliced country ham and steamed, grilled or sautéed asparagus spears dressed with balsamic vinegar and extra virgin olive oil.

Crush the garlic, a pinch of salt and all of the minced herbs with a mortar and pestle into a smooth paste and set aside. Butter four small, ceramic ramekins or custard molds. Put the milk and cheeses in a saucepan over medium-low heat. Turn the heat down to very low. As milk is heating, break up the cheese and stir it together. Put mixture in a blender and blend it for a few seconds until smooth. Add herb mixture and blend briefly. Pour cheese and herb mixture from the blender back in the pan used to heat the milk and cheese. Add the cayenne and stir together.

Beat the eggs thoroughly and add them to the herb and cheese mixture. Stir together gently, taking care not to create air bubbles that would create a rough texture in the finished custards. Fill the four custard molds equally with the egg and cheese mixture. Place them in a bamboo or metal steamer. Steam for 20 to 25 minutes — a bit longer for ceramic molds. The center of the custard should be slightly firm when touched with the tip of your finger. (If available, use a polar fleece glove to remove the custard molds from the steamer. They are more precise and safer than hot pads or tongs). Set the custards in a pan of cold water for 10 minutes to chill. Remove them from the cold water and run a sharp knife around the inside edge of the mold and invert it on an individual serving plate. Gently lift off the cups.

Crush the lemon zest, the reserved herbs and a pinch of salt to a smooth paste in a mortar and pestle. Mix in the lemon juice. Add olive oil and whisk the mixture into a smooth emulsion. Alternatively use a blender or food processor and process until smooth. Dribble equal amounts of the herb emulsion over each of the custards. Garnish each with a sprig or two of chive and a few tarragon leaves; place a violet on top of each and serve.

A simple, clean sauce for either of these entrées is an emulsion made in a separate pan of equal parts melted butter and fresh squeezed lemon juice, and a pinch of minced herbs such as parsley, chervil or tarragon, by themselves or mixed together, which allows the flavors of the custard to shine through.

BEVERAGE RECOMMENDATION

Good wines to enhance the custards served with any main course are Chandon's Carneros Blanc de Noirs; Monet's favorite, Veuve Clicquot Brut Champagne; a white Burgundy, such as a Grand Cru Montrachet; or a simpler, more affordable sparkling wine, such as Nino Franco Prosecco.

BRAISED TURNIPS

4 medium-sized shallots, peeled and finely chopped

2 tablespoons mild walnut oil or extra virgin olive oil

4 medium-sized turnips, peeled and quartered

2 cups stock of your choice

2 bay leaves

1 teaspoon finely minced fresh thyme

1 cup dry white wine such as Pinot Blanc

Salt and freshly ground pepper to taste

1 tablespoon minced curly leaf parsley

SERVES 4

The choice of which stock to use for the braising liquid depends on what entrée it is intended to accompany. For a poultry dish the best choice would be a rich stock made from the bird trimmings. To accompany a beef dish, beef stock. This increases the compatibility of the flavors. Ultimately though, these are personal, much like choosing wine. You may, for example, prefer braising both the turnips and beef in Root Vegetable Stock (p. 122) or veal and turnips in Mushroom Stock (p. 126). As long as it pleases you and your guests that's all that matters.

Heat the oil in a nonreactive pan over medium heat and sauté the shallots until lightly caramelized. Add the turnips, stock and bay leaves. Cover and simmer on low until the turnips are almost tender when penetrated with a paring knife. Add the thyme. Cover and continue simmering until the turnips are tender (about 30 minutes total). Remove the turnips with a slotted spoon. Add the wine; scrape and deglaze the pan residue. Reduce down to a near glaze. Stir often and lower the heat as it thickens so it won't scorch. Correct the seasoning with salt and pepper. Put the turnips back in the pan and coat them with the reduction.

Let the turnips rest for an hour or so before serving. To keep them moist and add more flavor, baste them occasionally with the sauce and cover. Sprinkle with the minced parsley. To serve, warm for a few minutes to release their flavors; plate and pour the sauce over the beautifully braised turnips.

Olives are admittedly not a local food to Utah but with the rapid climate change the lower elevations in the southern part of the State offer real possibilities for an olive industry. The rest is up to intrepid, enterprising growers.

MARINATED OLIVES

We like to eat food that comes from close to home, as much as possible. Olives and olive oil are important exceptions that we make to that guiding principle. This recipe is designed for an unusual canned olive. The brand is Graber (see resources). It is a large, tree-ripened, untreated variety grown in southern California on old trees. It is a little difficult to find in grocery stores but well worth the effort. It has a natural, mottled green color with flecks of brown and is not pitted, which helps it retain a rich flavor. The oily flesh has the ability to absorb an unusual amount of additional flavor. It is excellent as an appetizer, in salads or scattered over sliced tomatoes.

1 clove garlic, peeled

1 tablespoon minced and mixed fresh herbs such as thyme, curly leaf parsley, chervil, tarragon and flat leaf parsley

1/2 cup extra virgin olive oil

1 (15-ounce) can Graber olives

SERVES 4 TO 6

Crush the garlic and herbs in a mortar and pestle. Add the olive oil and thoroughly mix together. Alternately, place the garlic, olive oil and herbs in a blender or food processor and blend until smooth. Add the minced herbs and blend a little more leaving some of its texture.

Drain the liquid from the olives and cover them with the mixture in a nonreactive container for up to 3 or 4 hours. If marinated any longer they oxidize and their rich flavors drift out of focus.

POTATOES SOFIA

A robust dish richly scented with sautéed lovage, onion and carrot with a soft, creamy texture. It goes well with roasts and chops as well as grilled meats.

---

1 pound (4 medium-sized) organic new potatoes such as Yukon Gold or Pontiac Red

2 tablespoons extra virgin olive oil

2 tablespoons butter

1/2 medium yellow onion, peeled and finely chopped

2 medium carrots, diced 1/8 inch

1/3 cup fresh, finely chopped lovage

3 eggs

1 cup cream

1/2 cup feta cheese

2 quarts (about one bunch) chard loosely packed, stems removed

Spring water

Red wine vinegar

Salt and fresh ground black pepper to taste

SERVES 2 TO 4

Preheat oven to 400° F.

Gently simmer potatoes with their skins on until tender. Peel and slice 1/8 inch thick and set aside. Use a sharp, thin-bladed knife, rinsed clean in hot water between slices, so the slices don't break apart.

Heat olive oil and butter in a frying pan. Sauté onion, carrots and lovage, on medium-low. Cover and
let cook until soft. Set aside.

Beat eggs thoroughly, add cream and blend together. Crumble feta cheese into egg and cream mixture and fold together. (Final mixture should have some small feta cheese lumps.)

Cook chard in an inch or two of simmering spring water for a few minutes until tender, but still bright. Drain and set aside to cool. Squeeze out most of the water, chop and season with a little red wine vinegar, salt and pepper. Add it to the creamy mixture, and fold in the sautéed mixture.

Layer ingredients in a 9 x 5 x 3-inch ceramic baking dish, starting with the sliced potatoes. Season each potato layer with a little salt and pepper. Spoon a layer of the creamy mixture over the potato, repeating until all ingredients are used, ending with a layer of the creamy mixture, creating about 3 to 4 layers. Bake in preheated 400° F oven for about 45 minutes until the top is a light golden brown. The creamy mixture is set when a toothpick inserted in the middle comes out clean.

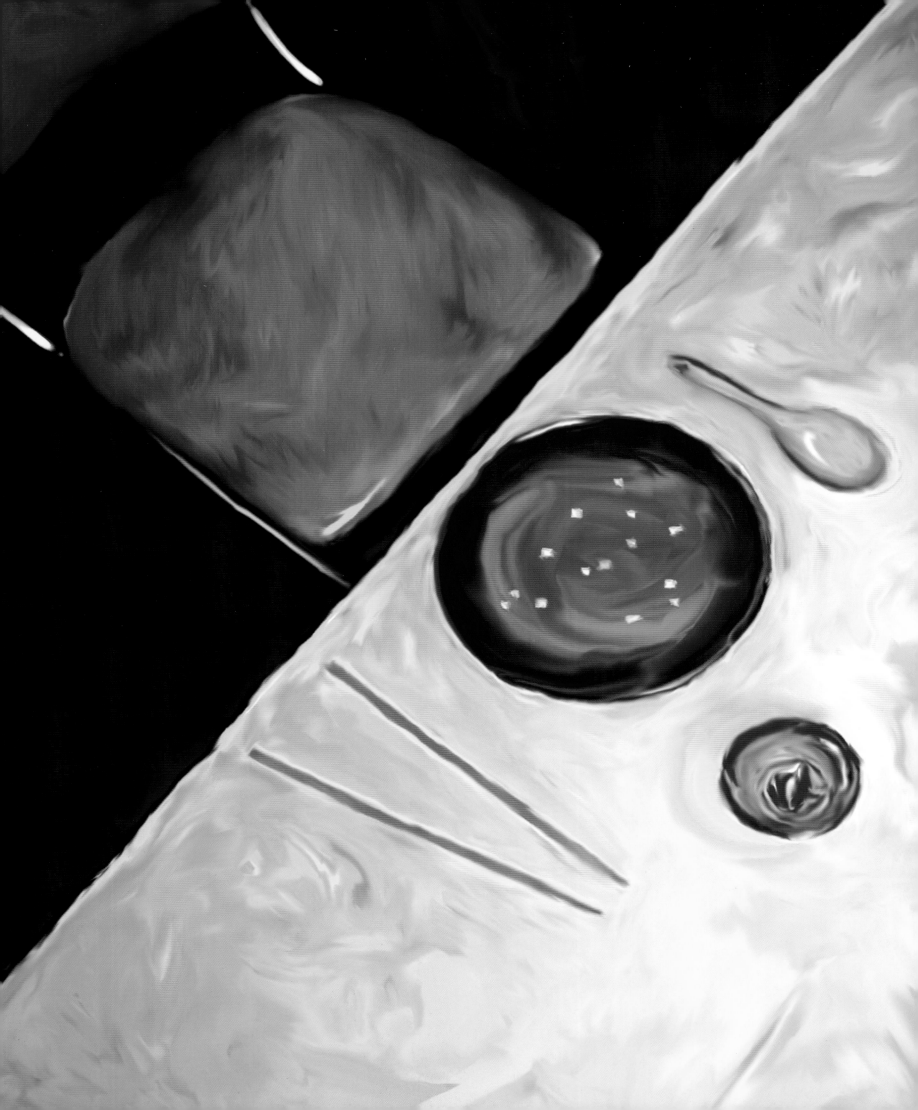

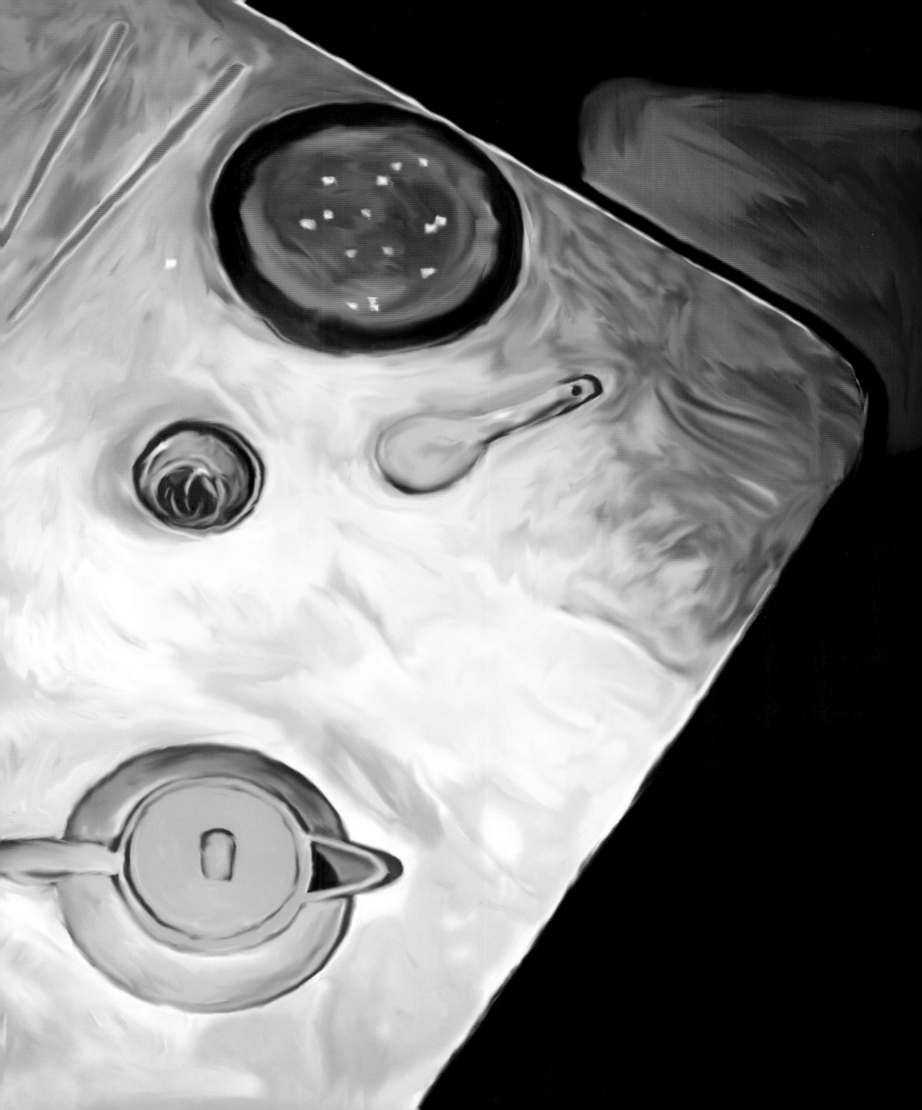

Risotto
(Traditional and Microwave)

Traditional (Miso):
The most traditional Italian risotto uses a large grain rice such as Arborio, along with veal stock and bone marrow for its primary flavors and textures. This nontraditional recipe has two versions. The most unusual uses pearled barley in place of rice. Both are made with miso broth instead of veal stock, and olive oil replaces the marrow. The barley version is rich with a chewier texture than rice. It has a smoky miso flavor. The second recipe has similar flavors but a creamier texture. Both have a burst of fruity elegance from olive oil added at the very end. Both are delicious with grilled fish filets or Barley Risotto Stuffed Poultry with Pine Nuts and Plum Sauce (p. 138).

3 heaping tablespoons barley miso paste or red miso paste

2 quarts spring water

1 yellow onion, chopped fine

1 or 2 cloves garlic minced

8 tablespoons extra virgin olive oil

2 cups dry, pearled barley or 2 cups Arborio rice for the second version

Bragg Liquid Aminos to taste (resources)

SERVES 6

Whisk the miso paste into the spring water in a 3-quart saucepan until smooth and bring to a simmer. In a 6- to 8-quart saucepan, sauté the onion and garlic in 2 tablespoons of olive oil, stirring over medium-low heat until soft and slightly caramelized. Add the uncooked grain of your choice to this mixture and stir together coating the grains evenly. The Arborio rice will form a white spot in the middle of the grain in about one minute to let you know that it is ready. Allow the mixture to almost stick to the bottom of the pan before adding a ladle of hot miso stock. Gently scrape and stir the bottom of the pot with a wooden spatula. Continue stirring gently until the broth is completely absorbed and the grain becomes sticky. This should take about 10 minutes. Add more miso broth. Repeat until all the broth is absorbed into the grain, but not dry. The risotto should have a creamy texture. Ideally you will have used all of the miso mixture when done.

The barley version will take about 30 to 40 minutes; the Arborio rice version about 20 minutes.

After the risotto has cooked and cooled a little, correct the seasoning with Bragg Aminos if necessary. Add the rest of the olive oil and gently stir it in. Serve immediately.

Microwave (Garlic and Sage):

I can hear the screeches for cooking such a hallowed dish in a microwave oven. But, I must say, it is the best use of that appliance I have come up with. Please try it before you decide.

The beauty of this method is twofold: it requires almost no stirring therefore requiring little of the cook's attention, which is easily the most demanding part of the traditional method. Because it is stirred very little the rice remains whole yet very creamy. Instead of the venerable Arborio rice I use a common, short grain white rice, such as Calrose, which works very well with this method.

1 cup white short grain rice

Olive oil as needed

2 cloves garlic crushed

A dozen or so sage leaves fresh or dry with stems removed

3 1/2 cups chicken stock reduced from 7 cups

SERVES 4 TO 6

Add the dry rice to a microwave safe container. Add about 1 tablespoon oil and stir to coat the rice evenly. (My preferred dish for this is an old Pyrex rectangular vessel that I've had for years. It measures 8 x 4 x 3-inch deep.) Crush a clove of garlic into the rice. Push a half dozen sage leaves into the mixture. Pour a cup of stock over it and stir everything together with a spatula, scraping down any rice grains on the side of the dish between each cycle.

Microwave ovens are famously unlike one another so I would recommend experimenting with this recipe before you cook it for guests. For the first cycle, set the timer for 5 minutes. Between cycles the rice can remain in the microwave oven for a minute or two as you finish up other chores. This method is quite flexible and forgiving. The rice will continue to absorb the broth and flavors and it will soften as it rests. Remove the dish from the oven and pour another half to full cup of stock over the rice, just enough to barely rise above the surface. Stir in with the spatula. Set the oven timer for 4 minutes or so. When it finishes, drizzle a tablespoon of oil over the rice and stir in more stock. Set the timer for, say, 3 minutes. Taste and tune the additions accordingly—a little more garlic and 2 or 3 leaves of sage. The total length of time for the complete process, including a few minutes of resting, is about 20 minutes.

For the last cycle crush a little more garlic, add the last of the sage leaves and the rest of the stock. Correct the seasoning with Bragg Aminos (see resources) if necessary. Set the time for 2 or 3 more minutes to finish. Allow risotto to rest for another minute or 2, take it out and drizzle a little olive oil overall and serve.

BEVERAGE RECOMMENDATION

The combination of a mild-fleshed, grilled fish such as pike or lake bass and the miso risotto go particularly well together with a good sake such as Hakutsuru Premium Sake, which is mineral rich with a delicate rice aroma. The garlic/sage version goes well with poultry and fits an Oregon Pinot Noir such as an inexpensive 2008 Mirassou or a pricier 2009 O'Reilly's.

PICNICS TO LIVE FOR

Roasted Vegetable Puree with Toasted Shallots

This side dish has rich, smoky flavor that complements a number of Southeast Asian dishes such as braised beef with orange or smoky, garlicky chicken satay. It's also delicious with Brown Sauce (p. 260).

Charring vegetables over wood or charcoal embers can give them a complex range of flavors which, depending on the wood, can include notes of caramel or toasted figs layered with a smoky sweetness (I never use self-lighting briquettes. They impart a petroleum taste and odor to food). Lump charcoal is the best choice. It's more expensive but gives a cleaner, more natural taste to the food. My second choice is a briquette that can be lit without the use of petroleum.

Some vegetables, especially fibrous ones such as scallions, are difficult to puree smoothly unless you have a food processor or a power blender such as a Vita-Mix (see resources).

However, with a little patience, using a reinforced strainer and a wooden spoon you can achieve a smooth puree from thoroughly cooked vegetables. Flatten the shallots with the side of a chef's knife. Strip away and discard any dry brown outer husks. Brush shallots and the other vegetables with a little olive oil and cook over a charcoal grill, turning as needed until golden brown.

Put them all in a two-tiered steamer with a tight lid and steam until tender. Coarsely chop and process the vegetables in a food processor or blender with the coconut milk. Continue processing as you add the peanut oil and lime juice. After the mixture is smooth, season it with salt and pepper to taste.

6 medium shallots or scallions with their root ends trimmed

1 butternut or other winter squash peeled and cut into 4-inch pieces

2 rutabagas or turnips, peeled and quartered

2 russet potatoes, peeled and quartered

Olive oil

1/2 cup coconut milk

4 tablespoons peanut oil

2 tablespoons freshly squeezed lime juice, strained

Salt and pepper to taste

SERVES 6

Bohemian Farms

In 2003 my wife Sofia, my brother Fred and I decided to revive some of the family farm to explore the local produce markets and to answer some of the questions brought to our attention by the creation of this book. If we were to base our recipes on what grows in this area, we wanted to know if there were new plant varieties that can be grown here in this part of the state. The local climate has warmed by several degrees Fahrenheit in the last 50 years. Other questions arose: What are the economics of being a small, local farmer? Can a local producer actually make a living doing this? I was also keen on the idea of breeding unique varieties of plants, something nearly impossible to do in a small urban garden. To have enough genetic accidents to work with, the numbers of plants involved in a genetic experiment would have to be much higher than one would have in a garden. Rather than dozens, we would need thousands. As we realized the things we wanted to accomplish, it became apparent that we would need to farm.

Our techniques were mostly based on the way the farmers in Spring Lake, the little farm community where I grew up, farmed before and during World War II. At that time the farmers used local manure rather than factory-made nitrogen, phosphate, potassium, herbicides and insecticides that my father's generation had opted for after the war. Our agricultural experiment lasted three years and answered most of our questions. It also opened many rewarding doors into our local food community. For two years we sold produce at our local farmer's market, sold directly to home cooks in a Community Supported Agriculture or CSA program, and supplied over 30 restaurants in our surrounding three-county area.

It was an experience about as rich as any I've ever had in my life. For one thing I don't think I ever felt as respected as I did from the chefs I delivered produce to during those years. To open large coolers with nearly perfect baby lettuces harvested with their roots packed in

I have farmed and gardened both conventionally and sustainably most of my life and seen the result of both methods and the effect they have on the soil. It is vast. The first is ultimately destructive and the second is a process of healing and nurturing.

two or three inches of ice water, or flats of vine-ripened, heirloom tomatoes harvested only hours before, and to see the looks on their faces was a reward beyond money. In some cases it was a look of instant conversion to the advantages of buying locally grown produce.

On the other hand, it was an up-close look at the harsh economic realities of small-scale local farming and the disadvantages of competing with agribusiness. Along with the sweet pleasure of farming came the bitter revelation that we would not be making money any time soon. As the three years passed it became apparent what small farmers face. Our first year we made barely over one dollar an hour for our time. The second year we went over seven dollars an hour and the third barely over ten. That was with an infrastructure paid for. We farmed land that we paid very minimal rent on and used farm equipment that was free of charge, and between my brother Fred, myself and my wife, we had a total of over a hundred years of experience growing nearly every crop ever grown in this region.

The crux of the problem for the local food movement is the farm bill. It defies common sense. It was put together by lawmakers who couldn't see further than the next election cycle. The cost to society of losing thousands upon thousands of family farms is much deeper than what the price of groceries at the supermarket would indicate.

Until the federal farm bill is untangled from its political web of favoritism and shortsighted goals, the small farmer in America is in real jeopardy of extinction and the local food movement is largely a romanticized fantasy struggling to survive on a badly slanted playing field against much larger players.

THRESHING WHEAT

{ SAUCES & CONDIMENTS }

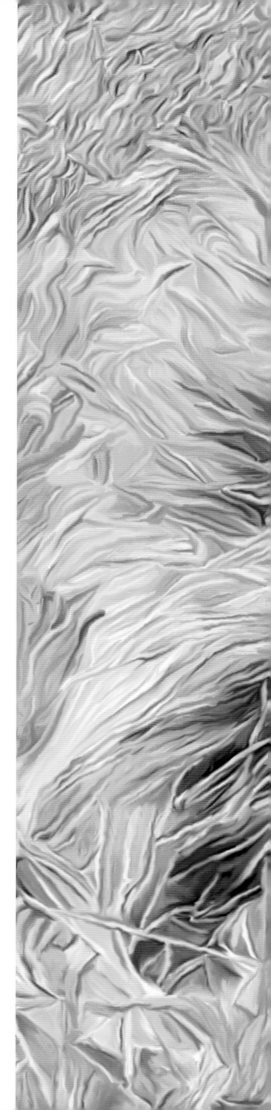

THRESHING WHEAT

At the tail end of the horse-drawn era when I was growing up in the country, farmers still used a binder to cut and bundle grain after it ripened in the late summer sun. Like so many farm machines from that era, it was a wonder of innovation—a kinetic, metal beast evolved from the imagination of man. Behind the straining triple team its silver teeth chewed a swath through the shimmering grain with mechanical precision.

After the late summer grain had been bundled, men would go through the fields with pitchforks and make "shocks" from six or seven bundles, creating what looked like miniature straw stacks. The shocks would then dry for a couple of weeks. Then on horse-drawn wagons bundles were hauled into the thresher, which traveled from farm to farm, and the grain was separated from its straw and chaff.

While the men worked themselves into a state of ravenous hunger, the women prepared one of the great bygone food spectacles of rural America—threshing day dinner. It took place at noon and what a meal it was! Spread across the table would be a variety of fine glass dishes filled with all kinds of pickles: pickled beets, sweet pickles, dill pickles, bread-and-butter pickles and two or three pickled relishes. The main course had one or two substantial dishes such as mutton stew with garden vegetables, roast beef with mashed potatoes and made-from-scratch brown gravy or stewed chicken with homemade noodles and thickened broth. There would always be hot yeast biscuits with homemade butter and an assortment of jams. There could be any combination of blanched vegetables such as string beans, corn on the cob or small sweet carrots, There was always a summer salad of whatever was ripe in the garden such as lettuces, English peas, lush tomatoes and scallions and for dessert a variety of pies, cakes and a hand-cranked freezer of ice cream.

Threshing grain, in those days, was an intoxicating experience—full of excitement, wonderful aromas, laughing, joke telling, story swapping, hard work and good food. It was a communal ritual of necessity done with great enthusiasm and as full of life as an Ernest Hemingway novel.

ONE QUART OF MAMA BETH'S DILL PICKLES

Most people never make pickles because they think it is just too daunting. In the dark, worried part of their mind lurks an imaginary vision of kitchen chaos that includes pressure cookers, an army of bottles, bushels of cucumbers, peppers, garlic and a sink overflowing with dirty pots and pans. So they retreat from the whole idea and just settle for the wimpy stuff from the grocery shelf. If you haven't eaten them, believe me, homemade pickles are so much better. They convey a promise of pure culinary art. This recipe also eliminates the chaos of large-scale pickling simply by scaling down the process. The beauty of making your own pickles is that you can create your own signature version by finding unusual ingredients from your garden, the farmer's market or supermarket — delicacies of the season in the place where you live.

This is a soul-satisfying project for a weekend. Since it is only one quart, treat yourself to a handsome antique bottle and spend an afternoon creating a piece of consumable beauty that you can leave on the kitchen cupboard while it cures. I love old canning jars, especially those with a delicate blue-green cast. They define another era when home canning was a regular part of life, like Sour Cream Butter (p. 20) and fresh baked bread hot from the oven.

FOR THE PICKLING LIQUID

3/4 cup apple cider, rice, balsamic, red wine, Champagne or Cognac vinegar or a mixture

Spring water to fill jar

1 heaping tablespoon of sea or kosher salt

FOR THE PICKLES

Enough baby cucumbers — about 10 to 20, depending on size — plus shallots, peppers, garlic cloves, peppercorns, bay leaves, juniper berries or other delicacies that you want to pickle, to fill a quart jar

3 or 4 unsprayed grape leaves or a dozen cherry leaves to keep the pickles crisp and snappy

MAKES 1 QUART

Carefully sterilize the equipment for preserving according to directions on p. 231.

Bring the vinegar and spring water to a simmer. Arrange the pickling ingredients in a sterilized jar. Add the salt to the simmering spring water and vinegar to dissolve. Pour into the jar over the ingredients up to within 1/2 inch of the top. Make sure the liquid covers the pickles. Some of them may have to be removed or rearranged with a sterilized fork to accomplish this.

Screw the ring on tightly over the lid, then lower the jar into a container of simmering water which comes 2/3 of the way up the jar. Cover. A tall cylindrical pan, such as an asparagus steamer, is ideal for a one-quart jar. Simmer for 5 minutes then remove the jar from the hot water so the pickles don't cook. Allow the pickles to cure for about one month to develop their flavors before opening the jar.

THRESHING WHEAT

Grandma Myer's Cucumber Relish

My grandma Myers was an artisan cheese maker and a serious farm cook. Her kitchen was a small food factory feeding upwards of 20 people on a regular basis. During canning season her kitchen became a home canning factory, making the most of the many seasonal surpluses growing in the fields and along the lanes as well as in the family's big kitchen garden. For her cucumber relish the garden supplied cucumbers, onions and bell peppers, both green and red (golden bell peppers were not around much in those days).

This is an old family recipe and an excellent all-purpose table relish. Like Sister Hill's Mustard Pickles (p. 232) its strength is its versatility. It can be offered with a variety of dishes such as potatoes, noodles, poultry and meat. On some country tables, even today, relishes of one kind or another are almost as important a condiment as salt and pepper.

FOR THE PICKLING LIQUID

3 cups sugar

1 quart Bragg Apple Cider Vinegar (see resources) or other good apple cider vinegar

1 1/2 tablespoons good salt

3 teaspoons mustard seed

1 teaspoon celery seed

2 tablespoons all-purpose flour

2 tablespoons butter

1 tablespoons turmeric powder

FOR THE CUCUMBER RELISH

12 large cucumbers

5 large yellow Spanish onions

2 green bell peppers

3 red bell peppers

MAKES APPROX. 14 PINTS

In a 12-quart kettle, combine sugar, vinegar, salt, mustard seed and celery seed. Bring to simmer. Make a paste of the flour, butter and turmeric. Add a little of the hot liquid to the paste and whisk together well, taking care to whisk out any lumps. Vigorously whisk the paste into the hot vinegar mixture again, taking care to whisk out any lumps. Simmer until the taste of rawness is gone from the flour mixture (about 10 minutes).

While pickling liquid is simmering, grind cucumbers, onions, green peppers and red peppers in a meat grinder using a coarse disk. Add ground vegetable mixture to pickling liquid. Bring to a simmer and cook for a minute or two more to sterilize vegetables.

While the relish is cooking, prepare equipment for preserving according to directions below.

» Place ladle, lids, tongs and funnel in large mixing bowl.
» Pour boiling water over all.
» Remove lids with tongs and place, rubber side down, on clean paper towels.
» Wash jars in hot, soapy water and rinse well. Place in a large pot of water. Bring to boil and sterilize for five minutes.
» Jars should be hot when filled, so you'll want to remove them from the hot water and fill just one or two at time. Remove with tongs and turn upside down to dry on paper towels for about a minute.
» While jar is still hot, fill with simmering cucumber relish to within one-half inch from the top of the jar.
» Clean rim of jar with dry paper towel before sealing tightly with lid and ring and set aside to cool. Lid will be indented when properly sealed. You may hear a pop as each jar seals.

Will keep for one year in a cool storage area.

SISTER HILL'S MUSTARD PICKLE RELISH

This is a classic country relish. Because of its versatility, variations of it were once very common on farm tables across America. It complements almost any savory dish including fried chicken, roasts and braises. For those who really care about the quality of what they eat and are willing to put forth the effort, mustard pickle relish is a great condiment. In addition to its versatility it is visually appealing with enough color to excite even the most jaded eye.

This relish can be made two basic ways: the first is the rustic version that requires roughly chopping the ingredients — it is the faster, less uniform method. The second is the refined version that requires cutting the ingredients more carefully giving the finished relish a finer, more uniform texture. Most farm women didn't have time to fuss with the more careful method. Either way, other than texture, the taste is about the same.

FOR THE PICKLE RELISH

1 cup Kosher or sea salt

10 medium young pickling cucumbers, unpeeled

10 small green tomatoes, cored

1 small head cauliflower

1 stalk of celery

2 red bell peppers

1 green bell pepper

4 cups small boiling onions, left whole

4 quarts spring water

MAKES APPROX. 12 PINTS

If you have an overabundance of large cucumbers and want a fine-textured relish, peel, slice lengthwise and seed the cucumbers, then slice them again, lengthwise to create four quarters. Slice them crosswise in even slices. Cut the other vegetables similarly for a more uniform version. Otherwise leave the peel on the cucumber as shown below.

Coarsely chop the cucumbers, green tomatoes, cauliflower, celery, red and green bell peppers. Leave the boiling onions whole.

In a nonreactive stockpot stir salt into spring water and allow it to dissolve. Turn off the burner. Put vegetables in the pot and cover with more water if necessary. Lightly stir to distribute the salted water. Leave mixture overnight. Drain well the next day and set aside in a large bowl.

FOR THE PICKLING LIQUID

2 tablespoons dry mustard

1 tablespoon turmeric

1 1/2 tablespoons celery seed

2 quarts Bragg Apple Cider Vinegar (see resources) or other good apple cider vinegar

1 tablespoon curry powder

2 cups sugar

1 cup all-purpose flour

1 quart water

In a small bowl, mix dry ingredients with 1 cup of spring water to make a paste. Whisk remaining spring water and vinegar into a paste taking care to whisk out any lumps and place in the stockpot. Simmer low heat until the rawness is cooked out of the flour, stirring occasionally (10 minutes or so). Add drained vegetables. Bring back to a simmer for an additional 2 minutes.

While the relish is cooking, prepare equipment for preserving according to directions below.

» Place ladle, lids, tongs and funnel in large mixing bowl.
» Pour boiling water over all.
» Remove lids with tongs and place, rubber side down, on clean paper towels.
» Wash jars in hot, soapy water and rinse well. Place in a large pot of water. Bring to boil and sterilize for five minutes.
» Jars should be hot when filled, so you'll want to remove them from the hot water and fill just one or two at time. Remove with tongs and turn upside down to dry on paper towels for about a minute.
» While jar is still hot, fill with simmering pickle relish to within one-half inch from the top of the jar.
» Clean rim of jar with dry paper towel before sealing tightly with lid and ring and set aside to cool. Lid will be indented when properly sealed. You may hear a pop as each jar seals.

Will keep for one year in a cool storage area.

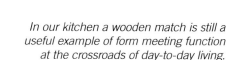

In our kitchen a wooden match is still a useful example of form meeting function at the crossroads of day-to-day living.

PICKLED BEETS

Pickled beets are a sweet-and-sour side dish with rich crimson color, flavors of clean summer earth, apple cider and tropical spices. They are especially beautiful when served with a complementary sprinkle of finely chopped chives or parsley. Perhaps because of their rural roots, homey flavors are a relative rarity in today's urban world and even the most sophisticated diners can be charmed by them. For an unusual variation add sweet or hot peppers and instead of cinnamon and cloves, found in the standard version, add mustard seed, allspice berries and juniper berries.

CLOVE AND CINNAMON VERSION

3 1/2 pounds fresh beets (16 to 24) preferably all about the same size

PICKLING INGREDIENTS

2 cups Bragg Apple Cider Vinegar (see resources) or other good apple cider vinegar

1 cup raw sugar

2 tablespoons sea salt

6 whole cloves

1 3-inch cinnamon stick

MAKES APPROX. 4 PINTS

*Make a spice bag out of two layers of cheesecloth, cut about 4 inches by 4 inches. Place seasonings on cheesecloth and tie with cotton string to form a pouch.

Wash beets. Do not peel. Trim off all but a short piece of the root and 1 inch of the stem. Doing so keeps the flavor and color in the beet. Simmer the beets in spring water in a nonreactive pan until tender but firm when pierced with a paring knife (about 30 minutes for medium-sized beets). Measure 1 cup of the cooking water, taking care not to stir up any grit that may have settled on the bottom of the pan. Cool beets in cold water, slip off their skins with your hands, trim off the top stems. Cut beets into quarters and set aside.

Put the cup of reserved cooking liquid, the beets, cider vinegar, sugar and salt in a clean, nonreactive saucepan. Place the cloves and cinnamon into a spice bag.* Add it to the saucepan. Bring mixture to a low boil, reduce the heat to a low simmer and cook for 5 minutes. Remove the spice bag.

While the beets are cooking, prepare equipment for preserving according to directions below.

» Place ladle, lids, tongs and funnel in large mixing bowl.
» Pour boiling water over all.
» Remove lids with tongs and place, rubber side down, on clean paper towels.
» Wash jars in hot, soapy water and rinse well. Place in a large pot of water. Bring to boil and sterilize for five minutes.
» Jars should be hot when filled, so you'll want to remove them from the hot water and fill just one or two at time. Remove with tongs and turn upside down to dry on paper towels for about a minute.
» While jar is still hot, fill with simmering beets to within one-half inch from the top of the jar.
» Clean rim of jar with dry paper towel before sealing tightly with lid and ring and set aside to cool. Lid will be indented when properly sealed. You may hear a pop as each jar seals.

Will keep for one year in a cool storage area.

(recipe continued on page 236)

THRESHING WHEAT

MUSTARD, ALLSPICE AND JUNIPER VERSION

3 1/2 pounds fresh beets (16 to 24) preferably all about the same size

PICKLING INGREDIENTS

2 cups Bragg Apple Cider Vinegar (see resources) or other good apple cider vinegar

2 tablespoons sea salt

1 cup raw sugar

4 sweet banana peppers or 2 spicy chiles such as jalapeno peppers, quartered, stemmed and seeded

12 medium shallots, peeled or 2 yellow onions, quartered

1 tablespoon mustard seed

1 tablespoon allspice berries

1 tablespoon juniper berries

MAKES APPROX. 4 PINTS

Follow the directions for preparing the beets from clove and cinnamon version. Put the cup of reserved cooking liquid, the vinegar, salt and sugar in a clean, nonreactive saucepan. Put the mustard seed, allspice berries and juniper berries into a spice bag and add it to the saucepan. Cook for 5 minutes over medium-low heat. Remove the spice bag and fill the hot sterile jars according to directions below. (An alternative is to take the seeds and berries out of the spice bag, divide them up and put them into the bottles. As the beets cure this will give them additional flavor and a darker color.)

CREAMY CAPER SAUCE

2 tablespoons Sour Cream Butter
(p. 20) or unsalted butter

4 tablespoons minced shallot
or red onion

4 tablespoons small capers, drained

1/2 teaspoon Prepared
Horseradish (p. 249)

1 cup crème fraîche, whipping
cream or half-and-half

1 tablespoon vermouth

Fresh lemon juice,
squeezed and strained, to taste

Spring water to thin if desired

MAKES APPROX. 1 CUP

This is a tartar sauce based on cream instead of mayonnaise. It can be thick or thin depending on your choice. Cream adds an elegance to fish dishes that are usually served with a mayonnaise-based tartar sauce.

Sauté the shallots in the butter on low heat until translucent (about 5 minutes). Add the capers and horseradish and stir in the cream and vermouth. Bring mixture to a simmer for the warm version. Leave uncooked for a thicker, room-temperature version. Add fresh lemon juice, stir in and serve immediately. Thin with a little spring water if desired or leave thick.

SPECIAL TARTAR SAUCE

1 cup of Walnut/Lime
Mayonnaise (p. 263)

1 tablespoon finely chopped
dill pickle

1 tablespoon capers

1 tablespoon mixed finely chopped
fresh herbs such as chives, tarragon,
chervil, and curly leaf parsley or dill,
chervil and flat leaf parsley

1 tablespoon finely minced shallot
or red onion

MAKES APPROX. 1 CUP

A luxurious version of tartar sauce. Excellent with Freshwater Fish Cakes with Shallots and Cilantro (p. 159).

Place ingredients into a small mixing bowl. Gently blend together and transfer to a serving dish.

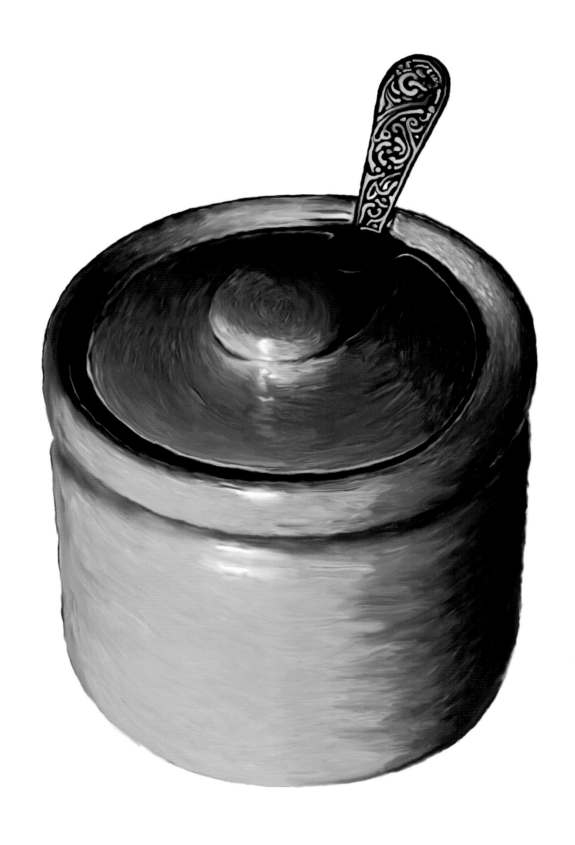

THRESHING WHEAT

MOTHER ALVEY'S MUSTARD

1/2 cup all-purpose flour (cornstarch can be substituted, which eliminates most of the curing time)

1/2 cup Coleman's dry mustard (in the spice section of most grocers)

1/4 cup sugar

3/4 cups Bragg Apple Cider Vinegar (see resources) or other good apple cider vinegar

1 teaspoon Dynasty hot Chinese mustard, or to taste (can be found in Asian markets)

MAKES 2 CUPS

Irma Alvey is my sister's mother-in-law and has been making this mustard as long as I can remember. It has legendary status in the family. It is my favorite mustard for a variety of dishes. It goes especially well with hamburgers and sausages. Its flavor is clean, dry, sharp and focused. It is a combination of English and Chinese powdered mustards blended with apple cider vinegar and flour to bind and tame it. Its heat can be adjusted by the amount of hot Chinese Mustard you use. I like to adjust the final mixture with a little salt, although it isn't called for in her recipe.

Combine all ingredients thoroughly. Place in the refrigerator for 7 days to cure. (This eliminates the raw taste of the flour and melds the flavors). Stir thoroughly once every other day, tasting each time until desired results are obtained.

ROSEMARY GARLIC OIL

1/2 cup extra virgin olive oil

1 small clove garlic, crushed

Leaves from 2 or 3 sprigs fresh rosemary

SERVES 4

This is a rich, fragrant oil. When brushed on thin slices of Home Bread (p. 51) with an offering of cheese, such as sheep's milk feta, topped with a leaf of baby arugula, a sliver of sweet onion, a few olives, a grind of black pepper paired with a glass of wine it is a good way to both stimulate and divert a hungry guest while you finish preparing dinner.

Combine ingredients using a mortar and pestle or blender to create a smooth paste.

BEVERAGE RECOMMENDATION

Any sparkling wine or fruity Zinfandel works equally well.

THRESHING WHEAT

Extra Classic Mint Sauce

This is a simple but very special sauce that was created for roast lamb. It is an old family recipe that came from my first wife's grandfather. He was the superintendent of the commissary for the Union Pacific Railroad.

"Papa" loved to tell stories about the golden age of the railroad, and the Union Pacific in particular, when its food was as good as any restaurant in the U.S. His explanation was that the railroad was constantly on the move through various food regions where producers supplied the train as it passed with the finest local products they had: Blue Point oysters, wild salmon, Dungeness crab, berries and apples in Washington, prime beef in Omaha, spring lamb in Colorado, wine, olives, citrus and fresh vegetables in California. The railroads also had the money to hire the best chefs and prided themselves on having a rolling wine "cellar," ranked, according to him, with the best terra firma cellars in the country.

3/4 cups Bragg Apple Cider Vinegar (see resources) or other good apple cider vinegar

1/2 cup alfalfa or clover honey

2 tablespoons crushed dried mint leaves

SERVES 8

Place all the ingredients in a small saucepan over low heat. When the sauce reaches a simmer turn the heat off immediately. Pour through a mesh strainer to remove any large pieces of stem or leaf, although a little mint leaf is good. Serve the sauce warm on the table in small individual pitchers or in a larger bowl that can be passed. A brown sauce made with lamb trimmings and bones is excellent served alongside the mint sauce to create a "double sauce" — my personal favorite.

GREEN TOMATO AND CARAMELIZED ORANGE JAM OR CHUTNEY

Rich caramelized orange peel makes this jam quite exotic, and it's a good way to use up green tomatoes at the end of the tomato season. It produces a euphoric effect when served on toast with Sour Cream Butter (p. 20), good coffee or steaming cups of Memory Tea (p. 314) in front of a crackling pine fire, shared with someone you enjoy.

The chutney recipe below it is another option — a richly flavored condiment for a variety of meats. When thinned with a little white wine or spring water it also makes a good barbecue sauce.

FOR THE JAM

6 to 8 medium Valencia oranges

2 tablespoon orange zest

8 cups chopped, green tomatoes

1/4 cup fresh squeezed lemon or lime juice

6 cups granulated sugar

MAKES 4 PINTS

Combine the orange sections, orange zest, green tomatoes and lemon or lime juice. Place in a 4-quart saucepan, and add a little spring water, to prevent scorching. Place over low heat until the juice from the fruit covers the mixture. Remove from heat and set aside.

In a second saucepan caramelize the sugar (see Dry-Caramelized Sugar below).

When sugar is caramelized, place a large metal colander or strainer, one larger then the saucepan, over the caramelized sugar to protect you from extremely hot splashes of sugar when you pour the orange and tomato mixture over the sugar. Remove saucepan from heat and allow the caramelized sugar to cool for few minutes. Slowly pour the orange and tomato mixture over the sugar mixture through the colander, then remove colander and stir mixtures together. Cook over very low heat, stirring frequently to avoid scorching as it thickens, until dark, bubbly and quite transparent, about 40 minutes. Pour into canning jars following directions below.

DRY-CARAMELIZED SUGAR

Because it requires low, steady heat and up to an hour of constant stirring for six cups of sugar, dry caramelizing also requires patience. White sugar will yield a mild flavor when caramelized. A metal disk under the pan is helpful in maintaining low, steady heat. If the pan is lined with steel, a medium-sized steel spatula is the ideal tool for stirring and scraping the bottom of the pan. If the pan is lined with tin, a flat-edged wooden spatula will do the job without scratching the tin.

Place the pan over very low heat, add one cup of sugar and begin stirring. After several minutes the pan will heat up and the sugar will begin to melt. When it is completely melted, slowly add another cup of sugar, stirring constantly. Repeat until all six cups of sugar have melted and turned a rich brown color.

(recipe continued on page 244)

While the jam/chutney is cooking, prepare equipment for preserving according to directions below.

» Place ladle, lids, tongs and funnel in large mixing bowl.
» Pour boiling water over all.
» Remove lids with tongs and place, rubber side down, on clean paper towels.
» Wash jars in hot, soapy water and rinse well. Place in a large pot of water. Bring to boil and sterilize for five minutes.
» Jars should be hot when filled, so you'll want to remove them from the hot water and fill just one or two at time. Remove with tongs and turn upside down to dry on paper towels for about a minute.
» While jar is still hot, fill with simmering fruit to within one-half inch from the top of the jar.
» Clean rim of jar with dry paper towel before sealing tightly with lid and ring and set aside to cool. Lid will be indented when properly sealed. You may hear a pop as each jar seals.

Will keep for one year in a cool storage area.

FOR THE CHUTNEY

3 cups Bragg Apple Cider Vinegar (see resources) or other good apple cider vinegar

2 cups currants

2 tablespoons ground ginger

2 tablespoons freshly ground black pepper

1 tablespoon cayenne pepper

3 cloves minced garlic

3 tablespoons sea salt

2 medium-sized yellow onions, chopped

MAKES APPROX. 4 PINTS

Combine all chutney ingredients in a 4-quart saucepan. Heat to boiling, then reduce to a simmer and cook until thickened, about 20–30 minutes. Add the Green Tomato Orange Jam to the chutney mixture. Bottle the chutney the same as the jam, according to preserving directions listed above.

FRESH FRUITED SYRUP

This is a simple way to add variety to syrups. It can be made, straight or mixed, with any number of ripe fruits such as cherries, peaches, apricots, oranges, apples, pears, plums, black raspberries. It is delicious on hot griddle cakes, crepes or ice cream.

1 cup light honey such as clover or alfalfa, or maple syrup

1 cup coarsely chopped fruit

MAKES 1 TO 2 CUPS

Place the honey and fruit into a nonreactive saucepan and put over low heat until the syrup reaches a low simmer. Turn off immediately. Allow to cool some before serving.

FRESH RIPE TOMATO SALSA

Good salsa is as fresh as a garden in summer. It adds flavor and color to eggs, fish, meats and beans. It's also good as a snack with tortilla chips.

1 to 3 chiles to taste, such as bell, Anaheim, poblano, chipotle, serrano, cayenne, habanero, from mild to hot in that order, roasted, skinned, seeded and chopped fine

2 garlic cloves, crushed

1/4 cup (packed), fresh cilantro leaves chopped

6 vine-ripe red tomatoes

1/4 cup chopped yellow Spanish onion

Lime juice to taste, strained

Salt to taste

MAKES 2 CUPS

To roast the tomatoes, place on a hot griddle until they brown a little, blister a little and soften inside. Skin the roasted tomatoes. Core the stem end of the tomatoes and coarsely chop them, whether they are raw or roasted.

Crush the ingredients in a coarse lava mortar and pestle or process in a blender just until they break down a little and combine. The texture is more interesting when it has some roughness.

WILD PLUM JAM

Red and yellow Potawatomi plums grow wild in many areas in the high Western desert. They are flavorful plums good for jam and jelly as well as tarts. This jam is wonderful on toast or to use as a glaze for a number of things such as grilled fowl, or for pie and tart shells before fruit is added. It is also good as a base for barbecue sauce.

12 cups of whole Potawatomi plums

8 cups of raw turbinado sugar (brown sugar may be substituted)

MAKES 6 PINTS

Wash, stem and pit the plums. Put them in a large nonreactive saucepan with a splash of spring water on a heatproof pad over low heat. After about 10 minutes they will release their juices and cover themselves.

Put the plums through a food mill or push through a strainer and discard the skins. Place the strained pulp back in the saucepan. Cook over low heat, stirring frequently, until the mixture reduces, thickens, darkens and mellows (about 1 hour). As the mixture gets closer to the finished stage, stir and scrape the bottom of the pan continuously with a spatula so the jam won't scorch. Toward the end, add the sugar and allow it to dissolve, blend and mellow a little for about 10 more minutes.

While the jam is cooking, prepare equipment for preserving according to directions below.

» Place ladle, lids, tongs and funnel in large mixing bowl.
» Pour boiling water over all.
» Remove lids with tongs and place, rubber side down, on clean paper towels.
» Wash jars in hot, soapy water and rinse well. Place in a large pot of water. Bring to boil and sterilize for five minutes.
» Jars should be hot when filled, so you'll want to remove them from the hot water and fill just one or two at time. Remove with tongs and turn upside down to dry on paper towels for about a minute.
» While jar is still hot, fill with simmering fruit to within one-half inch from the top of the jar.
» Clean rim of jar with dry paper towel before sealing tightly with lid and ring and set aside to cool. Lid will be indented when properly sealed. You may hear a pop as each jar seals.

Will keep for one year in a cool storage area.

THRESHING WHEAT

PREPARED HORSERADISH

Making your own horseradish offers several advantages: It can be processed to your own liking, from coarse to fine, using higher quality salt and better vinegar. For example, the clean taste of rice wine, the fruitiness of apple cider or the delicate sweetness of white wine vinegar. The absence of chemical preservatives also has advantages. It is healthier without the chemical harshness that sensitive palates can taste. If you've not tasted homemade horseradish you are in for a treat.

Horseradish is an essential condiment for all cuts of beef, including steaks, prime rib and pot roast. In the fall, homemade horseradish is sometimes available in good farmer's markets. If you have a blender and horseradish plants it is surprisingly simple to make.

1 1/2 cups fresh horseradish rounds

1 cup white wine vinegar to taste

1 tablespoon sea salt

MAKES ABOUT 2 CUPS

Horseradish roots grow deep, so it's easier to dig them when the ground is soft and damp. Any remnants left in the ground will grow into another plant. This is OK unless you're trying to keep them isolated in a particular area. Dig them out of the ground and spray the dirt and mud off them with a hose. Take them in the house and scrub them well with a vegetable brush. Rinse them thoroughly. Cut off the side shoots with a sharp paring knife. Peel the bigger roots with a potato peeler. Cut the root crosswise with a chef's knife into 1/4-inch cross sections (rounds) and reserve.

Put a cup of vinegar in a blender and add salt. Blend on medium-high. Add horseradish rounds, a few at a time, through the top opening of the blender. Continue to blend until the desired consistency is reached. If necessary, correct the seasoning with salt, allow it to dissolve, then taste and correct for both salt and vinegar.

If you want less vinegar, after processing, you can reduce the amount by putting the mixture in a strainer set over a stainless steel or ceramic container to drain off excess vinegar. Reserve the vinegar for the next batch or for vinaigrettes for a fresh horseradish flavor.

Store the processed horseradish sauce in a tightly covered glass jar in the refrigerator. The volatile elements in horseradish are quite corrosive, so before putting the lid on the jar, cover the top of the jar with several layers of plastic wrap. Prepared horseradish will last up to a year stored in the refrigerator.

CHILE OILS

I keep small bottles of chile oil in my pantry to add heat and flavor to various dishes. Chile oil is easy to make and indispensable for a range of dishes. There are a seemingly endless variety of chiles from mild to hot, large to small, sweet to tart and tannic. There are probably close to 100 chiles used in Mexican cooking alone.

Chiles are easy to grow with seedlings from your local nursery or you can grow them from seed in pots before setting the plants in the ground a few weeks later. Seek out different varieties at your farmer's market or grocer and save their seeds so you can grow them yourself. Dry them or roast them over wood in a charcoal broiler for added flavor. Combine them and blend them with various oils. They can be a wonderful addition to your culinary tool kit adding rich layers of heat and flavor to a variety of foods such as corn dishes, sauces, beans, soups, stews, casseroles, meatloaf, eggs. If you use them only occasionally you may want to keep them in the refrigerator so they won't oxidize and become rancid. If stored at room temperature with a tight-fitting lid they will remain quite fresh for a few weeks.

---

1 cup mild oil such as corn, safflower or soybean

Fresh or dried chiles to taste such as cayenne, jalapeno, habanero, guero, poblano, chipotle, Anaheim

MAKES ABOUT 1 CUP

NOTE: Wear rubber gloves and avoid rubbing your eyes when you work with any chiles.

Combine oil with crumbled dried or chopped fresh chiles in a mortar and pestle or a food processor. Grind, blend or process the mixture until silky smooth to minimize the solids from settling in the bottle. This makes it easier to mix the contents with a shake or two, dispersing the solids throughout the oil before each use. Chile seeds add heat, so for milder oils you may wish to remove some or all of the seeds before processing the chiles into oils. Some may require straining through a fine mesh strainer.

"The Genius of The Genius of Chile"

Homage to the chile pepper whose secrets extend
back beyond the Americas, beyond words, stoves
and cooks all the way back to the big bang.

How did the chile pepper figure out how to excite us?

How did its journey land it in the midst of intellectuals
who escaped the wrath of tyrants—

like Trotsky escaping Lenin when he fled to Mexico City

to live with Diego and Frida's essence

when both were painting with earthly abandon?

It spiced the food of genius—

as it did countless times before.

Ground Cherry Jam with Wild Honey

With nine sisters, my mother's family considered foraging for wild foods to be a family outing as well as a first step in making some of their favorite foods. Late summer to late autumn was an especially rich time for foraging. Wild plums and ground cherries were favorites for jam. Mint for Extra Classic Mint Sauce (p. 241) and rose hips for tea. The tradition of foraging was handed down to our family where I grew up with my five siblings on the same farm. Like my mother's family, we considered ground cherries to be very good for jam. They are both sweet and tart with a uniquely wild flavor. They grow on small bushes close to the ground especially in grainfields where they ripen after the grain is harvested. They are much like miniature tomatillos. Each berry is about the size of an extra large pea and comes beautifully wrapped in a little, pale green, paperlike sheath much like ones that wrap the tomatillo.

If you can't find ground cherries for this recipe substitute tomatillos, which usually appear at the supermarket or farmer's market in high to late summer. The wild ground cherry has a unique flavor lacking in tomatillo jam, but they are similar.

I prefer to use local honey to make this jam but you may want to experiment with different sweeteners such as sorghum or fructose, each of which can affect flavor and the way it sets up. Try a small batch first.

Young children love to pick ground cherries. It is a good way to introduce them to foraging wild foods. Although I've never seen it, some people are supposedly sensitive to ground cherries that aren't fully ripe. To help you decide which are ripe, look for the characteristic loose husk that indicates full ripeness.

12 cups of ripe ground cherries or tomatillos, chopped

Wild honey to taste (about 3 cups), (brown or Turbinado sugar, sorghum or fructose may be substituted)

Splash or two of spring water

MAKES 3 TO 4 PINTS

Put the ground cherries in a 2-quart saucepan. Add a little spring water so they won't scorch and set over low heat. Cook until the cherries release their liquid and become juicy. Over a heatproof pad or on extra low heat, add the honey and cook until translucent (about 60 minutes). Every five minutes or so stir and scrape the bottom of the pan with a heat proof spatula. If you want a richer jam, let it cook for up to 2 hours. It will reduce further, caramelize, turn richer and darker but will have less fruit flavor. You have to watch the darker version very carefully to avoid scorching. It is my favorite of the two.

While the jam is cooking, prepare equipment for preserving according to directions below.

» Place ladle, lids, tongs and funnel in large mixing bowl.
» Pour boiling water over all.
» Remove lids with tongs and place, rubber side down, on clean paper towels.
» Wash jars in hot, soapy water and rinse well. Place in a large pot of water. Bring to boil and sterilize for five minutes.
» Jars should be hot when filled, so you'll want to remove them from the hot water and fill just one or two at time. Remove with tongs and turn upside down to dry on paper towels for about a minute.
» While jar is still hot, fill with simmering fruit to within one-half inch from the top of the jar.
» Clean rim of jar with dry paper towel before sealing tightly with lid and ring and set aside to cool. Lid will be indented when properly sealed. You may hear a pop as each jar seals.

Will keep for one year in a cool storage area.

THRESHING WHEAT

Two Green Tomatillo Salsas, One Fresh and One Cooked

This sauce can be made with raw or cooked tomatillos for a sauce different both in flavor and texture. Either way it is one of the most common and arguably most classic of the Salsa Verdes. Both versions are best enjoyed as soon as you make them. If you're preparing your salsa ahead of time, cover and refrigerate until serving.

10 or 12 ripe tomatillos

Spring water to cover tomatillos (for the cooked version)

1/2 cup spring water for the raw version

2 or 3 mild chiles, such as Anaheim, roasted, skinned, seeded and chopped

1 or 2 cloves garlic crushed

1/4 cup firmly packed cilantro chopped

1/4 sweet white Maui or Vidalia onion, chopped

1 tablespoon strained lime juice

Salt to taste

MAKES 2 CUPS

For the raw version chop the tomatillos and put them into a blender with the 1/2 cup of spring water and all the other ingredients. Blend until smooth. If you prefer a rougher texture blend all ingredients except the tomatillos until smooth and then add the tomatillos. Blend a little, leaving them rougher than the other ingredients.

For the cooked version, cover the tomatillos with spring water in a saucepan and simmer for a few minutes until the tomatillos turn a lighter green. Remove the tomatillos from their liquid and reserve both. Put 1/2 cup of the cooking liquid in a blender with all the ingredients except the tomatillos. Blend until almost smooth then put the tomatillos in and blend until the desired texture is reached.

BEVERAGE RECOMMENDATION

Match with Pink Lymanitas (p. 317), Limeade with Lime Zest and Honey (p. 318) or good Mexican beer.

Two Tomatillo Chutneys, One Fresh and One Cooked

FRESH CHUTNEY

A light chutney, with flavors of India and Mexico interacting like two exotic dancers, it's good with grilled meat, fish, eggs and vegetables. When used as a condiment, it is a nice touch to fill small individual dishes for each diner.

1 cup fresh tomatillos, chopped

2 poblano peppers, roasted, skinned, seeded and chopped, or 1 green bell pepper prepared the same way

1/2 sweet white onion, chopped

1 clove garlic, crushed

Lime juice to taste

1 tablespoon raw sugar

Salt to taste

1/4 cup chopped fresh mint leaves

Fresh ground red or black pepper to taste

MAKES APPROX. 1 PINT

Process everything but the mint leaves and pepper in a blender until nearly smooth. The mint can easily dominate the flavors so you should add a little at a time. Blend, then taste. Grind a little pepper over the sauce before serving.

COOKED CHUTNEY

This is a very aromatic chutney. It is not as versatile as fresh chutney, but it pairs very well with wood-grilled meats. Tomatillos replace two of the ingredients used in most chutneys—a tart ingredient, like green tomatoes and a sweet ingredient like pears or apples. To accomplish this, use tomatillos that range from firm and tart to soft and sweet.

The tomatillo I like to use for this recipe is the quite common Toma Verde. It can get as big as a golf ball and ripens to a yellow, sweetly aromatic, slightly flattened fruit. Try other varieties if you can find them. Sometimes unusual varieties are available in farmer's markets during the fall season. Requesting unusual produce from farmers is like casting your vote or putting in an order. Sometimes it can be enough to encourage a farmer to plant something new.

1 red bell pepper

3 quarts of coarsely chopped tomatillos ranging from firm, green and tart to soft, yellow and sweet

1 cup dried black currants

1/2 cup pitted prunes, chopped medium

1 medium yellow Spanish onion, chopped fine

1 pint Bragg Apple Cider Vinegar (see resources) or other good apple cider vinegar

1 tablespoon mustard seed

1 teaspoon ground cloves

1 teaspoon ground allspice

2 cloves crushed garlic

1 1/2 cups full-flavored honey such as Tupelo or elderberry (available in natural food stores)

1 tablespoon lime zest

Salt to taste

MAKES APPROX. 3 PINTS

Place the pepper over an open flame and char its skin until quite solid black on all sides. Place it in a paper bag to sweat for 15 minutes. Remove it from the bag. Scrape off the blackened skin, pull off its stem and slit it lengthwise. Open the pepper and scrape the seeds from the interior. Save any flavorful liquid from the interior. Finely chop pepper.

Put all ingredients in a large nonreactive saucepan over low heat. Bring to a simmer and stir often. Cover with a lid that is slightly ajar. It should take about one hour to reach the right consistency. As this mixture cooks and thickens it can scorch easily; so watch it carefully and stir and scrape the pan often, especially after it begins to thicken.

While the chutney is cooking, prepare equipment for preserving according to directions below.

» Place ladle, lids, tongs and funnel in large mixing bowl.
» Pour boiling water over all.
» Remove lids with tongs and place, rubber side down, on clean paper towels.
» Wash jars in hot, soapy water and rinse well. Place in a large pot of water. Bring to boil and sterilize for five minutes.
» Jars should be hot when filled, so you'll want to remove them from the hot water and fill just one or two at time. Remove with tongs and turn upside down to dry on paper towels for about a minute.
» While jar is still hot, fill with simmering chutney to within one-half inch from the top of the jar.
» Clean rim of jar with dry paper towel before sealing tightly with lid and ring and set aside to cool. Lid will be indented when properly sealed. You may hear a pop as each jar seals.

For keeping chutney on the shelf for extended periods, bottle it while hot in sterilized pint jars. Will keep for one year in a cool storage area.

Endless Savory Soup Sauce

This soup sauce is a pungent, savory sauce with the approximate consistency of yogurt. It is designed to add flavor, color and interest to savory soups. It was inspired by the classic Italian pesto sauce and its French cousin, pistou.

This recipe can be endlessly modified to complement a wide variety of soups. It can be floated on the surface of the soup just before serving or it can be stirred in. It can be added by each guest at the table or by the cook before it is served. In place of or in addition to this soup sauce, a dribble of good extra virgin olive oil, pecan oil, walnut oil or hazelnut oil and a grind or two of black, white or red pepper or nutmeg also add a nice touch just before serving.

Personally, I think the creation of a soup sauce should be preceded by the creation of the soup. Of course it can also be done the other way around. My preference is matching the more quickly created sauce to the soup — which usually takes more time. Think of the process as music. It can be contrapuntal or harmonious, atonal or syncopated. It should add additional pleasure to the soup without overpowering or distracting from it. It can be similar in character or opposite. It can include a punctuation of heat from chiles, horseradish or mustard. The best way to get it right is to taste and adjust, taste and adjust both soup and sauce.

Most cooking is an additive process. Proceed with clarity and patience especially when ingredients are finely ground or liquid. Impulsive behavior in the kitchen can rarely lead to a stroke of genius, but more often leads to a disaster or somewhere in between. This is especially true of adding salt. It takes a few minutes for it to dissolve so it's important to wait until it does before adding more. A lot of good food has been ruined by oversalting.

1 clove raw garlic (roasted garlic, pickled garlic, oil-cured garlic)

1 anchovy, rinsed with water and blotted dry (sardine, smoked trout, smoked salmon, pickled herring)

1 tablespoon chopped capers (dill pickle, sweet pickle, green or black olives)

1 tablespoon minced shallots (red onion, chive, green onion, leek)

2 tablespoon pine nuts (English walnuts, black walnuts, almonds, pecans, macadamia nuts, brazil nuts, hazelnuts, all can be use raw or dry toasted in a dry skillet over medium heat while stirring or shaking)

1 tablespoon lemon juice with a little zest (lime juice/zest, grapefruit juice/zest, finely chopped kumquats

4 tablespoons olive oil (safflower oil, walnut oil, hazelnut oil or sunflower oil)

Black pepper (white pepper, nutmeg, mace, cinnamon, juniper berries, allspice, cardamom, cayenne pepper, chipotle pepper)

1 or more tablespoon finely chopped vine-ripened tomato

1 or more tablespoon finely chopped vine-ripened tomatillo

1 tablespoon minced fresh herbs straight or mixed such as tarragon, thyme, chervil, parsley, cilantro, sage, rosemary, dill or mint

Salt to taste

MAKES 8 TO 10 SERVINGS

Intermittent tasting is especially important when making something as complex as soup and soup sauce. The combination of the two can quickly take you into the realm of the infinite. In a lifetime, one could never accurately duplicate a past soup or soup sauce anyway, so just enjoy the uniqueness of each dish and learn what you can each time you do it.

The ingredients in parenthesis are suggested additions or replacements. And of course it can also easily be altered by omitting ingredients.

Add all but the minced herbs to a blender or food processor, or process with a mortar and pestle to a fine, creamy paste, or leave texture as desired. Taste and add, if desired, more of one or more ingredients to correct and fine-tune flavors.

A pinch or more of the minced herbs can be added earlier and processed to a paste with the other ingredients to add additional flavor. The bulk of the herbs however should be added after it has been processed once and then processed the second time only until the desired texture is reached. Season with salt.

Brown Sauce, with Notes on Integral Sauce

Most of the great sauces used in the modern kitchen are a gift to civilization from the collective genius of French chefs down through the ages. In the classical French repertoire of brown sauces there are about two dozen: Sauce Africaine, Aigre-Douce, Bigarade, Bonnefoy, Bordelaise, Bourguignonne, Charcutiére, Chevreuil, Chaud-froid Brune, Chateaubriand, Chasseur, aux Champignons, Duxelles, Diable, aux Fines Herbes, Grand Veneur, Italienne, Lyonnaise, Madère, Périgourdine, Périgueux, au Porto, Robert, Poivrade and Piquante. The variations are an adjustment to different types of food and specific recipes from different regions.

Throughout this book I have recommended using Brown Sauce for different recipes of mine, from meat loaf made with elk to dressing corn cakes. I always adjust my basic recipe for brown sauce to fit the food it accompanies, taking my cues from the ingredients in the dish. Short of devoting yourself entirely to becoming a saucier, I recommend starting with a basic brown sauce, like the one on the following page, and experimenting from there. The first step is to learn to make proper Meat Stock (p. 124).

My recipe is a versatile sauce that can be made with mushroom (p. 126), root vegetable (p. 122) or meat stock (p. 124). The stock can be reduced down to 25 percent of its original volume before adding it to the brown sauce. This saves time in the final preparation. Brown Sauce goes well with a range of beef or red meat game entrées, but with variations it can be adjusted to other dishes.

Threshing Wheat

1 yellow onion, finely chopped

1 carrot, finely chopped

1 stalk celery, finely chopped

1/4 cup clarified butter

1/4 cup all-purpose flour

1 quart double stock

1 or 2 vine-ripened tomatoes chopped, or 1 cup canned tomatoes

1/4 cup parsley, finely chopped

1 tablespoon tarragon, finely chopped

4 tablespoons good dry red wine

Salt and fresh ground white pepper to taste

Pinch of cinnamon

MAKES 3 CUPS

There is nothing, however, in the realm of dark savory sauces with more flavor than what is known as an integral sauce made with drippings from a roast or cuts of meat sautéed on top of the stove. The basic method for a quick integral sauce is to remove the meat to a platter and pour off the fat from the pan. Put the pan on a burner over medium heat and deglaze what remains in the pan with a splash or two of red wine, scraping all of the flavorful bits into the wine. Add a pat of butter to the hot liquid. Put in a pinch of finely minced herbs chosen to enhance the particular dish you have prepared. For example, for beef it could be thyme and parsley or tarragon and a dab of Dijon mustard. Tip the pan, whisk the ingredients all together then return the pan to the heat to reduce the mixture a little. Whisk again vigorously for a few seconds. Slice the meat and divide among individual warmed plates. Pour the sauce over the meat.

For greater volume, simply add brown sauce to the integral sauce when heating. Adding brown sauce to an integral sauce yields a greater volume of an intense flavor. Ladle the sauce under the meat and drizzle some across of the vegetables if desired.
The flavors of the integral sauce and the brown sauce are elevated by combining them.

Sauté the onion, carrot and celery in the clarified butter until soft. Add the flour. Stir and cook over medium heat until the mixture turns golden brown (about 10 minutes). Add the stock, tomatoes, parsley, tarragon and wine. Simmer over low heat until the mixture reduces by about half and is the consistency of heavy cream (about 2 hours). Skim the surface for any scum that rises to the top. Stir only occasionally. Too much stirring will lighten the color. Strain and season with salt and fresh ground white pepper. Add a very small pinch of cinnamon and stir in. Strain again once or twice through a fine strainer, such as a chinois.

For those who would like to pursue the subject of sauce-making further, I recommend *Sauces* by James Peterson.

THRESHING WHEAT

WALNUT/LIME (OR MINTED) MAYONNAISE

Walnut oil and fresh lime, including the zest, make a rich and unusual mayonnaise that is delicious with full-flavored dishes such as wood-broiled meats. The minted version is excellent with Lamb Burgers with Garlic and Mint (p. 182). There is also a roasted garlic version below that is very good with garlic-mint lamb burgers.

These four versions are good with blanched vegetables. New potatoes in their jackets, tiny green beans, fava beans, carrots, baby beets with their greens and immature summer squashes preferably with their blossoms still attached are all enhanced by this mayonnaise.

To keep the blend from breaking up, always let mayonnaise ingredients reach room temperature just before making.

---

1 teaspoon lime zest or 2 tablespoons fresh mint, minced

Salt to taste (about 1/4 teaspoon)

2 tablespoons fresh lime juice, strained

2 egg yolks

1/2 cup fresh, mild walnut oil

1/2 cup corn oil or safflower oil

Cayenne pepper to taste

1 head of garlic for the aïoli version

MAKES ABOUT 1 CUP

Crush the lime zest with a pinch of salt to a smooth paste with a mortar and pestle. Add the lime juice and stir it all together. In a separate bowl, whisk the egg yolks and lime juice mixture together and add the rest of the salt. In another small bowl, mix the two oils together. Drop by drop, whisk the oil into the egg mixture. It will start to emulsify and thicken almost immediately. After about 1/4 of the oil has been added, you can gradually speed up the addition of the oil, but do not add the oil too rapidly or it won't be fully absorbed. When all of the oil has been incorporated, stir in the cayenne. Immediately put the mayonnaise in the refrigerator to cool until served. Because it is made with raw eggs you should use this mayonnaise as soon as possible. Even when refrigerated, it shouldn't be kept for more than two days.

FOR THE GARLIC VERSION
Roast a head of garlic wrapped in aluminum foil in a 350° F oven for 1 hour. When it is finished, depending on how garlicky you want it, squeeze the garlic from a few of the cloves into a mortar and pestle and grind it into a smooth paste with a little oil. Incorporate the garlic mixture into either of the finished mayonnaises.

ROASTED CORN RELISH

This is a great summer table relish that's good with grilled fowl, grilled meats and grilled fish. You can make it with raw or roasted corn. For added flavor, roast and baste the corn with coconut milk over a wood fire. Roast until it is a barely golden color. Cut the kernels off the cobs. Take care not to allow the corn to dry out. The relish has a homey flavor with an exotic twist of coconut and visual appeal of red, yellow and green flecks.

2 cups corn kernels (about 4 ears of corn) raw, or roasted and basted with coconut milk

1/2 cup coconut milk for basting

1/2 teaspoon Coleman's dry mustard (in the spice section of most grocers)

1/2 teaspoon sea salt

3 tablespoons citrus honey or clover honey

1/4 cup strained lime juice

1 tablespoon minced cilantro leaves

1 tablespoon minced Thai or sweet basil leaves

1 teaspoon minced fresh mint leaves

1 heaping tablespoon finely chopped chives

1/2 cup finely chopped sweet white onion

3 tablespoons red bell, or for more spice a hotter red pepper such as a red banana pepper or red jalapeno pepper seeded and chopped fine

MAKES APPROX. 1 QUART

Roast corn and cut kernels off, or simply cut kernels from raw corn. Set aside in a nonreactive bowl. Whisk together a dressing of mustard, salt, honey and lime juice until smooth. Place the cilantro, basil, mint, chives, onion, pepper (of your choice) and the corn in a bowl and toss together with the dressing. Chill in refrigerator for an hour and toss every 15 or 20 minutes before serving. It is even better left refrigerated overnight to mellow and allow the flavors to penetrate the vegetables.

THRESHING WHEAT

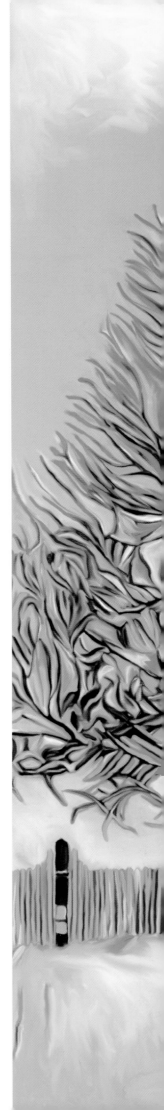

THE FLOWERS COTTAGE

{ DESSERTS }

THE FLOWERS COTTAGE

People's Park rebellion garden is often given credit for marking the official beginning of the modern organic movement. Of course the world of media influence and the credit it bestows often belongs to the most famous entity, and that wouldn't be an obscure plot in my backyard in the Avenues of Salt Lake City. But to me, that's where it all began.

Let's start with the story of how I found my bit of paradise, a little farm in the urban clutter. I had graduated art school in 1966. My teaching certificate landed me a job on the Oregon Coast, where my wife, two children and I lived, starved for the interaction of friends back in Utah. After nine months, we were back in Zion. We needed a place to live. Having been away from the family farm for seven years, I began feeling a pronounced craving for soil. My hands wanted to dig into earth. I was attempting to be a responsible adult with a job and a house, but I knew that within that responsibility scheme, I needed a place where we could grow a garden.

As the designated house hunter, I literally criss-crossed my way across the valley, starting at the south end of Salt Lake Valley, past the Kennecott Copper mine and the Oquirrh Mountains to the Capitol building. Four or five hours at a time I combed the entire city, dirt roads, suburban sprawl and all. I really had no idea what I was looking for, just a vague yearning for a little rural oasis to call my own.

Why I thought I would find something I would like in the densely packed houses of the Avenues, I don't know. The Avenue streets run east and west interspersed with lettered streets running north and south, starting with "A Street" and progressing to "V Street." Dreadful apartment houses stood like pockmarks throughout the district. But back in the day, this was where wealthy polygamists and the titans of industry like Thomas Kearns rooted homes to show off to the community. To this day the lower Avenues are lined with some of the state's most extravagant homes, mostly restored for high-end offices of prestigious corporations.

Among this elegance and jumbled aesthetics, I turned onto 5th Avenue, and it appeared like a vision. Oh my God. It was obvious this was our house, a wood-frame Queen Anne that hadn't been painted for decades. Yet it had a feeling of neglected dignity; it didn't really need the paint.

There was no for-sale sign but I whipped over to the curb and parked. My pulse picked up noticeably as I knocked on the door. No answer.

Then, just as I turned to leave, the neighbor showed up on the doorstep next door and glared over at me, the supposed trespasser. I asked about the owner of the house. "If you're interested in buying it," he quickly snapped, "it's not for sale."

"Oh, OK. Do you know the owner's name?" I asked, undeterred. "It belongs to the Flowers family," he shot back before disappearing into his house.

Seville Flowers was a respected biology professor at the University of Utah, where I had earned my art degree. I didn't know much about him, only in the way of friends of friends who rented from them, so I looked up the Flowers name in the phone book. To my relief there were only two. When I finally got ahold of him, he was friendly, but to the point. "Let's meet at the house tomorrow after school," he said.

When I arrived the next day and walked across the front porch, the sounds of an all wood house creaked under my feet. I knocked on the solid old door and heard footsteps almost immediately. I had butterflies in my stomach. When Dr. Flowers opened the door I was standing face to face with the illustrious professor. He was a small man, probably not much over five feet, with a kind, weathered face. He greeted me with a warm handshake.

The interior of the house was amazing. It looked as if no one had touched anything for years. It was stuffed with Victorian artifacts of all kinds. Immediately behind him in the hall was a large black nickel plated stove. A big china cupboard stood in the corner of the dining room behind a

big, round oak dining table, where he invited me to have a seat. There was a radio with a large freestanding speaker with a needlepoint cover. It was as if I had stepped onto the movie set of an old English film circa the late 19th century. It could have been where Aubrey Beardsley lived in London in his short but romantic life. It had a hundred years of patina overlaid with a decade or more of benign neglect, a result of his younger sister Maude's insistence on doing everything herself and her long progressive loss of eyesight. Until the day they took her to the rest home, she had insisted on heating the house with coal from an old shed behind the house, just as her family had during the years she had grown up there, from 1893 when the family moved into the newly built home.

"It's apparent to me that you're supposed to have this house" were the first words he spoke. "What do you want to do?"

I stammered back weakly, "Rent it, I guess."

"How does $40 a month sound?" he said. Even in 1967 that was cheap. "That sounds fine," I said. I pulled my wallet out of my back pocket and opened it. There, amazingly, lay two twenty dollar bills, my last until payday. It was a surreal moment scripted by the benevolent hand of fate. Few things in life, I thought, ever work this well.

Next day the kind professor sent a second note. "We've hit a snag. Meet me at the house tonight right after school." My mind raced through dozens of possibilities which repeated like a cruel, self-imposed loop for the next few hours until we met.

This time there was an air of regret from Dr. Flowers and I didn't like the way it sounded.

"After we talked yesterday I went home and called a family meeting with the two other members of the family. They were both upset with me. They said I'd made a bad deal," he revealed. "First the $40 a month has to be split 3 ways and that's after the water and sewer bill is paid. So this is what they are willing to accept: We can't rent the house to you but we will sell it. We don't think the place has much value so we're willing to sell it for the value of the lot. We think that's about $10,000. We'll carry the contract at 6 percent, which we think is more than fair. However, we will need $70 a month. Can you handle that?" I nodded my approval. Then he went on. "We can call a thrift store and have them remove all of the contents of the house if you want." I told him that wouldn't be necessary. Then he gave me one last nugget of advice. "If I were you I would tear out all of these complex redwood moldings and replace them with small, thin, modern moldings so your wife won't have to waste so much time dusting."

I thanked him, amazed at the difference of our perceptions, and then we stood up, shook hands on the deal and started toward the front door. Then with a completely unexpected look of horror he turned and said, "I'm sorry but I forgot to ask for a down payment." I replied nervously, "I gave you my last $40 yesterday for the rent." Then he administered the final grace note. "OK," he said. "Let's call that the down payment."

So that was the deal, maybe the best of my life. The gods of providence had smiled down on us big time.

We now had our own place to live in, at a price that was less than an apartment would cost. Plus, we finally had a place to plant a full-scale garden. Our dream of an urban farm was coming true.

But as we anticipated creating a space for our lives, other things were waning. By spring my wife and I came to realize our incompatibility and watched with mixed feelings as our marriage dissolved, ravaged by the culture storms of that unsettled era. She moved out with the children and I found myself alone in the great house with all its space.

As if in some act of healing, I opened my mind to the creative possibilities an empty house can offer. At the suggestion of a photographer friend, one bedroom became a darkroom. The laundry shed was converted into a guest room for fellow bohemians who happened to be traveling through town on their way to San Francisco or east to a commune or concert in Colorado or the Fillmore East in New York City.

Much to the curiosity of the neighbors, counter-culture had landed in their neighborhood and by spring that would include an urban vegetable garden, the first any of them had seen in this neighborhood. As far as I was concerned, I was now the new owner of one of the coolest New Age digs anywhere. It even smelled of incense, the old-fashioned kind, little black cones so sweet you could smell them across the room before they were lit.

Spring came, and as the ground warmed up and the processes of nature came alive, my thoughts turned to the 2,000 or so square-foot patch of land behind my house. It was the dawning of the Age of Aquarius and the year was filled with New Age optimism. It all seemed too good to be true. I began to realize that I had purchased, along with a place to grow food, my secret weapon. Now I could avoid the starving part of being an artist and explore my passion for growing at the same time. And I was free to garden organically the way my parents and grandparents had before the chemical madness swept over the world of agriculture.

The garden had been lying fallow for years and was covered with dry weeds and copious amounts of pigeon droppings from cages above. One morning as I was making tea I looked out the kitchen window to see my latest guest, Julian Babcock, a hitchhiker from the farm country of Ohio. Lo and behold, he was scattering the pigeon droppings around the dirt with my garden spade, turning the ground like a real farm boy. This garden that was taking place in this outpost of counterculture was a full year ahead of the People's Park rebellion garden in Berkeley, far ahead of the Reagan massacre that took place in that very city the following spring.

The People's Park rebellion happened only blocks from UC Berkeley. The uprising was covered by the news media like a duck attacking a June bug. The story broke from coast to coast with the fervor of a prison riot, which in a sense it was. So a year later, as we put in our second garden, we watched in disbelief as we learned of the murder and mayhem in Berkeley. After the dust settled and the blood was washed from public view, without realizing it we witnessed the beginning of another California

first, the New Age of organic agriculture. "California is where it all starts," as the saying goes, but if by chance it actually doesn't it usually gets the credit anyway because that is where the eyes of the nation are waiting and watching to see what its future holds.

Revolution was in the air and not only in California. If any other American city was ripe for a revolution, as unlikely as it might sound, it was Salt Lake City, roughly 800 miles to the east of where the Berkeley massacre took place. Salt Lake City was always dominated by Mormonism like Catholicism dominates the Vatican. The pressure that domination created built up over a period of decades and anyone paying attention would have noticed it building towards what came next. Like a diamond being formed in a crucible of heat and pressure, Salt Lake City gave birth to its own jewel of a renaissance.

In a remarkable show of brilliance, this outlier of American culture, this Mormon outpost that people seem to love to make light of, went kaboom! with the birth of 3D computer graphics as well as the humble birth of a family of optical processes that grew into "optical effects," later merging into "digital effects." So, too, our house and its garden developed in the late 1960s. Early experiments gave way to light shows, my newest passion. Collaborators and artistic guests were sustained with food that came from our backyard garden.

This outpost in the desert, however, was not new to transformational technologies. By the time the sixties came along it had already been the location of one of the world's most astonishing engineering feats, the quiet birth of the age of modern irrigation. It was forged out of necessity in the harsh desert environment. From the simple act of diverting a small creek flowing down a nearby canyon to a hastily plowed field scattered with grain, Mormon irrigation technology quietly appeared on the world stage, then grew over the next century into one of the most remarkable events in the history of the new world. From it sprang pretty much every modern irrigation technique and every hydroelectric dam in the modern world.

"And the desert shall bloom like a rose" (Isaiah 35:1). And so it did, and the industrious bees' home, the beehive, became the state symbol. At the same time, Salt Lake City became the center of the largest desert civilization in the history of the world. It all began on that hot day in late July 1847. And in my mind our humble quarter-acre lot in the Avenues Historical District was somehow connected to it all. It still is, quite literally, connected to the same City Creek stream of water that was flooded onto the fields that fateful day when the first wagon train entered the Salt Lake Valley. My great-great grandfather, Amasa (pronounced Amasee) Lyman, a Mormon apostle, was among that amazing group of pioneers.

From the beginning my garden served as our private farmer's market as well as my personal agricultural laboratory. Over the years, it saw an ongoing series of urban farm experiments: at one time we had 15 colonies of Italian honeybees, a hutch of rabbits, a milking nanny goat and various breeds of chickens. But we still didn't have the animals necessary to make enough manure for our garden, so we made use of a variety of external resources like manure from a dairy farm at the south end of our valley.

We brought in rock dust from a limestone quarry in Utah County, close by my family's farm where I grew up. We gathered tons of bagged leaves from the streets of Salt Lake City in the autumn and enriched our soil with red rock minerals from various parts of Utah. With all of the available organic inputs, it made sense to recycle them through the garden. Otherwise they would have gone to waste.

Looking back over the 43 years our garden has been producing, I have seen sweeping changes in America's culture, including a growing interest in urban farming and a generation that eschews the use of chemicals to grow vegetables. People raise their own chickens, keep hives, or make an effort to support something local.

One wonderful irony of my way of farming and that of this generation of New Age farmers is that even though they are, in sum, arguably the most creative and progressive of any generation, they chose to follow the wisdom of the world's farmers of the past centuries. Despite the so-called "advancements" in production and higher yield of the reductionist methods of modern agricultural chemistry, these New Age minds value something else, something more environmentally acceptable. They eschew the modern techniques as environmentally unacceptable. It gives one great optimism.

THE FLOWERS COTTAGE

The sweeping interest in urban farming today makes its more and more clear that we can't separate people from the land with political decrees and technological advances, put them in crowded cities and expect them to forget the millennia-old bonds that we have with the land. The spirit of farming, of living on the land and the joys it brings to the nature-hungry souls of humanity, will eventually overcome bad government policy and technology's efforts to unitize consumers around the world. The most effective way to transcend the flaws of the modern food chain is to plant a garden. In that humble act lies nothing less than the survival of the soul of humanity.

TRISTAR CAKE

The wild part of the highly revered TriStar Strawberry's genetics was obtained from a wild strawberry found in the mountains east of Salt Lake City only miles from the Strawberry Ranch where I spent some of my favorite years.

This is a moderately rich dessert that combines the best of our region. Freshly ground wheat flour, sea salt and spring water for the cakes. Sour Cream Butter (p. 20), honey, local strawberries and whipping cream to finish the assembly.

1 cup strawberries

1 cup alfalfa or clover honey

1/2 recipe of Luxuriously Simple Crepe (p. 47), reserved on a warm plate and covered with a clean towel

Powdered sugar for serving

Fresh strawberries to garnish

1/2 cup whipping cream

Sugar to taste

1/2 teaspoon vanilla

SERVES 8

Put strawberries into a small saucepan and pour honey over them. Mash the strawberries and honey together and bring them to a simmer over low heat. Remove pan from heat, cover and set aside to macerate for 10 minutes. Force strawberry mixture through a sieve and reserve.

Brush each crepe on both sides with honey-strawberry syrup until all are saturated.

To serve, stack 6 crepes. Cut the cake in 8 pie-shaped wedges. Dust with a little powdered sugar if desired. Top each serving with a fresh strawberry and serve with a generous dollop of sweetened whipped cream.

Rustic Raspberry Tart

This is a simple but elegant tart made with my favorite fruit. I make the crust with local wheat flour, Utah pecans and the freshest berries I can find. The Bear Lake region of Utah produces some of the best red raspberries in the United States.

This tart sweetened with honey and served with rich vanilla ice cream makes a wonderfully decadent dessert.

1/4 cup shelled pecans

1 1/4 cup whole-wheat pastry flour

1/4 teaspoons salt

6 tablespoons cold butter cut into 1/4-inch pieces

Cold spring water as needed

2 cups of fresh ripe red raspberries

1/4 cup raspberry, alfalfa or clover honey

1 tablespoon honey to glaze crust

SERVES 6 TO 12

Preheat the oven to 400° F.

Put the pecans in a dry blender or food processor and process until they resemble the texture of cornmeal. Mix the pecan meal, flour and salt in a large mixing bowl. Quickly rub the butter and flour mixture together with your hands until it resembles coarse cornmeal. If you overwork the mixture the butter will get warm and melt, making the mixture oily and the crust hard. If your hands are warm put them under cold water then dry them. Add a sprinkle or two of ice water if needed, so the mixture will stick together. Shape the dough into a ball and put it back in the bowl. Cover the bowl with a cloth and refrigerate while you pick through the berries.

Put the raspberries in a mixing bowl and drizzle half the honey over them. Gently mix together with your hands. Roll the dough out on wax paper or on a lightly floured surface in a circular shape about 1/8 inch thick. Transfer the circle to a flat baking sheet. Brush the dough with 1 tablespoon of warm honey. Lay the berries out on the dough leaving 2 to 4 inches clear around the edge. Pour the last tablespoon of honey over the berries. Wrap the edges of the dough up and around the berries. Pinch the dough together in a few places to seal. Place the baking sheet in the oven. Bake for 30 to 40 minutes until the crust is nicely browned. Serve each piece with a scoop of good vanilla ice cream or a dollop of whipped cream.

BEVERAGE RECOMMENDATION

Cognac, such as Martell complements the rich nutty crust and velvet smoothness of the cream.

CARAMELIZED FRUIT

Much lighter than a traditional fruit pie but still full of flavor. If the fruit is in good condition it can be left unpeeled. Serve plain or with a dollop of whipped cream sweetened with maple syrup. Both versions are enhanced by a good grating or two of nutmeg.

2 pounds or a variety of ripe cherries (pitted and halved) or apricots, apples, pears, peaches, or plums which have been stemmed, cored, pitted and/or peeled and sliced lengthwise about 1/4 inch thick

1 cup good port wine or apple juice

1/4 cup of sugar (or to taste) for fruits that are a little tart

Pinch cinnamon

1 cup heavy cream, chilled and whipped

Maple syrup to taste

Grating of nutmeg

SERVES 4 TO 6

Preheat oven to 500° F.

Bring fruit and port or apple juice to a simmer in a small uncovered saucepan. Add sugar and cinnamon. Cook on low, basting the fruit often with the liquid, until fruit softens a little and the liquid reduces to about half. Transfer to preheated oven. Cook until fruit edges start turning dark brown (about 20 minutes). Cool for 5 to 10 minutes. Divide among 4 plates and serve warm with a dollop of whipped cream sweetened with maple syrup, if desired. Grate a little nutmeg over each serving.

BEVERAGE RECOMMENDATION

A good port such as a Sandeman Port Vau 1997.

Mama Beth's All-Purpose Pie Dough

2 cups all-purpose
unbleached flour

1/2 teaspoon salt

1/3 cup sugar

3/4 cup chilled lard or
1 cup chilled butter

Spring water to make
the mixture stick together

A few drops of vanilla for the
lard version (vanilla subdues
the lard flavor)

MAKES 2 CRUSTS

Mix the first 4 ingredients together until crumbly. Sprinkle with spring water and mix until soft enough to roll out into a nice crust. Mother used up to 1/3 cup spring water and said it didn't have to be cold and the dough didn't have to be refrigerated. What amazes me is that she would break rules that are considered gospel by most bakers and her crusts were still as tender as any I've ever tasted.

MAMA BETH'S LEMON SOUL

1/2 cup sugar

4 tablespoons cornstarch

Zest from one lemon

1/8 teaspoon salt

1/2 cup strained lemon juice

2 egg yolks (reserve whites for meringue)

2 cups spring water

1 1/2 tablespoons butter

1 teaspoon Bragg Apple Cider Vinegar (see resources)

1 recipe pie crust dough for one pie (p. 277)

MAKES ONE 9-INCH PIE

Preheat oven to 425° F.

Mix sugar and cornstarch together. Crush zest and salt together with a mortar and pestle to form a paste. Pour lemon juice into mortar and stir. Place egg yolks in a mixing bowl, add lemon mixture to egg yolks and beat well. Combine lemon/egg yolk mixture with sugar mixture. Stir until blended. In a 2-quart saucepan, bring spring water to a simmer. Using a wooden spoon slowly add lemon/sugar mixture to the water and stir continuously until thickened (about 5 minutes). Add butter and vinegar and stir thoroughly. Set aside to cool. Make meringue (see recipe below) while lemon mixture cools.

Line a 9-inch pie plate with pie crust dough. Cut off any excess dough spilling over the rim. Using your thumb and forefinger, flute edges around rim of crust. With a fork, prick the sides and bottom of the crust in a few places to allow steam to escape. Bake in a 425° F oven until lightly browned (about 12 minutes). Remove from oven and allow crust to cool. Pour cooled lemon mixture into baked pie crust shell. Cover with Mama Beth's No Fail Meringue and bake in a 425° F. oven until meringue peaks are golden brown (about 10 minutes).

MAMA BETH'S NO-FAIL MERINGUE

1 tablespoon cornstarch

2 tablespoons cold spring water

1/2 cup boiling spring water

3 egg whites

6 tablespoons sugar

Pinch of salt

1 teaspoon vanilla extract

TO COVER ONE 9-INCH PIE

Blend cornstarch and cold spring water in saucepan. Add boiling spring water and cook, stirring until thickened and translucent. Set aside until completely cool. Beat egg whites until they form soft peaks. With mixer running, add sugar one tablespoon at a time. Beat in salt and vanilla. Fold cornstarch mixture into the egg whites and beat at high speed until firm.

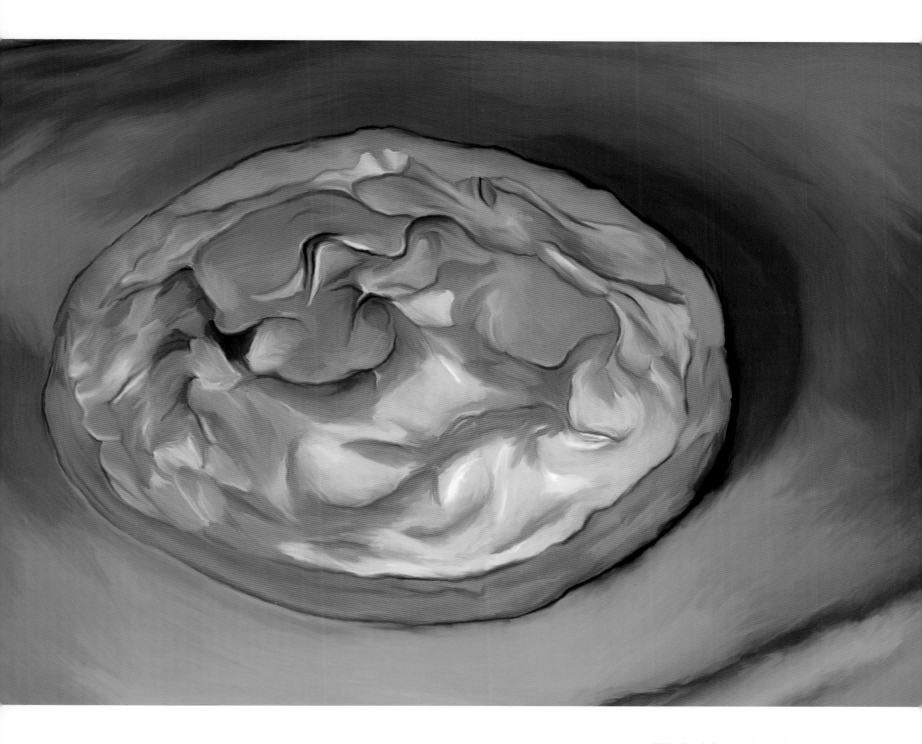

With the deftness of an old master
My mother would spread meringue
Over her lemon soul
With its simple crust
Then burnish it to gold
In the oven's heat

MAMA BETH'S MINCEMEAT PIE

A richly satisfying pie, redolent with spice, citrus and layers of complex sweetness. Sofia and I like it best warm with good Cabernet Sauvignon and vanilla ice cream.

1 quart boiled, shredded then ground deer meat (Mother used the neck from the venison but other venison meat will suffice. Ground beef is an acceptable substitute.)

2 cups raisins

1 cup currants

2 cups brown or raw sugar

1 tablespoon salt

1/2 cup molasses

1/2 cup Bragg Apple Cider Vinegar (see resources)

1 cup good Cabernet Sauvignon

2 oranges cut into pieces, seeded, and coarsely ground (Mother used a meat grinder for this, but you can chop these oranges with a chef's knife.)

Cinnamon to taste

1 cup ground suet (The fat that surrounds the kidneys of beef. You will need to ask your butcher for this ingredient.)

1 quart peeled, seeded and chopped, red apples

1 recipe pie crust (p. 277)

1 tablespoon cream

Sugar to sprinkle over the top

MAKES 4 QUARTS

Preheat oven to 350° F.

Place all ingredients in a large nonreactive saucepan. Bring to a simmer and cook, stirring constantly, until the apples are tender (20 to 30 minutes). Bottle and process in a covered simmering water bath for at least 20 minutes.

Pour 1 quart of mincemeat into a pie plate that has been lined with one-half recipe of pie crust. Roll out the other half for the top. While the top piece is still on the board, create a decorative pattern by piercing its top with a small sharp knife. Place pie crust over the pie and seal the edges of the two layers either with the tines of a fork, or with your fingers. Piercing the top layer allows the gases to expand and escape, preventing the pie from bursting. Brush the top with a little cream. Bake for 30 minutes at 350° F. Sprinkle with sugar after you take pie out of the oven.

THE FLOWERS COTTAGE

MAMA BETH'S RHUBARB PIE

This is a simple classic — the best kind.

All-Purpose Pie Dough (p. 277)

5 cups fresh-cut red rhubarb sliced into 1/4-inch slices

1 cup white or brown sugar

2 large eggs

2 tablespoons raw tapioca

1 cup heavy whipping cream

Sugar to taste

1/2 teaspoon vanilla extract

MAKES ONE 9-INCH PIE

Preheat oven to 350° F.

On a lightly floured surface, roll out pie dough to about 1/8-inch thick. Place the dough in the pie plate and trim the edge. Mound the rhubarb into the unbaked shell. Whisk sugar, eggs and tapioca together and drizzle evenly over rhubarb. Bake in a 350° F oven for 35 to 40 minutes. Serve with sweetened whipped cream flavored with vanilla.

BEVERAGE RECOMMENDATION

Excellent with a good bottle of Tokay, such as a five- or six-year-old 5 Puttonos Aszu. This is a luxurious dessert wine, rich with complex fruit, butter and caramel. It achieves a remarkable balance with the pie.

Rum Raisin Butter Nut Pie

This is a luxurious version of the raisin pie that was popular with the early Mormon settlers when fresh fruit wasn't available. Serve warm with heavy cream.

1 recipe of pie dough (p. 277)

1 cup raisins (packed)

Spring water to cover raisins

Spring water to increase volume to 3 cups

2 tablespoons strained lemon juice

3 tablespoons cornstarch

1/2 cup Muscovado dark brown sugar (see resources) or regular dark brown sugar

3 tablespoons butter

1/2 cup chopped pecans

4 tablespoons dark Puerto Rican rum such as Myer's Dark

1 or 2 tablespoons cream

White sugar

MAKES ONE 9-INCH PIE

Preheat oven to 350° F.

Put the raisins in a 2-quart saucepan and cover them with 1 inch of spring water. Bring to a boil, then immediately turn the heat down to a very low simmer. Simmer for 1 hour. Pour the raisins through a sieve into another saucepan. Measure the liquid. Add enough spring water to make 3 cups. Put the raisins back in the saucepan with the liquid. In a small bowl, mix the lemon juice, cornstarch, sugar and a little of the raisin liquid together until smooth. Add this mixture to the raisins and cook, stirring continually for a few more minutes until thickened. Remove from heat. Add the butter, pecans and rum and stir to incorporate.

Line a 9-inch pie dish with half of the dough. Trim the edges. Pour the raisin mixture into the dish. Roll out the rest of the dough for the top. While it is still on the board, use a small knife to create a simple decorative pattern. These vents will allow the expanding gases to escape. Place the top crust over the filling and seal the edges of dough together using your thumb and forefinger. Brush the top with cream and bake for 30 minutes. Sprinkle with a little granulated sugar after you take pie out of the oven.

BEVERAGE RECOMMENDATION

Serve with good tawny port such as Whiskers or Old Benson.

THE FLOWERS COTTAGE

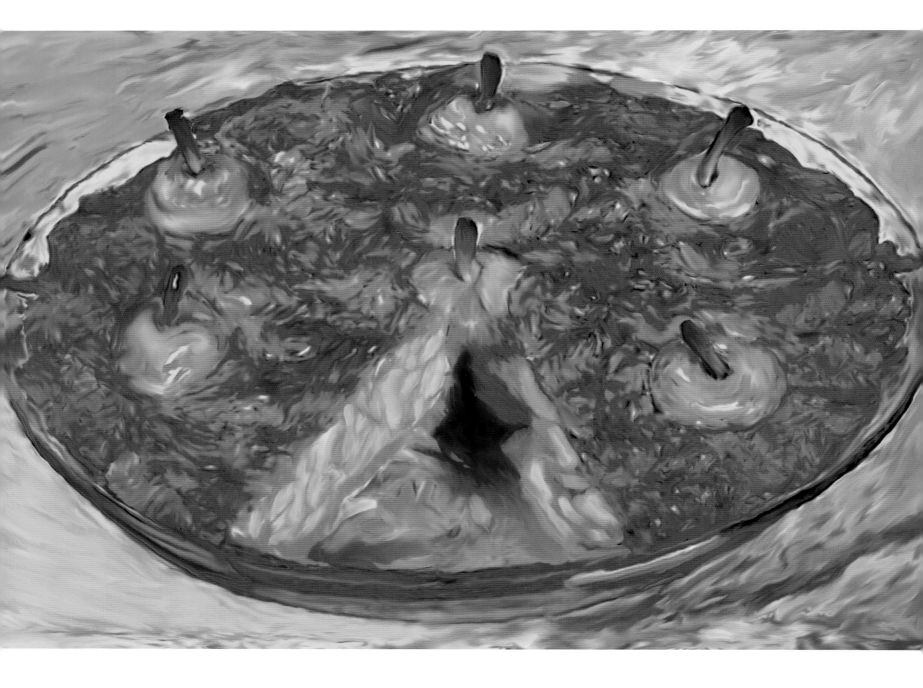

*Here is a pie so sensuous that I almost blush
to see its form, let alone taste its rich flesh
lying in the melt of vanilla ice cream.*

PEAR PIE

FOR THE BOTTOM CRUST

1/2 cup almond flour ground in a blender from whole, raw almonds and sifted

1 cup whole wheat pastry flour or all-purpose flour

2 to 3 tablespoons Muscovado dark brown sugar (see resources) or regular dark brown sugar

1/4 teaspoon salt

1/4 pound cold butter

Ice cold spring water as needed

Wild Plum Jam (p. 247) or apricot jam as needed for glazing

FOR THE FILLING

7 small Anjou or Bartlett pears (approximately 4 cups)

1/8 teaspoon ground cloves

1 cup Muscovado dark brown sugar or dark brown sugar

1 tablespoon lime or lemon juice

4 tablespoons dark rum

FOR THE TOP CRUST

1 cup finely ground almonds

1/4 cup whole wheat pastry flour

3 to 4 tablespoons Muscovado dark brown sugar or dark brown sugar

Pinch of ground cloves

1 teaspoon lime or lemon zest

Pinch of salt

2 tablespoons butter

1 tablespoon Wild Plum Jam or apricot jam

MAKES ONE 9-INCH PIE

The almond crust with citrus peel gives this pie an unexpected flavor that harmonizes nicely with the pear filling which is rich with tropical overtones of clove and rum. It may be served warm with whipped cream sweetened with rum and ground cloves, or with vanilla ice cream.

Preheat oven to 375° F.

Bottom Crust: Mix the first 4 ingredients together. Quickly rub the butter into the dry mixture until its texture resembles cornmeal. Sprinkle ice cold spring water into the mixture and work it until it sticks together. Pat into a ball and roll out the dough on a lightly floured surface. Place it in a 9-inch glass pie dish that has been buttered and lightly dusted with flour. Liberally brush the inside of the crust with some of the jam. The jam glaze creates a moisture barrier that helps keep the crust from getting soggy. Cover the outer 1/2-inch edge of the crust with a carefully cut circular ring of aluminum foil to keep it from burning. Bake it in a preheated 375° F oven for 15 minutes. Remove from oven and let it cool while you prepare the filling and top crust ingredients.

Filling: Slice about 1 inch from the top of each pear leaving the stem and skin attached. Set aside. Mix the cloves, sugar, lime or lemon juice and 3 tablespoons of rum together. Reserve 1 tablespoon of rum for the whipped cream. Peel, core and slice the rest of each pear 1/8 inch thick and lightly mix them with the sugar mixture. Let the mixture sit for 30 minutes or more then drain well in a large strainer set over a 2-quart saucepan (5 minutes). Set pears aside. Heat the drained liquid to a boil and reduce it to the consistency of cream. Set aside. Put the pear mixture into the baked crust. Arrange the pear tops on top.

Top Crust: Mix all dry ingredients together. Cut the cold butter into the dry ingredients until it resembles cornmeal. Sprinkle the mixture over the pear filling and around the pear tops and gently pat it down. Stir the jam into the reduced liquid and brush over the top of the pie. Place in a 375° F oven and bake until it browns nicely (45 to 60 minutes). Protect the outer 1/2-inch edge again with the same foil or it will burn.

BEVERAGE RECOMMENDATION

Pear Brandy, Brandy, Port or Tokay all go well with this pie.

286

Ahhh the Noble Pear

Like Marie Antoinette's Breast

Ripened by the vigorous bloom of youth

Stimulating secret memories of old men

Chocolate Espresso Muscovado Bourbon Cake

This is an intensely rich and moist special-occasion cake. For a nice variation add 1/2 cup of black currants or chopped pecans.

1/2 cup strongly brewed espresso

1/2 cup currants or chopped pecan meats, optional

1/4 cup spring water

2 tablespoons good Bourbon whiskey such as Maker's Mark

1 cup almond flour made from whole, raw almonds, ground in a blender or food processor and sifted

2 tablespoons Muscovado dark brown sugar (see resources) or regular brown sugar

1 teaspoon baking powder

1 cup chocolate chips such as Ghirardelli's Double Chocolate Chips

1/2 cup sweetened condensed milk

4 tablespoons butter, plus additional butter for the cake pan

Wax paper to cover bottom of cake pan

2 egg whites

1/8 teaspoon cream of tartar

1 teaspoon vanilla extract

2 egg yolks

Powdered sugar for serving

MAKES ONE 9 X 4 X 2-INCH CAKE

Preheat oven to 350° F.

Make the espresso and set aside. Cover the currants, if using, with spring water in a small saucepan. Simmer on low for about 5 minutes. Add the whiskey, simmer for another minute and set aside to cool. Put the almonds in a blender and blend on medium speed until they resemble the texture of cornmeal. Sift and repeat if necessary. Mix the almond meal, sugar and baking powder together and set aside. In a double boiler or a metal mixing bowl over a pot of hot, but not boiling water, place the chocolate chips, the sweetened condensed milk and the butter together and allow to heat slowly, stirring occasionally.

Butter a 9 x 4-inch loaf pan evenly. Leave room for the batter to rise about 50 percent. Measure a sheet of wax paper and fit it into the bottom of the buttered pan. Set pan aside. When the chocolate is almost melted (about 10 minutes) beat the egg whites and cream of tarter until stiff but not dry and set aside. Add the vanilla and the egg yolks to the melted chocolate mixture and stir quickly to blend. In a large mixing bowl add the almond meal mixture, melted chocolate mixture, espresso, the softened currants or dry nuts (if used) and mix together well. Fold in the egg whites, taking care not to overwork them or they may dissolve and lose some of their volume. Pour into the wax
paper—lined cake pan and bake in preheated oven for 45 minutes.

Remove the cake from the oven and allow to cool completely while still in the pan. Place cake in the refrigerator and chill well before attempting to remove it from the pan. Carefully run a sharp knife around the cake's edges and invert onto a cake plate. Peel off the wax paper. Dust the cake with a little sifted confectioner's sugar.

BEVERAGE RECOMMENDATION

With the black currant version serve a well-aged Cabernet Sauvignon. With the pecan version a Fino or Amontillado Sherry with a dry, nutty richness indicated by its amber color. Another sweeter pairing with either version is a good, wood-aged tawny port such as Whiskers or Old Benson, both from Australia.

THE FLOWERS COTTAGE

CORNMEAL ALMOND CAKE

1/2 cup currants (optional)

1/2 cup spring water

1/2 cup Madeira wine,
preferably Malmsey

1 cup yellow cornmeal

1 cup raw almond meal

1 level teaspoon salt

1 egg well beaten

1 tablespoon fresh walnut oil
plus a little for the pan (any mild oil
can be substituted)

1/2 cup elderberry honey (alfalfa or
clover honey may be substituted)

Enough powdered sugar to dust the
top (approximately 1 tablespoon)

MAKES ONE 9-INCH CAKE

A richly flavored cake with a crumbly texture; good dunked in a glass of
Malmsey Madeira served to each guest.

Preheat oven to 400° F.

If using currants, cover them with the spring water and simmer for 2 or 3 minutes. Add the
wine, remove from heat and set aside. (If you don't use currants add the spring water and wine
to the dry ingredients.)

Process a cup of raw almonds in a blender or food processor until finely ground. Leaving chunks of
almond in the meal can add a pleasant crunchiness to the cake if you like. Otherwise, pour
the almond flour through a sieve to remove the larger chunks. Mix the cornmeal, almond meal
and salt together. Stir in the egg, currants if using, water, wine, oil and honey.

Line the bottom of a 9-inch springform pan with parchment. Brush with a little walnut oil.
Pour in the batter. Bake at 400° F for 30 to 40 minutes until a toothpick inserted in the center
comes out clean. Cool. Slice into wedges. For a nice visual flourish, place a small, pretty leaf
on a slice of cake. Put a teaspoon of powdered sugar in a fine meshed sieve and dust it over
the leaf. Remove the leaf before serving.

Fantastic Almond Shortbread

Nothing compares with the rich, rustic flavor of absolutely fresh-ground whole grain. It just requires a grain grinder (see resources).

This simple, richly flavored shortbread can be cut into small squares for cookies or larger pieces for cakes. As a cookie it complements a variety of desserts. Larger portions can be topped with sugared berries and sweetened whipped cream to create a very special shortcake.

1/4 pound butter

Sugar to taste (4 level tablespoons for medium sweetness)

2/3 cup freshly ground whole wheat flour or whole wheat pastry flour

1/3 cup freshly ground raw almond meal (Process whole raw almonds in a blender or food processor until mealy; sift through medium strainer to remove chunks. Reprocess chunks.)

Powdered sugar for dusting (optional)

MAKES 8 COOKIES OR
4 SHORT CAKES

Preheat oven to 350° F.

Cream the butter and sugar together until fluffy and smooth. Add the flour and almond meal slowly while beating until completely incorporated. Form into a 1/2-inch-thick layer in a buttered Pyrex 8-inch square baking dish or pat the dough out on a baking sheet and bake for 20 minutes.

Cut shortbread into pieces while warm. After they have cooled, dust them with a little sifted powdered sugar, if desired, before removing them from the baking dish. It is best to leave them in a glass dish. Or if using a baking sheet, remove them from the baking sheet and place them on a small ceramic plate. Either way, cover with plastic wrap so they will not dry out. The shortbread will stay fresh for 2 or 3 days.

BEVERAGE RECOMMENDATION

Perfectly matched with a glass of late harvest Jacob Gerhardt Rheinhessen.

Decadent Hazelnut Butterscotch Pudding

A luxurious dessert when served in small bowls with a dollop of whipped cream sweetened with sorghum syrup or maple syrup, a sprinkle of crushed hazelnuts and a snifter of good whiskey on the side.

2 to 3 tablespoons spring water

3 level tablespoons cornstarch

1/4 cup butter

1/4 cup of Muscovado dark brown sugar (see resources) or regular dark brown sugar

1 cup cream

1 cup milk

2 or 3 pinches of salt

2 tablespoons hazelnut liqueur, plus 4 tablespoons to pour over the finished pudding

1/2 cup cream

1 tablespoon Appalachian sorghum (sorghum can be found in natural foods stores), maple syrup or white sugar for the whipped cream

Few drops vanilla extract (for use with white sugar version)

4 hazelnuts, crushed fine

SERVES 4 TO 8

Mix the spring water and cornstarch together with a whisk and set aside. It should be about the thickness of heavy cream. In a heavy saucepan, melt the butter and brown sugar over medium-low heat. Stir continuously to allow the mixture to darken somewhat. The darker it gets the richer the flavor will be. Be careful not to burn it or it will become bitter. While stirring continuously, add the cream. Continue to stir the mixture to just to the boiling point. When it all melts together, slowly add the milk and salt. Stir in the cornstarch mixture and add it to the pudding.

Stir and cook over medium low until the mixture simmers gently for a minute or two. Take it off the heat, add 2 tablespoons of hazelnut liqueur and blend it together. Let the pudding cool a little then divide it among 4 small bowls. Place a tablespoon of hazelnut liqueur on the top of each pudding to keep it from forming a skin. Put the bowls in the refrigerator for at least 1/2 hour before serving so the pudding can set up.

In a separate bowl whip the cream and sweeten it. When serving, put a dollop of whipped cream on each pudding and dust each with one crushed hazlenut.

BEVERAGE RECOMMENDATION

Serve George Dickel No. 12 whiskey in brandy snifters or large red-wine glasses, so you can enjoy the rich, maplewood perfume which echoes the silky textures and buttery flavors of the pudding.

JEANNE RAINEY'S DATE PUDDING

This dessert has been in our friend's family for generations. Years ago when we tasted it, it quickly became one of our favorites. It is rich, satisfying and goes perfectly with unsweetened whipped cream and a small glass of Petite Syrah.

Butter

1 cup chopped pitted dates

1/2 cup chopped walnuts

1 cup sugar

1 teaspoon baking powder

8 finely crushed saltine crackers

1 teaspoon vanilla

3 eggs, yolks and whites separated

Heavy whipping cream

MAKES 2 CRUSTS

Preheat oven to 350° F.

Butter a 9 x 9-inch glass baking dish. Set aside. In a mixing bowl, stir dates, nuts and dry ingredients together. Add vanilla and slightly beaten egg yolks. Mix together well.

Beat egg whites until fluffy, but still soft and silky. Gently fold egg whites into mixture, incorporating completely. Pour into prepared baking dish and bake for 30 minutes. Date pudding will turn golden brown on top and will be soft to the touch. It will crack and fall a bit as it cools.

Whip cream and refrigerate until serving (unsweetened is best—the pudding is sweet enough) Serve warm or at room temperature, topped with whipped cream.

THE FLOWERS COTTAGE

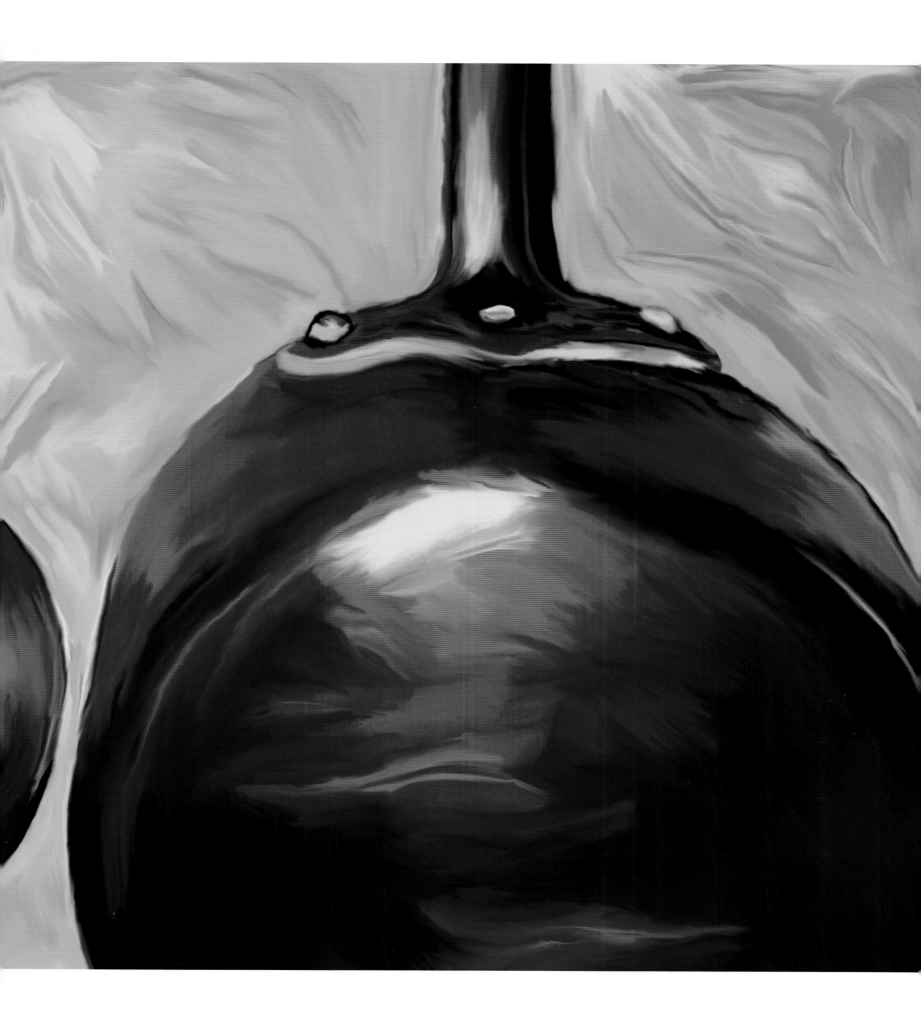

TRIPLE PEACH DESSERT

This is an unusual and festive dessert featuring ice cream with a rich almond flavor derived from peach leaves. The final presentation is a cool riot of color. Orange colored peach puree is topped with a scoop of sage-colored ice cream, circled with white whipped cream, topped with a red raspberry and dusted with dark flecks of rich, mocha-like peach-kernel pepper. Serve with Fantastic Almond Shortbread Squares (p. 290).

---

1 cup milk

40 medium-sized fresh, unsprayed, washed peach leaves

10 egg yolks (reserve whites for other uses)

3/4 cup Muscovado sugar (see resources) or regular dark brown sugar

2 cups heavy cream

FOR THE PUREE

6 fully ripe peaches

Chestnut honey or sugar to taste

FOR THE WHIPPED CREAM

1 cup heavy cream

1 heaping teaspoon powdered sugar

1 level teaspoon vanilla extract

FOR THE PEACH PEPPER

6 peach pits

MAKES ABOUT 1 QUART

For the Ice Cream: Blend the milk with the peach leaves in a blender or food processor. Turn off the machine and allow the leaves to thoroughly macerate in the milk for 2 or 3 minutes until the color stops changing. Press the resulting green mixture through a coarse strainer followed by a fine strainer. Discard the leafy pulp. Set the milk mixture aside.

In a 2-quart saucepan thoroughly whisk together the egg yolks, sugar and 2 cups cream. Place the saucepan over low heat and keep the mixture below a simmer, stirring continuously using a heatproof rubber spatula. Keep the heat very low as the mixture thickens. Do not allow the mixture to simmer or it will curdle. As the mixture heats up it will begin to cling to the spatula. As you stir, make sure you are reaching into the corners of the pan to prevent scorching. Remove from the heat. Mix the peach leaf mixture into the custard mixture and strain through a very fine chinois as many times as needed to remove any trace of fiber. It should be as smooth as velvet and taste a little extra sweet. (Freezing will reduce the sweet taste.)

Pour into an ice cream maker and process. The ice cream can be served soft, or if you prefer, cover the container with plastic wrap, replace the lid and put it in the freezer for an hour or two to make it firm.

For the Puree: Peel peaches and remove their pits. With a wooden spoon, press the peaches through a medium sieve twice. (Or the second time through a tamis.) Stir in honey to taste. Keep the mixture slightly on the acidic side as it pairs better with the creaminess of the ice cream and whipped cream.

For the Peach Pepper: Carefully remove the peach kernels from the pits. This will require protective eyewear, a seriously good nutcracker or a hammer and pliers to hold the pits.

Crack the pits open on a solid surface. (I use a brick on our butcher block.) Crack them gently but firmly trying to keep the kernels as whole as possible. Dry roast the kernels in a 400° F oven until they color slightly and become a bit brittle (about 5 minutes). Watch them carefully and stir them each time you check them, to prevent burning. Remove kernels from the pan and crush them thoroughly with a rolling pin. Scrape into a dish and set aside.

For the Whipped Cream: Whip the cream into soft peaks. Beat in the powdered sugar and vanilla. Spoon into a pastry bag with a decorative tip and set aside.

For the Final Assembly: Place a large spoonful of peach puree in a soup bowl (if possible, one that harmonizes with all of the dessert's colors). Use approximately 1/6 of the puree for each serving. If necessary, shake the bowl a little so the puree flattens out to the sides of the dish. Place a large scoop of ice cream in the middle of the puree. Pipe a circle of whipped cream around each scoop. Place a raspberry on the top of each scoop and dust with the crushed peach kernels.

BEVERAGE RECOMMENDATION

A good Cognac such as Martell.

Caramel Banana Ice Cream

This is a rich, buttery ice cream that goes well with chocolate cookies.

1 tablespoon butter

1 ripe banana, sliced into 1/4 inch rounds

1 cup white granulated sugar (total)

1 cup milk

10 egg yolks

2 cups cream

1 vanilla bean

1/4 teaspoon salt

MAKES 1 QUART

Place a heavy 1-quart saucepan over medium heat. Add the butter. When it is melted, add the bananas and toss well to coat. Mash the bananas as they cook and soften. Turn the heat high enough so the mixture begins to brown. At this point, remove from heat and set aside.

Put 1/4 cup of the sugar in a second heavy 2-quart saucepan over very low heat. Stir the sugar gently and continually with a wooden spoon until the heat builds up and the sugar begins to warm. After about 5 minutes the sugar will begin to melt. Keep stirring until the sugar is melted and has turned a golden brown, then stir in the remaining sugar a tablespoon at a time. Stir in each addition until it melts and becomes an integral part of the brown liquid. It will turn a nice chestnut brown when all the sugar is fully melted and mixed together. It will begin to take on a pleasant bitter aroma when it gets to this point. The color will tell you when it is done.

Warm the banana mixture over low heat and add it to the caramelized sugar mixture. Stir them together thoroughly. Add 1 cup of warm milk and stir over low heat until everything is melted and completely blended. Cool a little, then place the mixture in a blender and blend on medium speed until smooth. Set aside.

In a separate saucepan add the egg yolks, cream and salt and whisk together until smooth. Cut the vanilla bean in half, lengthwise and scrape the seeds from the bean into the mixture. Add the bean to the pan and place the mixture over low heat. Stir continually with a wooden spoon. As the mixture thickens it will begin to coat the spoon. Be careful to keep the heat on low at this stage or the mixture will curdle. If necessary lift the pan above the heat occasionally as you stir. When the mixture coats the spoon it is done. Remove from heat immediately.

Discard the vanilla bean pod. Mix the strained egg custard mixture into the banana mixture. Stir the combined mixtures together then strain again through a strainer or chinois. Refrigerate this mixture until it is completely chilled. Place the mixture in an ice cream freezer and follow the manufacturer's directions. When the ice cream is firm, remove the paddles, cover the canister with plastic wrap and replace the lid.

Freeze for 2 hours.

BEVERAGE RECOMMENDATION

Ice Muscat such as Vin De Glacier from Bonny Doon Vineyards.

PINK ECSTASY (ICE CREAM SHAKE)

1/2 cup Cabernet Sauvignon
or other dry red wine

2 cups vanilla ice cream
(amount may vary depending
on density of ice cream
and thickness desired)

SERVES 2

Dry red wine harmonizes beautifully with vanilla ice cream in this quick little shake that will make you smile. As always, the end result will be only as good as its ingredients. Serve with Fantastic Almond Shortbread Squares (p. 290).

Place ingredients into a blender and process until smooth.

ICE CREAM FIABON

2 cans coconut milk
(available in Asian food stores)
look for the thickest you can find

1/2 cup pure maple syrup,
or to taste

1 banana (optional)

1 teaspoon vanilla extract (optional)

MAKES ABOUT 1 QUART

Using ingredients from the Southern and Northern hemispheres, this is a special ice cream that celebrates the union of my Indonesian-born wife and me. Like our relationship it is richly flavored, yet pure and simple. It goes well with lemon desserts such as Mama Beth's Lemon Soul (p. 278) or Chocolate Espresso Bourbon Muscovado Cake (p. 288) or fresh ripe berries, such as blueberries, red raspberries or blackberries.

Blend all the ingredients thoroughly in a blender. Follow the manufacturer's directions for your ice cream maker. If you prefer a soft ice cream eat it as soon as it is removed from the ice cream maker. If you prefer firmer ice cream, remove the paddle and place the canister of ice cream in your freezer for an hour or more. If stored in the freezer, allow ice cream to soften a little before serving.

PINE NUT ICE CREAM

2 cups shelled pine nuts

4 cups spring water

1 cup Muscovado dark
brown sugar (resources)
or regular dark brown sugar

Pinch of salt

3 tablespoons cornstarch

MAKES 2 QUARTS

This ice cream is made with pine nut cream instead of dairy cream. It has the rich flavor of pine nuts with a creaminess that rivals dairy ice cream. It is delicious with fresh fruits — raspberries, pears and peaches, as well as fruit pies or tarts. It is also good served with other flavors of ice cream.

Process the pine nuts with the spring water, sugar and salt in a food processor or blender until completely smooth (about 1 minute). Add the cornstarch and blend in briefly. Pour into a 2-quart saucepan and heat to a low simmer, stirring constantly with a wooden spoon. Cook until it thickens enough to coat the back of the spoon (8 to 10 minutes). It will scorch easily, so scrape the bottom of the pan every minute or so with a spatula. Completely chill the cooked mixture in the refrigerator then process in an ice cream freezer as directed.

BEVERAGE RECOMMENDATION

Yalumba Tawny Port from Australia.

An Artist's Kitchen

A Most Memorable Experience

A few years ago, I had a most memorable experience while rafting the Green River with friends. As we rounded a bend in the river at about 10 a.m. one morning, we passed a massive pyramid of stone. It looked like it was 2,000 feet high or more. The sun's side angle put its face in dramatic relief. The detail was astounding. At every level of scale it was perfect, primal Egyptian. As I pondered what I was seeing it occurred to me that the Egyptian aesthetic, like most others back through history, came not from a formalized, intellectual process so much as direct inspiration from nature. That day and that massive pyramid on that great river was one of the most beautiful things I have ever experienced. The next day we took out at the little town of Green River, Utah, where close by, along the river's edge, fields of melons ripened in the late summer sun into some of America's finest.

FARMING WITH INTEGRITY

Farming, when done with true integrity can be a deeply satisfying experience. For one thing it means putting more back into the soil than you take out so there is a sense of honesty with the process. It also means having an appreciation of what has gone into this most universal of human endeavors—the thousands of years of plant breeding, farming techniques handed down from hundreds of previous generations and the hard-won evolution of the farmer's tools. All of these are things that can so easily be taken for granted. It also helps the farmer to know what the potential of his produce is in the kitchen. I find that being a cook greatly enriches the farming experience and that the opposite is just as true.

I have farmed and gardened both conventionally and sustainable most of my life and have seen the results of both methods and the effect they have on the soil. It is vast. The first is ultimately destructive and the second is a process of healing and nurturing.

Music

UK2 band. From top, left to right: Richard Taylor, Eric Muhler, Flavia Cervino Wood, Jon Davis, Harold Carr, Kenvin Lyman, Sonny Wolf

Music has always been an important part of my life. As I was growing up on an isolated ranch in the forties, music, ironically, was special because of our primitive technology. We owned an old Arvin battery radio that we could listen to only on Saturday night, the night of the Grand Ole Opry. Batteries were precious in our isolation so they had to be carefully preserved. The Grand Ole Opry was the pinnacle of our collective musical experience in those days and it still resonates on some level. Something that was important then and still exists in my life is live music. It is part of our family tradition. Mother taught us to play the ukulele and sing harmonies. That tradition still lives in my life; only now other instruments have taken the place of the ukulele.

Even before Duke Ellington's prescient observation that there are only two kinds of music—good and bad—I've always had a love for other music, classical, jazz and world music, when it showed up. These days, considering the present place music has evolved to, my favorite music for my light shows is jazz because it's more abstract, leaving more room for interpretation. My own music, on the other hand, stays simple like the way I cook, with a few ingredients freshly gathered, like new musical ideas, simply prepared and served with honest wine.

In 1960 I learned to play drums and my friends asked me to join their cover band The Nighthawks. It was a way to pay my way through college and it gave me a taste of the day-to-day music business, traveling on the road with other band members, setting up night after night and playing in smoky bars. Eventually we all lost interest and went on to do other things.

In the early seventies I realized I could write songs. That was a powerful discovery and has driven my music ever since. In 1973 I recorded my first album, *Eagle Ridge,* in another process of self-discovery that opened the door to a new world. Fast forward through 35 years of media projects: All of the band members that played on that album except the piano player Kevin Lewis are still living and agreed to work on my new album, included in this book, as the UK2 Band.

Besides recording, my other favorite expression for music is to play with whoever shows up for supper. After we finish eating, we gather around the hearth or the light show and lay it down. It is a source of endless pleasure, living on the edge of the creative unknown and one of my favorite ways to surf life's molecules.

LIGHT SHOWS

What do light shows have to do with food? The answer involves one foot in the past and one in the creative future. In the past, people thought of an evening's entertainment as something more than dinner and after dinner as more than sweets. Today I think of it as prime time for performance art. For one thing there are less calories involved and more excitement. Musicians and poets are among our favored guests because they easily can be accompanied by a visual performance (light show), turning the evening into something completely unique. I have included the light show in our lives for so long that it has become a family tradition, giving the evening a romantic air of the avant-garde.

Above all, a great deal of importance is placed on originality. To me, combining a visual performance with, say, jazz, a poetry reading, an aria, a dance, or whatever else is happening in the realm of the performance, is one of the most exciting ways to make art and to cap the evening.

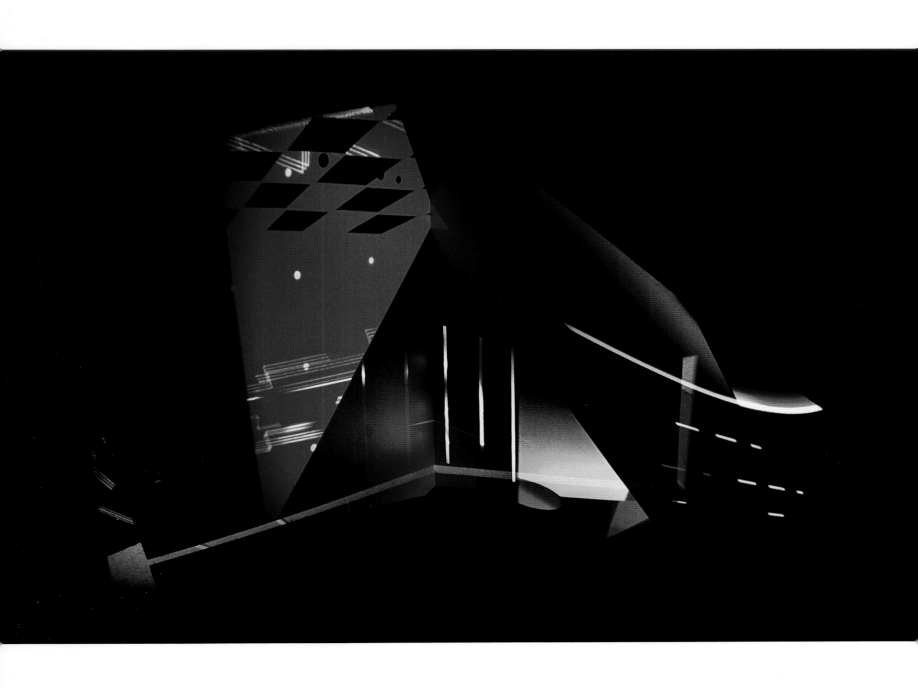

A Few Favorite Beverages

{ BEVERAGES }

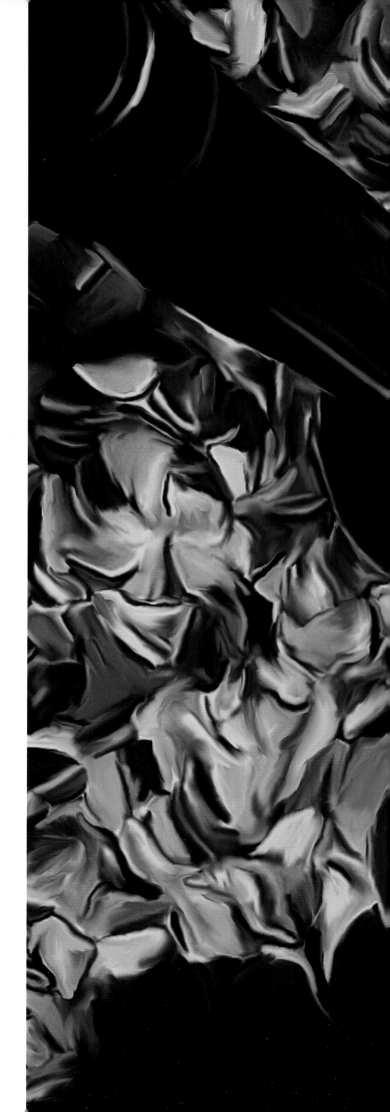

A FEW FAVORITE BEVERAGES

On these pages are my visual interpretations of some of the wines we tested and matched with the recipes in this book. During this process I was struck by the parallels between the language of the winemaker and the painter: Here the bottle with its contents and often iconic label play the role of the painter's model. For additional props I chose various wine glasses with poured wine and the bottle's cork or sparkling wine muzzle—all of which I think are beautiful objects themselves.

Fabric materials were chosen as backdrops because of their endless richness of folds, textures, and the way they interact with light. The rich patterns of light and colors reflecting from the fabric backgrounds express the vineyards and their surrounding environments with their endlessly changing colors and textures of land and sky and the qualities of their grapes, the often beautiful, and sometimes profound, wines made from them.

311

CHOCOLATE NUT MILK

1/2 cup raw pecans or walnuts

2 cups spring water

1 small pinch of salt

1/2 to 1 cup semi-sweet chocolate chips such as Hershey's special dark

Malt powder to taste (optional)

SERVES 2

Put pecans or walnuts and spring water in blender and blend until smooth. Pour mixture into a small saucepan and add other ingredients. Bring to a simmer, stirring continually. Pour back into blender and blend until silky smooth.

Serve in coffee cups. Garnish if desired with crème fraîche, whipped cream, grated chocolate, cinnamon, grated nutmeg or a twist of orange peel.

The Italians figured out how to make good coffee by first figuring out how to make a good coffee pot then refining both to perfection.

MEMORY TEA

For me the combination of wild mint and wild catnip when brewed into tea gives off aromas that stimulate deep memory. They remind me of childhood, shady groves, vacant lots and old cellars, sometimes stimulating primeval memory, like ancient places in the collective mind when people lived simple lives close to the earth like hobbits. To get the full effect you must use the wild versions. The large scale, farmed, neatly packaged, grocery store versions lack deep flavors, the soul of the plant. When gathering wild herbs, be careful they are not along ditches or fences that have been sprayed. If possible, cut enough to last a full year. Each fall, before the first frost, we pack a picnic lunch and make a day of it, filling large, plastic bags with freshly cut mint and smaller bags with catnip. As soon as we get home we spread them out on a clean surface allowing them to fully dry in the sun so they don't mold. Once they are completely dry we rub the leaves off their stems and put each in their own container with a tight lid.

Serve with Fantastic Almond Shortbread Squares (p. 290) or good toast spread with Sour Cream Butter (p. 20) and homemade jam or wild honey. Make a ritual out of the preparation and serving, elevating it to your own special experience.

---

2 tablespoons dried wild spearmint or peppermint leaves

1 tablespoon dried wild catnip leaves

5 cups of spring water

MAKES 5 CUPS

Heat spring water to boiling. Pour it over the leaves in a teapot and allow it to brew for 5 minutes before serving. Offer wild, clover or alfalfa honey.

SOMEWHERE INSIDE OF ME I AM ASIAN
IN MY CELLULAR MEMORY MY HAND KNOWS HOW TO HOLD A POT OF
BOILING WATER LIKE A TEA MASTER

AND WITH MY ANCIENT EYE I SEE THE SAME UNIVERSAL BEAUTY THAT
WAS THERE WHEN CHANOYU WAS AS YOUNG AS MOLTEN LAVA

PINK LYMANITAS

In the mid-1980s, my brother Jay and I worked on several advertising campaigns as illustrators for the head office of Coca-Cola in Atlanta. The project's creative team would fly into Salt Lake City to work with us. At the end of one of our projects we were able to host them for dinner at my house. To accompany our à la Mexican dinner we served my version of the classic Mexican Margarita. They heartily approved.

One of the team members who had come to dinner that night called a few weeks later to request the recipe. I told him I would be willing to trade it for the Coca-Cola recipe. Unfortunately, my request was denied. I gave it to him anyway. They named it the "Lymanita" and said, due to their efforts, it was being served in various watering holes around Atlanta. One of the most charming aspects of this drink is its color — a delightful combination of light and dark greens and the delicate pink from the addition of blended raspberries.

For me salt (see resources) is particularly important for a good margarita as it coats the rim where the taste can either enhance or detract from the drink.

---

3 or 4, 1 x 1/2-inch strips of lime zest cut with a potato peeler before limes are halved for juicing; reserve

1/4 cup of fresh-squeezed lime juice

2 to 4 tablespoons orange or lime blossom honey to sweeten

1/2 cup orange liqueur such as Mandarin Napoleon or Grand Marnier

1/2 cup tequila such as Cuervo Reserva

1 cup fresh raspberries

1 cup crushed ice made from spring water

Deep-mined, Utah Salt (see resources) or sea salt to rim the glasses

4 1/8-inch slices of lime for garnish

MAKES 2 LARGE DRINKS

Put the lime juice in a blender and turn it on low. Pour the honey in a thin stream into the blender. Stop the blender and taste. Repeat until you achieve the desired sweetness. It takes almost an equal amount of honey to counteract the acid in lime juice. It will eventually reach a balance where the mixture will neither taste acidic or sweet. This is the proper balance for the mixture. (It is a critical point of judgment and should be remembered for the next batch.)

Mix equal parts sweetened lime juice, orange liqueur and tequila — a kind of secular Mexican Trinity if you will. Add the raspberries. Turn the blender on high. Puree, then strain the mixture to remove the seeds before slowly adding ice, one or two cubes at a time. Blend until they are absorbed. Repeat until the liquid starts to reach the slush stage but no further. Too much ice will weaken the drink's flavor. Using a wedge of lime skin bent backwards into a crescent shape, circle the rims of Margarita or Martini glasses to extract the oil that will moisten and perfume the rim. Pour the salt into a small saucer. Dip the inverted glass into the salt. Carefully pour the blended mixture into each glass. If there are more lime strips left, squeeze the oil across the surface of the drink. Dispose of the spent strips and garnish each drink with a wedge of lime placed on the rim.

LIMEADE WITH LIME ZEST AND HONEY

This is a delicious summer beverage and a good drink for children. It's perfect for accompanying summer meals such as hamburgers or grilled tuna melts. Personally I like it strong. I like to add ice to the ingredients without the water. Then I let the ice melt awhile before serving. This way the ice provides all or most of the necessary water and it is nicely chilled from the first sip. The zest adds intensity and enhances the rich citrus flavors.

Most citrus fruit flavor is in the peel in the form of oil. Zest can be used for many things from braises to ice cream. It's a pity to discard unzested citrus peel. A simple way to retain this valuable commodity is to completely zest a citrus fruit before juicing it. Extra zest can be stored in a sealed container and kept in the freezer for later use. It can also be dried, placed in a glass jar and kept on the pantry shelf in a sealed container.

2 cups lime juice from 8 to 16 limes

Zest from 8 to 16 limes

Alfalfa or clover honey to taste

1 quart crushed ice

Spring water to taste

MAKES 1 TO 2 QUARTS
OR 8 TO 16 SERVINGS

Put the lime juice and about 1/3 of the zest into a blender and blend at high speed until the zest is incorporated. Strain the mixture through a fine sieve to remove any zest granules. Pour the strained mixture back in the blender and turn it on low. Slowly add the honey in a thin stream. Turn the blender off and taste. Add the spring water and correct the sweetness. It should be quite sweet because the cold of the ice will reduce its apparent sweetness.

Pour the mixture into a serving pitcher and fill the pitcher with ice. Let the mixture rest for awhile before serving to allow some of the ice to melt. If it is too strong at serving time, add spring water to taste. If it isn't strong enough or sweet enough after you add the water, correct by pouring in a little spring water or lime juice in the blender and blend in honey. Add to the iced mixture and stir to mix. Fill the glasses with additional ice, then pour in the limeade. Garnish with a thin slice of lime.

THE BACK LANES AROUND
OUR FARM WERE LINED WITH
WILD ROSE HIPS AND FLOWING
WELLS THAT PRODUCED
ENDLESS AMOUNTS OF
CRYSTAL CLEAR WATER
AND THICK STANDS OF
WATERCRESS. FRUIT GREW
EVERYWHERE. WILD YELLOW
AND RED POTAWATOMI PLUMS
AND EVEN THE OCCASIONAL
MULBERRY TREE LINED THE
LANES. PEAR, PEACH, APRICOT,
APPLE AND CHERRY TREES
GREW IN WELL-TENDED
ORCHARDS OR WOULD DEFY
THE ODDS AND GROW ALONG
THE SIDES OF IRRIGATION
DITCHES WHERE YOU COULD
HELP YOURSELF TO THEIR
CONTRARIAN BOUNTY.

A FEW FAVORITE BEVERAGES

Rose Tea

This tea is nice for those who appreciate subtlety. Besides the quality of ingredients, which can't be overemphasized, the most misunderstood aspect of making hot teas is the temperature of the water. Granted, the time a tea steeps can be important but water temperature is usually what people get wrong. For this tea, 190° F is the proper temperature — not boiling, which, depending on the altitude, is around 212° F.

For this recipe you should use unsprayed, aromatic rose petals. The wild, yellow rose is our rose of choice for both ice cream and tea. We make ice cream with fresh rose petals and tea with dried. Fortunately, this yellow rose grows along the interior fences away from the roads in the fields on our family farm. Collecting those on the perimeter fences along the sides of the road exposes people to the dangers of chemical sprays where various governing agencies honestly believe spraying is a good idea and blindly continue the program. And so it is with the consumption of wild edibles that grow along most of America's roads. It isn't recommended.

The rose is a cousin to the apple and quite naturally complements apple desserts. A good combination is Rose Tea with an Apple Dessert such as Caramelized Fruit (p. 276) with Rose Petal Ice Cream. An easy way to make Rose Petal Ice Cream — if you don't have the time to make it from scratch — is to chop a handful of fresh rose petals and stir them into vanilla ice cream. Put the mixture back in the freezer for a few hours to give the petals time to infuse before serving.

Dried rose hips to taste, about 4 or 5 tablespoons

Dried rose petals to taste, about 4 or 5 tablespoons

4 or 5 cups of spring water

Mild honey, such as clover or alfalfa to taste

MAKES 4 OR 5 CUPS

Using a quick read thermometer bring the spring water to 190° F. Place the rose hips and petals in a mortar and lightly crush with a pestle. Add them to the teapot and pour hot spring water over them. Allow them to steep for 10 to 15 minutes to achieve their full flavor. Strain into cups and offer a mild honey or raw sugar to sweeten if preferred.

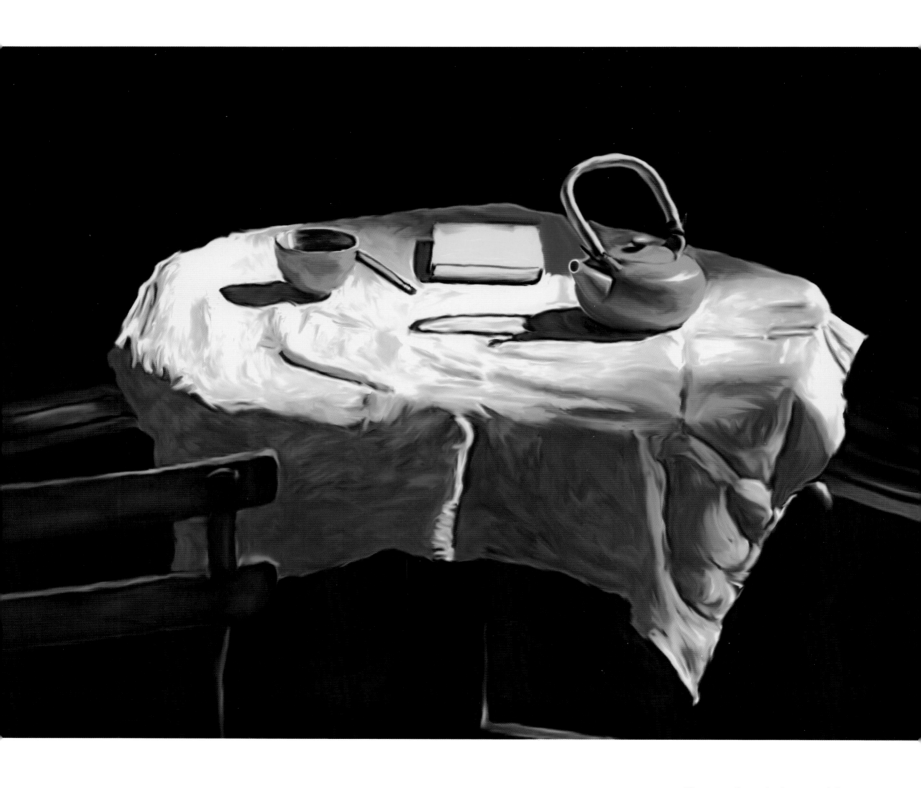

There are times in the rays of the morning's early light when a cup of tea, a pencil and pad of paper give flight to the loftiest ideas.

A FEW FAVORITE BEVERAGES

THE BEST TOMATO JUICE

During the tomato season, if you have access to good, vine-ripened tomatoes, it is easy to make the best tomato juice. With a modern, powerful blender (see resources) you can quickly purée whole, raw, garden-fresh tomatoes, skin, seeds and all if you like or, for a more traditional consistency and texture, you can blend the tomatoes just enough to break up their cell structure then push them through a strainer to remove the skin and seeds. With either method, you can make a fresher tasting juice than you could ever get from a can or bottle. It is also easy to customize your juice with your choice of favorite flavors. Good tomato juice is an excellent beverage with a sandwich, slice of dill pickle, a few olives and handful of chips.

---

3 or 4 vine-ripened tomatoes, all of one variety, or a mixture

Good salt and a grind of fresh black pepper to taste

Lemon or lime juice if desired

A few drops of Worcestershire sauce if desired

Dash of Prepared Horseradish if desired (p. 249)

Stick of leafy celery from a celery heart

MAKES 2 SERVINGS

Core and cut tomatoes into pieces that fit into the blender. Place all the tomatoes inside the canister and cover. Blend on medium for a few seconds or a minute or two depending on the style of juice you prefer. Strain it if you like. Add salt to taste and black pepper if desired.

Taste and add lemon or lime juice to taste (optional). Sprinkle in a few drops of Worcestershire sauce to taste (optional). Add horseradish to taste and blend slightly (optional).

Pour over ice and garnish with celery.

We have a small red wine vineyard that provides grapes for our own personal wine. My wife and I calculate that we can make about half of the wine we drink from about 30 vines. The first phase is to see which vines do well on our soil in this climate. Because of our day-to-day preference for red wine, we have planted Grenache, Tempranillo, Cabernet Sauvignon, Zinfandel and Petite Syrah. Our goal is to make wine to match our food in style and quality.

A FEW FAVORITE BEVERAGES

SMART FARMING

With the exception of the Wasatch Front, where we get an average annual 16 inches of rainfall, Utah is a true desert with an annual average rainfall of 10 inches. This puts the state in a continual zero-sum tug-of-war with the powers of nature, more specifically the power of osmosis.

The 1902 Reclamation Act guaranteed Utah farmers cheap, subsidized water, no matter what the cost to the American taxpayer. Those costs are high and going up. Alfalfa, the state's traditional crop of choice, is a stark example. An acre of alfalfa needs somewhere between slightly less than three acre feet of water per crop (with an average three crops per year) to over six acre feet, depending on what irrigation system is used. The cost of this water to the American taxpayer is greater than the return to Utah farmers. Part of the irony is that in a state where free-market capitalism is much in favor, large government water subsidies to farmers have always been eagerly accepted.

As it is practiced today, agriculture contributes a mere one percent to Utah's economy. Alfalfa can make a farmer $500 or so per acre on a good year. Without heavy subsidies, the state's alfalfa industry would experience a rapid collapse simply because it would be more cost effective to import it than to grow it. One possible answer to this untenable situation is to find a smarter way to farm.

Next door, the state of Colorado may have come up with a solution — wine grapes. Colorado estimates each acre of wine grapes has a synergistic effect on the state's hospitality industry of about $175,000 per year and, serendipitously in this arid region, mature wine grapes require only about 20 percent as much water as alfalfa.

When vineyards are planted and made into wine, people start coming from the urban areas to rural destinations where they spend a few days and leave behind a lot of money. Compared with pretty much anything that can be legally grown, this is a mind-boggling amount. The general pattern is quite predictable: after the vineyards come the wine makers then the chefs who establish a variety of eateries. The best of them create food designed to match the local wines. To city dwellers in the surrounding areas and tourists this is an irresistible combination that leads to increased visitors with an unusually high rate of return. Next is the need for hotel accommodations, bed and breakfasts, motels and campsites. The locals are hired to work in the various businesses. Young people who never thought it possible to make a career in their hometown find a variety of new career paths available to them.

On the one hand in fiscal year 2007 Utah sent $42,390,925 outside the state to buy wine from producers around the world. On the other hand the State, until 2007, levied a 53% tax on all Utah wine production. Wine producers around the world pay an average of less than 10% to cover approximately the same taxes worldwide. This tax made it virtually impossible, before the new tax changes, for Utah's producers to compete on the world market. The State's rationalization for this breach of free-market principle was that the tax on producers goes directly into the State's education system, which, they claimed, justified such an repressive tax. If raising money for Utah's school system is so important the wine industry will be able to make a vastly greater contribution to the State coffers if the industry is reasonably taxed and allowed to grow.

A common fear among Utah legislators was that increased wine production in the State would encourage people to drink more but further research showed that drinking patterns are quite stable. Any adult in the State who wants to buy wine or spirits has easy access to liquor stores throughout the state. Allowing more wine production to take place here will not alter its availability only the amount of money that will remain in the State. It will also bring millions of dollars into depressed rural economies around the State and in my opinion help usher in a new culinary era.

It has been difficult to arrive at a definition of what Utah food really is. Unlike most of the great culinary traditions around the world Utah's lack of a wine industry emasculated what was once a vigorous food tradition based on the many ethnic influences of the thousands of the mostly European converts brought into the Mormon church in its early years. It was during those years that a wine industry flourished in the State. As the church leaders aged and became more socially conservative winemaking was outlawed in the State. The inevitable result was a slow but steady decline in the evolution of what was becoming a unique food tradition. Nothing stimulates the appetite and enjoyment of food like the inclusion of wine at the table and on the other hand nothing kills a wine-based food tradition faster that outlawing wine.

There are no wines that match food better than the ones grown in the area where food is produced and prepared. Think of the great culinary traditions of Europe: from Alsace to the slopes of Mount Etna in Sicily there are hundreds of local wines linked to local food traditions. The key to understanding why local wines work best with local food is to understand that they evolved together over time. The winemakers adjust their techniques to achieve a wine that works with the local food and vice versa. As the years pass the two achieve a harmony that is unique to a region. In Alsace the most famous and successful marriage of food and wine is between what they consider to be there best wine made from one of the six noble grape varieties that flourish in that region. Riesling and the heavily German-influenced foods of the same region: including a variety of smoky meats, sauerkraut and sausages. This is only one example of many brilliantly successful combinations. Because of their lengthy coevolution they are, some would say, a match made in heaven. Another equally famous food and wine region is Burgundy. Burgundian food would have little meaning without its local wine: from the dry Chablis to the rich sensuous Romanée Conti. Burgundy is one of the greatest wine regions in the world. It is an ancient Province and its food reflects the same sophistication and depth that its wines do and together they have conquered the respect of the world.

Many books have been filled with the legendary combinations of local foods and their wines. This is the foundation of a tradition that the State of Utah can look forward to as it begins the exciting process of exploring a new wine region. I can think of few things in the world of food more exciting. And with the old tax structure lifted I think a new age of wine and local food is about to begin.

RESOURCES

Black Walnuts

www.black-walnuts.com
phone: 888-429-6887

Blender

Not all blenders are created equal. Here are two home blenders with commercial power:

Vita-Mix: www.vitamix.com
phone: 800-848-2649

Blendtec: www.blendtec.com
phone: 800-253-6383

Bio-K+

www.biokplus.com
phone: 800-593-2465

Bragg Liquid Aminos & Bragg Apple Cider Vinegar

Bragg Liquid Aminos is my favorite soy sauce with none of the chemical and added salt found in most commercial soy sauces. It has a cleaner more focused taste with no bitterness.

Bragg Apple Cider Vinegar is a wonderful, raw, unfiltered, organic vinegar with the mother still in the bottle.

www.bragg.com
phone: 800-446-1990

Graber Olives

A buttery, canned, raw California olive that will absorb flavor better than any olive I have ever used.

www.graberolives.com
phone: 800-996-5483

Grainmaster

This grinder is one of the best. It is available through the mail, lasts for years and repays its price many times over.

www.pleasanthillgrain.com
phone: 800-321-1073

Muscovado Sugar

A sugar from the island of Mauritius, grown on volcanic soil, which gives its flavors a dark, rich intensity.

www.indiatree.com
phone: 800-369-4848

Pavel's Original Russian Yogurt

Pavel's is easily my favorite commercial yogurt, made by a family-owned business in San Leandro, California. It has a delicate curd made of nothing but milk and cultures with none of the fillers and additives found in most of today's commercial yogurt.

www.pavels.net
phone:510-352-1474

Pinkeye Beans

Mitchell Farm
phone: 801-756-2882

Real Salt

Our favorite salt comes from Redmond Mineral in Redmond, Utah. An exceptionally clean-tasting, ancient, pre-pollution, deep-mined sea salt sold under the name of *Real Salt.*

www.realsalt.com
phone: 800-367-7258

Rose Water

Organic Bulgarian Rose Water.

www.bulgarianroseotto.com
phone: 312-528-9161

Wild Rice

www.nativeharvest.com
phone: 888-274-8318

Big poaching pot

Twelve-inch diameter 20-quart stainless steel pot with lid. This pot is very inexpensive, usually less than $30, because it has a simple 1 layer bottom. It is good for poaching and making stock but not much else as things scorch in it very easily. A good source is at a brewer's supply store. (An oversized pot is an excellent way to poach a medium-sized bird such as a chicken, duck or pheasant). I have a 20-quart, 12-inch diameter pot exclusively for this one purpose. It has two main advantages: one is that it yields extra stock and the other is the ease at which a fully cooked bird can be removed with a colander leaving it in one piece and in excellent condition.

10-inch zinc plated steel spikes (nails)

This is a useful tool for conducting heat into a stuffed cavity, i.e., a boned stuffed chicken, turkey or saddle of lamb where it is difficult to conduct enough heat to raise the stuffing temperature to its proper level. These spikes are plated and smooth as opposed to a hot-dipped spike that is rough and unsuitable for this purpose. Spikes made of aluminum are not satisfactory either as they are not nonreactive. Steel spikes that are not zinc plated are also not satisfactory as they can impart an oxidized iron flavor and rust easily. They can be obtained from any good hardware store.

Acknowledgments

Like most people I am largely a reflection of the influences I have absorbed throughout my life, and so I lift my glass to those things and to the people who shaped me, with special thanks to the following:

Elizabeth Myers Lyman, my mother, who taught me about unconditional love and an unwavering devotion to the things that always mattered most to her, including the preparation of thousands upon thousands of heartfelt meals for family, friends and whoever happened to be around at mealtime, including hoboes and strangers picked up on the road.

Grant Mason Lyman, my father, who taught me discipline and the richly textured techniques of ranching, farming and gardening.

My older brother Fred, who steered me toward a love of art and life's finer things.

My brother Jay, who backed me up as an artist but never got the credit he deserved.

My other siblings: Jennie Ruth, Brent and Ross, with whom I shared those thousands of farm meals, laughs, tears and conversations.

My children, Bowen, Peter and Angie, who allowed me to learn cooking at their expense. Actually, they had no choice.

My other daughter, Katherine, who I didn't get to meet until she turned 30, who lives in the woods of Michigan with her husband Chad and their daughter Nadia.

My grandchildren, Nadia, Orion and Elizabeth and her sons Max and Angel.

My godson Cedar, his sister Rayna and their mother Marinda Coleman. My offspring and theirs represent the future of our family's culinary legacy.

My first wife, Linda, who was my second cooking teacher, and her Grandfather ("Papa"), who, as the head of the commissary for the Union Pacific Railroad during its heyday, introduced me to a whole new world of fine food.

Mikel Covey, a kindred spirit, fellow artist and "The King of Soup," who raised the standard for me in the kitchen, and his wife Traci O'Very Covey, a great couple with whom my wife Sofia and I experienced unsurpassed meals.

All the cooks and chefs I am inspired by through one kind of media or another, including Richard Olney, Alice Waters, Julia Child, Jeremiah Tower, Thomas Keller, Charlie Trotter, Emeril Lagasse, Jamie Oliver, Martha Stewart, Lynne Rossetto Kasper, Alton Brown and Henri de Toulouse-Lautrec in his book *The Art of Cuisine.*

The peerless lifestyles of Claude Monet and all the original French Impressionists who fearlessly blazed a broad path into a bold future of art, wine, food and conviviality the likes of which was never seen before and probably never will be again.

Paul Cézanne, Vincent Van Gogh, Paul Gauguin, Django Reinhardt, Arthur Rimbaud and Amedeo Modigliani, who showed me how, with enough faith and hard work, an indifferent world can never overrule the artistic gifts of the gods.

All the sustainable growers, foragers, poets and artists, cooks, bakers, winemakers, writers, actors, composers, musicians, filmmakers and dancers who devote themselves to a life often ignored or ridiculed by the very societies they enrich with their priceless treasures.

The inventors, builders, engineers and scientists who have expanded our view of the way we grow and prepare our food.

The great chefs and cooks of history that invented the many dishes and methods of preparation of the modern kitchen that we regularly take for granted.

All those who have and still labor in anonymity in whatever field they happen to find themselves. How many of today's treasures of the creative process have been attributed to someone other than their rightful inventor?

My generation which bravely and shamelessly labored for, among other things, spiritual freedom, peace, civil rights, equality of the sexes, respect for human sexuality and all members of the human tribe, new dance, theatrical, visual and musical forms, a healthier environment, alternative medicine, holistic consciousness, sustainable agriculture, a respect and new awareness for the culinary and viticultural treasures of the past and a new vision for their future.

Robert Redford and his long-running environmental work for all of us, and the Natural Resources Defense Council he so tirelessly supports, and their combined work to protect the environment and countless animals that don't have a voice in the politics of our self-absorbed world.

Bob Dylan, who inspired me to be a songwriter.

Richard Taylor, with whom I experienced many great visual breakthroughs and the vagabond's life performing light shows on the road in the sixties and seventies.

Pepper and Denise Provenzano, who trusted me and saved us from the wolf time and time again.

Gerald Purdy, my first art teacher, who believed in me.

My wife, Sofia, the love of my life, who knows what I think before I do and encourages and influences me in more ways than I can comprehend, who shares my values, my art, our table and bed.

And finally, to the gods of sun, soil, rain, genetics and all the mysterious forces and miracles of life—and here's to more!

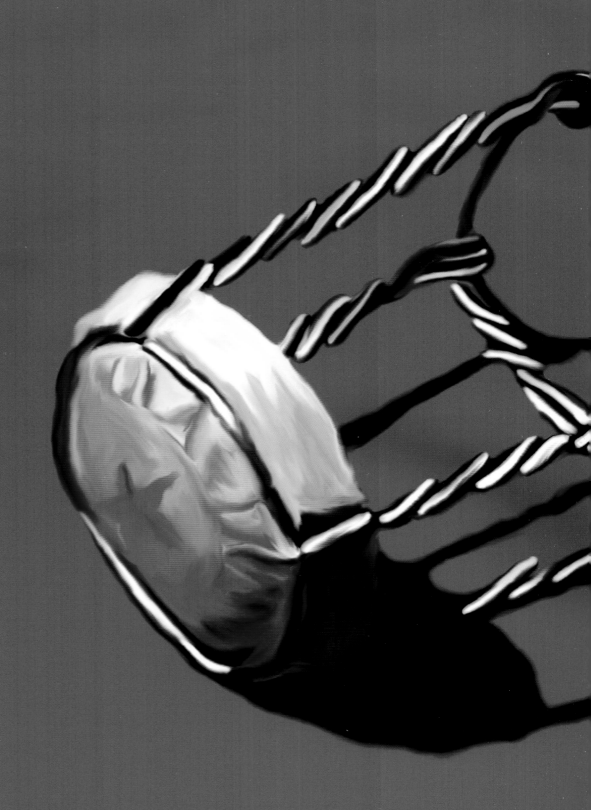

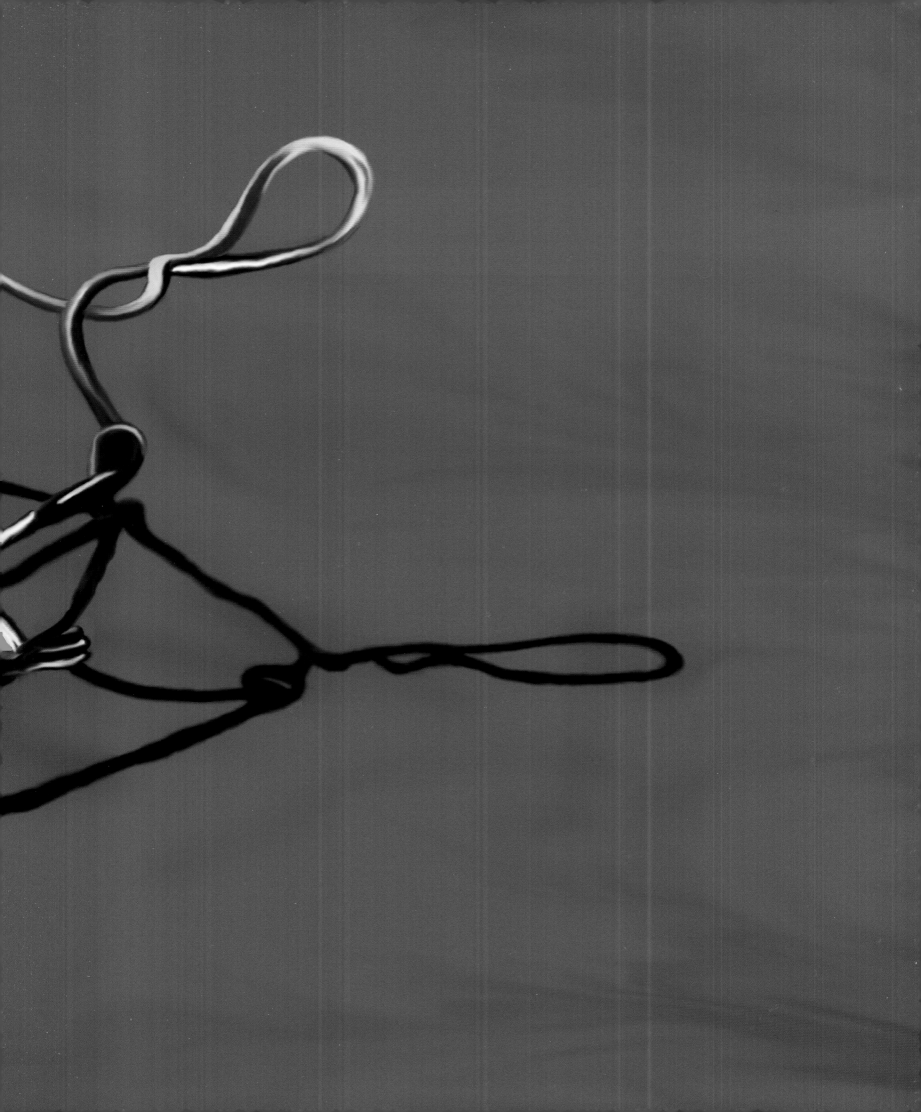

A NOTE TO THE READER

If you have read through this book you understand that this is not just a cookbook. It is the manifesto of a very special and beloved man, a man who shared his life, his experience, his talents, and his love without any thought of glamor or desire for special recognition. Kenvin was a wide-ranging, creative dynamo, for deep in his heart was a work ethic born and nurtured in the mountain ranges of Utah. He drew his inspiration from generations of Mormon pioneer ancestors—farmers and ranchers, and from his bohemian peers. The habit of crossing vocational and professional lines without hesitation became a hallmark of his life's work. Kenvin came to our lives with his soul reaching toward the light in the stars. His journey does not end with departure from this planet. Kenvin's light show continues beyond this universe.

This book would not have come to light without the dedication and love of numerous friends. I join Kenvin in raising my glass to: Richard Taylor, who stood by Kenvin from the early stages of Kenvin's career as a partner and continues to ensure that Kenvin's light will shine on. Gibbs Smith for his unwavering belief in this book. Virginia Rainey and Susan Massey for their endless editing, testing and guidance. Vanessa Chang, who brought Kenvin's voice out on paper. Kelly Schaefer, whose design complements Kenvin's so well. Scott Aucutt for making sure all this hard work will be printed correctly and for creating the special font in this book from Kenvin's handwriting. Julie Howell for her advice and support. Mikel Covey, for his professional guidance, who inspired Kenvin's cooking and art. Christopher Baker for his keen eye in bringing the poetry to this book. Pepper Provenzano for polishing the draft and for his and Denise Provenzano's guidance. And finally to Fred Lyman, more than a blood brother to Kenvin, for turning on the first light show in Kenvin's soul. —Sofia

I DEFINITELY SPENT TOO MUCH TIME CHASING
MONEY, BUT FORTUNATELY AT SOME POINT I
REALIZED THAT I COULD EITHER CONTINUE ON
THAT PATH OR GO TO MY GRAVE WITH DIGNITY.

Farewell Kenvin Lyman

The gulls wheel and cry.
The frigate birds hang upon the sky.

Ahoy there! Ahoy!
Drop your anchor back,
Let the chain run out.
The tide is certain against you.
Come back ashore!
Can't you hear the town bell tolling?

Ahoy! Ahoy there!
Wind up your sails.
Square your yards.
The wind runs ashore
And it will surely blow you back.

You cannot sail away.
You cannot!
At least give us one more turn
About the bay,
Just one more turn!

But the frigate birds
Have cut the distant sky,
And the gulls have wheeled away,
And the ship's already hull down
Over the limn of the planet,
Scudding before the light,
Down, to the other side.

Farewell Kenvin Lyman.
Fare Well, Kenvin Lyman.

—Christopher Baker

ILLUSTRATIONS

AN ARTIST'S KITCHEN

NOTES

Published by
Gibbs Smith
P.O Box 667
Layton, Utah 84041

Orders 1 800 835 4993
www.gibbs-smith.com

Design concept by Kelly Schaeffer
Final Production Design by Aucutt Design, Inc.

Printed and bound in China

Gibbs Smith books are printed on either recycled, 100% post-consumer waste, FSC-certified papers or on paper produced from
sustainable PEFC-certified forest/controlled wood source. Learn more at www.pefc.org

Library of Congress Cataloging-in-Publication Data

Lyman, Kenvin, 1942–2011, author.
Kenvin : an artist's kitchen : food, art & wisdom of a bohemian cowboy /
recipes, stories & artwork by Kenvin Lyman. — First Edition.
pages cm
Includes index.
ISBN 978-1-4236-0330-6
1. Cooking, American—Western style. 2. Local foods—Utah.
I. Lyman, Kenvin, 1942–2011, illustrator. II. Title.
TX715.2.W47L96 2013
641.5978—dc23
2012038141